Stanley Cavell

Stanley Cavell has been one of the most creative and independent contemporary philosophical voices. At the core of his thought is the view that skepticism is not a theoretical position to be refuted by philosophical theory but a reflection of the fundamental limits of human knowledge of the self, of others, and of the external world that must be accepted. Developing the resources of ordinary language philosophy and the discourse of thinkers as diverse as Wittgenstein, Heidegger, Thoreau, and Emerson, Cavell has explored the ineliminability of skepticism in philosophy, literature, drama, and the movies.

This volume includes major new accounts of Cavell's contributions to ethics, the theory of action, the philosophy of mind and language, aesthetics, Romanticism, American philosophy, Shakespeare, and film and opera.

The appeal of this volume will be unusually broad and will include students of literary studies, American studies, film theory, cultural studies, music, and art history, as well as philosophy.

Richard Eldridge is a professor of philosophy at Swarthmore College.

Contemporary Philosophy in Focus

Contemporary Philosophy in Focus offers a series of introductory volumes to many of the dominant philosophical thinkers of the current age. Each volume will consist of newly commissioned essays that cover major contributions of a preeminent philosopher in a systematic and accessible manner. Comparable in scope and rationale to the highly successful series **Cambridge Companions to Philosophy**, the volumes do not presuppose that readers are already intimately familiar with the details of each philosopher's work. They will thus combine exposition and critical analysis in a manner that will appeal both to students of philosophy and to professionals and students across the humanities and social sciences.

FORTHCOMING VOLUMES:

Paul Churchland edited by Brian Keeley
Donald Davidson edited by Kirk Ludwig
Ronald Dworkin edited by Arthur Ripstein
Jerry Fodor edited by Tim Crane
David Lewis edited by Theodore Sider and Dean Zimmerman
Alasdair MacIntyre edited by Mark C. Murphy
Hilary Putnam edited by Yemima Ben-Menahem
Richard Rorty edited by Charles Guignon and David Hiley
John Searle edited by Barry Smith
Charles Taylor edited by Ruth Abbey
Bernard Williams edited by Alan Thomas

PUBLISHED VOLUMES:

Daniel Dennett edited by Andrew Brook and Don Ross
Robert Nozick edited by David Schmidtz
Thomas Kuhn edited by Thomas Nickles

Stanley Cavell

Edited by

RICHARD ELDRIDGE
Swarthmore College

CAMBRIDGE
UNIVERSITY PRESS

PUBLISHED BY THE PRESS SYNDICATE OF THE UNIVERSITY OF CAMBRIDGE
The Pitt Building, Trumpington Street, Cambridge, United Kingdom

CAMBRIDGE UNIVERSITY PRESS
The Edinburgh Building, Cambridge CB2 2RU, UK
40 West 20th Street, New York, NY 10011-4211, USA
477 Williamstown Road, Port Melbourne, VIC 3207, Australia
Ruiz de Alarcón 13, 28014 Madrid, Spain
Dock House, The Waterfront, Cape Town 8001, South Africa

http://www.cambridge.org

First published 2003

Printed in the United States of America

Typefaces Janson Text Roman 10/13 pt. and ITC Officina Sans   *System* LaTeX 2$_\varepsilon$ [TB]

A catalog record for this book is available from the British Library.

Library of Congress Cataloging in Publication data
Stanley Cavell / edited by Richard Eldridge.
    p.   cm. – (Contemporary philosophy in focus)
Includes bibliographical references and index.
ISBN 0-521-77025-4 – ISBN 0-521-77972-3 (pbk.)
1. Cavell, Stanley, 1926–   I. Eldridge, Richard Thomas, 1953–   II. Series.
B945.C274 S73   2003
191 – dc21   2002071483

ISBN 0 521 77025 4 hardback
ISBN 0 521 77972 3 paperback

Contents

Contributors

STANLEY BATES is Professor of Philosophy and Chair of the Philosophy Department at Middlebury College. His main areas of philosophical interest are ethics and aesthetics, and he is currently working on a study of moral perfectionism.

J. M. BERNSTEIN is University Distinguished Professor of Philosophy at the New School for Social Research. His most recent work is *Adorno: Disenchantment and Ethics*, and he has edited and written an introduction to *Classic and Romantic German Aesthetics*. He is completing a book of essays on modernism and painting.

ANTHONY J. CASCARDI is Professor of Comparative Literature, Rhetoric, and Spanish at the University of California, Berkeley. His books include *Consequences of Enlightenment, The Subject of Modernity*, and *Literature and the Question of Philosophy*. He is the editor of *The Cambridge Companion to Cervantes* and is currently at work on the topic of aesthetics and agency.

WILLIAM DESMOND is Professor of Philosophy and Director of the International Program in Philosophy at the Institute of Philosophy, Katholieke Universiteit Leuven (Louvain), Belgium. He has written on metaphysics, aesthetics, and the philosophy of religion. Among his works are *Being and the Between* (1995) and, most recently, *Ethics and the Between* (2001). His *Art, Origins, Otherness: Between Philosophy and Art* is scheduled to appear in 2003.

RICHARD ELDRIDGE is Professor of Philosophy and Chair of the Philosophy Department at Swarthmore College. He is the author of *On Moral Personhood: Philosophy, Literature, Criticism and Self-Understanding; Leading a Human Life: Wittenstein, Intentionality, and Romanticism*; and *The Persistence of Romanticism*. He edited *Beyond Representation: Philosophy and Poetic Imagination*. His *An Introduction to the Philosophy of Art* is forthcoming from Cambridge University Press.

TIMOTHY GOULD is Professor of Philosophy at The Metropolitan State College of Denver. He is the author of *Hearing Things: Voice and Method in the Writing of Stanley Cavell* and has written a series of articles tracing connections between Kantian analyses of pleasure, sublimity, and freedom and Romantic efforts to realign and redeem our words and the world. He has written about aftermaths of Kant and the Romantic in such regions as the Gothic, Marx, Nietzsche, feminism, and modernism. He is at work on a manuscript tentatively entitled "Traces of Freedom: An Archaeology of Kant's Aesthetics" and another entitled "Prophets of the Everyday."

STEPHEN MULHALL is Fellow and Tutor in Philosophy at New College, Oxford. His research primarily focuses on the writings of Wittgenstein, Heidegger, and Kierkegaard. His recent publications include *Inheritance and Originality* (2001) and *On Film* (2002).

WILLIAM ROTHMAN received his Ph.D. in philosophy from Harvard University, where he wrote his dissertation on the aesthetics of film under Stanley Cavell's supervision. He is the author of *Hitchcock – The Murderous Gaze*, *The "I" of the Camera*, *Documentary Film Classics*, and (with Marian Keane) *Reading Cavell's The World Viewed: A Philosophical Perspective on Film*. He is series editor of the Studies in Film series published by Cambridge University Press. For many years he taught film history, criticism, and theory at Harvard; he is currently Professor of Motion Pictures at the University of Miami.

Stanley Cavell

1 | Introduction: Between Acknowledgment and Avoidance

RICHARD ELDRIDGE

In an early essay, Stanley Cavell writes that the problem of the ordinary language philosopher – a problem from which he himself takes his bearings – is "to discover the specific plight of mind and circumstance within which a human being gives voice to his condition."[1] What can this mean? What is a *plight of mind and circumstance*? How does *giving voice* constitute a response and address to a general human condition that is instanced in a specific way?

Since it is a plight *of mind* that is in question, it is already evident that Cavell must be concerned with something more than simply a physical or biological state of being a human being, even if the mind is itself inextricably lodged in both bodily and cultural circumstances. Nor is the problem of giving voice simply that of unburdening oneself of an idiosyncratic emotion: *giving voice* implies not brute discharge alone, but further a making intelligible of how the human condition is present in one who has been moved to speak. Nor will just any speech do; *giving voice* implies an achievement of expressiveness that is beyond the communication of bits of information about the material world.

Instead, to be moved to give voice to a plight of mind and circumstance – to manage that achievement – is to express a specific sense of just how, here and now, one's human capacities for free and fluent voicing and action are somehow both enabled and inhibited by one's culture and one's life with others as they stand. One seeks, as Cavell elsewhere puts it, "freedom of consciousness, the beginning of freedom, ... freedom of language, having the run of it, as if successfully claimed from it, as of a birthright."[2] One seeks to have one's performances – one's uses of concepts in thought, in utterance, and in action, which are all internally related – be both one's *own* as expressions of one's independent personality and desire, against the sways of the common, and reasonably *endorsable*, by both others and oneself, as valuable expressions of common possibilities and necessities.

This is no small task, and Cavell emphasizes the persistence of the effort to achieve such expressiveness, as against both simpler, dogmatic recipes for its achievement and (what he sees as) naturalist-quietist scantings of the adventure of the human. Rather than sketching and defending any definite account of human flourishing, Cavell notes that there are certain "arguments that must not be won" and that philosophy might be conceived of as "the achievement of the unpolemical, of the refusal to take sides in metaphysical positions."[3]

This is not a refusal to take sides or to enact commitments as such, but rather "a refusal of, say, disobedient to, (a false) ascent, or transcendence"[4] as a ground of commitment. Against false ascent, Cavell poses *philosophy as descent*, the necessary faithfulness of philosophy to the common and the ordinary, as the only available loci of repertoires of language, thought, conceptual life, and human action. But it is also true that "the (actual) everyday [is – or can be experienced as, for Cavell, following Wittgenstein –] . . . a scene of illusion and trance and artificiality (of need)."[5] *Philosophy as ascent* is also called for. Hence what is pursued, in and through the pursuit of fully expressive action, aiming at exemplariness of voicing, is an eventual or transfigured ordinary, a fit common habitation for the human.

Since, however, one takes one's own bearings and possibilities of thought, action, and expression from within the ordinary as it stands, as a scene of both possibilities and (false) necessities, of both affordances and inhibitions, it follows that philosophizing, the effort to enact more humanly expressive possibilities, will be "a spiritual struggle, specifically a struggle with the contrary depths of oneself."[6] One will find oneself, at times, pursuing a thought, vision, or course of action that is not generally shared, hence seeking abandonment of or departure from the common. But then one will also find oneself, at times, recoiling from the solipsistic madness of apocalyptic vision and returning to the common, accepting it as cure.[7] Neither movement, in Cavell's perception, can be complete or final. What is left, to adapt Dieter Henrich's useful characterization of Friedrich Hölderlin's stance, is the thought "that conscious life is at once shaped and unbalanced by the basic *conflicting* tendencies orienting it. And the formative process of life aims at finding a balance and a harmony amidst this strife, in which no one tendency is entirely suppressed or denied in its own right."[8] For Cavell, as for Hölderlin, these conflicting basic tendencies include at least the pursuit of independent selfhood and the pursuit of communion, community, love, and the common. Seeking both, one is left between *avoidance* (of others, of the common, of what is common with others in oneself, as decayed, vulgarized, inhibiting, and empty) and *acknowledgment* (of others, of the common, of what is common with others in oneself, as what alone enables thought, recovery, conversation, and restoration).

To find oneself in such a plight is, in Cavell's reading, central to what it is to be "a creature complicated or burdened enough to possess language at all."[9] Not everyone will feel or accept this, will feel or accept the burden or complication of seeking expressive freedom and the run of language, thought, and action. The demands of daily life or of sheer survival are too pressing for some to notice this plight; others are reasonably distracted by scientific, political, artistic, intellectual, and other problems that are genuinely absorbing. But then it is also true that these problems themselves may include problems of human aspiration that touch on this plight of mind, that those who are pressed or absorbed in daily life may suffer from quiet desperation, silent melancholy, or distractedness, all covertly legible in their pursuits and entertainments, and that in certain nights of the soul a sense of this plight may come to consciousness, even if it is then often reasonably suppressed in the name of decency, work, or common life.

We come to language as something that is already there before us in the practices of our elders. The criteria for calling something what it is are there in practice before we are, and we cannot come to thought and linguistic practice without them. This fact has both positive and negative sides. "I have to accept [criteria], use them," if I am to enter into linguistic and conceptual practice at all, but "this itself makes my use of them seem arbitrary, or private – as though they were never shared, or as if our sharing of them is either a fantastic accident or a kind of mass folly."[10] Their presence and availability in practice are not grounded for me in any kind of unmediated knowledge of ultimate realities and of the relation of words to them. If words and the criteria for their use then seem ungrounded or arbitrary, I can feel my own dawning powers in their exercise to be uncertain. My exercise of these powers may seem liable to drift away from others' and then to repudiation, and I can wish to do better. I can indulge in a fantasy of absolute power in my uses of (to me) primitive words, fully grounded in necessarily private acts of inner "recognition." Or I can indulge in a fantasy of powerlessness or "necessary inexpressiveness,"[11] in which my uses of words occur "according to laws of nature" in and through me, without implicating me in responsibility for their finding or missing understanding in any audience.

Yet these fantasies of cognitive omnipotence and of necessary inexpressiveness come to nothing, can't be worked out. "We cannot really imagine . . . , or rather . . . there is nothing of the sort to imagine, or rather . . . when we as it were try to imagine this we are imagining something other than we think."[12] The discovery of either private, perfect, absolute "inner recognitions" or fully law-governed natural processes in me cannot be stated within ordinary language without returning us to the very scene of risks and responsibilities we had sought to escape. Ordinary criteria *"are* the terms in which *I relate what's happening,"*[13] and I must draw on them if I am to think and speak at all. This is not to deny that there can be innovations in language in the form of new technical terms or new turns of metaphor. It *is* to deny that language as such could have such bases in individual acts or events apart from the common. Public words and the criteria for their use *are* there before us, and they *are* the only things we have to go on. In Stephen Mulhall's useful summary, Cavell's thought is that

> if the ground of the inheritability of language, the basis of the continued ex-
> istence of the speech community and its members, is the capacity of human
> beings to see and hear themselves in the words and deeds of other human
> beings, then the continuance of that community cannot be guaranteed ei-
> ther by nature or by grammar; it rests solely upon our capacity to take and
> maintain an interest in one another and in ourselves.[14]

Though we can succeed in taking and maintaining such an interest, we can also fail, and we can feel the responsibility for success or failure to be an undue burden. Hence we live, in Cavell's perception, in simultaneous satisfaction with and disappointment in criteria and the ordinary,[15] engaged in "a continuous effort at balance,"[16] between escape into independence and personal assertion, on the one hand, and return to accommodation, habit, and domestication on the other. The reason for this joint disappointment and satisfaction is that there is within us "the human drive to transcend itself, make itself inhuman."[17] "Nothing could be more human" than "the power of the motive to reject the human,"[18] than to seek somehow – whether in perfect individual cognitive omnipotence (even if within a narrow domain) or in perfect submission to the ordinary and natural – to perfect one's satisfactions and overcome one's disappointments. "The threat, or the truth, of skepticism [is] that it names our wish (and the possibility of our wishing) to strip ourselves of the responsibility we have in meaning (or in failing to mean) one thing, or one way, rather than another."[19] There is inherent in the human and "inherent in philosophy a certain drive to the inhuman . . . [that is] somehow itself the most inescapably human of motivations."[20]

For beings who are freighted with such wishes and responsibilities, aris-
ing in and through engagement with the ordinary, the ordinary itself is, in a phrasing Cavell adapts from Heidegger, "at bottom . . . not ordinary; it is extra-ordinary, uncanny."[21] For Cavell, "the uncanniness of the ordinary is epitomized by . . . the capacity, even the desire, of ordinary language [that is, of we who use it] to repudiate itself."[22] Nothing within ordinary thinking

or linguistic practice *guarantees* its continuation; how it goes on is up to us, we who are initiated into it and go on within and from it, and this can seem terrifying. Yet ordinary thinking and linguistic practice are necessary media for the presence of things to discursively thinking, judgmental subjects, and we do not have the power to alter prior patterns of language and thought *tout court*. These patterns have a certain sway over us, and this too can seem terrifying. Both "the repudiation of the world" as a scene of perhaps false necessities, and of perennial risks, and "its revelation of the world" are "internal to" ordinary language.[23] As discursive, acting, judging subjects, we wish for more – more mastery, more grounding, more surety – from the ordinary. Yet the ordinary (together with its possible successors) remains the only scene for our lives as such subjects. We are hence in relation to the ordinary both at home and not at home; it is uncanny. "The human necessity of the quest for home and the human fact of immigrancy are seen together as aspects of the human as such."[24]

Inhabiting our relation to the ordinary, therefore, are opposed drives toward both its acceptance and its overcoming. The ordinary and our relation to it in turn enable – and may even present themselves as requiring – the working out of both drives. It is possible, and sometimes necessary if solipsistic madness is to be foregone and thought and reasonable action are to be continued at all, to consent "to become intelligible."[25] Acknowledgment of the common – both the current common and the perfected common that can arise out of it alone – is possible. To refuse that acknowledgment altogether and instead to insist on pure independence of thought is to fall into skepticism not as insinuating possibility, but as mad discovery, or to fall even further into the all-too-human avoidances and rages of Othello and Lear. In Wittgenstein's phrasing, "Knowledge is in the end based on acknowledgment"[26] of the common, of what is among us. Acknowledgment is available, and there is no thought or reasonable action without it. Even genius, whatever departures from the common it enacts in an exemplary way, must be "the name of the promise that the private and the social will be achieved together,"[27] that a perfected ordinary will be the site of return and redemption. The remarrying pairs canvassed in *Pursuits of Happiness*[28] arrive at such an achievement, and it is – sometimes – a genuine possibility of significance for us.

But then too a certain avoidance – what Cavell, following Emerson, calls "aversiveness" or "daring to say"[29] – is also possible and sometimes necessary. "Emerson calls the mode of uncreated life," in which we are dominated by a fallen social world and seem to ourselves not to be authors of our lives, " 'conformity.' . . . Each of the modern prophets [– Cavell lists

Mill, Nietzsche, Marx, and Freud as well as Emerson –] seems to have been driven to find some way of characterizing the threat to individual existence, to individuation, posed by the life to which their society is bringing itself."[30] In the face of such threats, there are times to be "the one who goes first"[31] to refigure what the ordinary might better be. In either case, in moments of either acknowledgment or avoidance on the path of thinking,

> [w]hat I require is a convening of my culture's criteria, in order to confront them with my words and life as I pursue them and as I may imagine them; and at the same time to confront my words and life as I pursue them with the life my culture's words may imagine for me: to confront the culture with itself, along the lines in which it meets in me.
> This seems to me a task that warrants the name of philosophy.[32]

To undertake the task of philosophy is then to attempt to speak, in a phrase of Kant's that Cavell adapts to describe the efforts of both the critic of the arts and the ordinary language philosopher, "with a universal voice."[33] Centrally, this attempt will take the form of making what Cavell calls *a claim of reason*, a claim about what *our criteria are*. One will find oneself saying *what we would say when*: "this is what we call an accident as opposed to a mistake, or this is what we call justice, or love, or knowledge." Such claims of reason are lodged as reminders and vehicles of reorientation – to and on behalf of both others and oneself – when the applications of the concepts expressed by these words are somehow both dimly available and yet attenuated or disputed. As Wittgenstein puts it, "When I think away the normal language-game with the expression ..., then I need a criterion of identity for it."[34] Such utterances are *claims* all at once to self-knowledge (of what one would say when), to community (to what *we* would say when), and to reason (to what it makes sense to say when).[35] "The philosophical appeal to what we say, and the search for our criteria on the basis of which we say what we say, are claims to community. And the claim to community is always a search for the basis upon which it can [be] or has been established. ... The wish and search for community are the wish and search for reason."[36]

Such claims to reason that embody efforts at reorientation of both self and community are distinctive of philosophy and philosophical criticism: the heirs, one might say, of necessary truths as constituting what is distinctive about philosophy. Unlike, however, necessary truths as traditionally conceived – that is, as objects of a fixed intellectual discovery that is always ratifiable by anyone – these claims, for Cavell, can fail in their inherent aim of refiguring rational community. "It may prove to be the case that I am wrong [in making such a claim], that my conviction isolates me from all others, from myself."[37] This is a standing risk for the modernist philosopher – affiliated with the modernist artist's risk of fraudulence in seeking new routes of artistic work[38] – as one who lives in a modern community "in which history and its conventions can no longer be taken for granted,"[39] if they ever quite wholly could.

But such claims can also succeed, as Austin's treatments of accidents versus mistakes and losing control of oneself versus succumbing to temptation perhaps above all demonstrate. We can then find ourselves, with ourselves and one another, possessing our own criteria and knowing what we would say when. The magic of philosophy (and of art) lies in the achievement of this reorientation in practice, where and when it can be achieved, and in acceptance of the thought that here or there it will, always, have to be reachieved again. Without their relation to subjectivity, its standing possibilities of disorientation and inexpressiveness, its standing risks of fraudulence and trust,

> art and the criticism of art [– and, given the analogies, philosophy and the criticism of philosophy –] would not have their special importance nor elicit their own forms of distrust and gratitude. The problem of the critic, as of the artist [– and the philosopher (of a certain kind) –], is not to discount his subjectivity [– and need for new routes of expressiveness and perception –] but to include it; not to overcome it in agreement, but to master it in exemplary ways. Then his work outlasts the fashions and arguments of a particular age. That is the beauty of it.[40]

In a justly famous, perhaps even notorious, passage at the end of the opening section of Chapter 4, "Self-Consciousness," of *The Phenomenology of Spirit*, Hegel writes that we have reached a great "turning point." Our thinking about who and what we are at this point "leaves behind it the colourful show of the sensuous here-and-now and the nightlike void of the supersensible beyond, and steps out into the spiritual daylight of the present."[41] What this turning point turns out to involve, very roughly, is the absorption of essentially epistemological questions by essentially political, historical, artistic, and religious questions. Allowing for the foreignness of the idiom, in Chapters 1, 2, and 3 of the *Phenomenology* the topics are all ones that would be familiar to contemporary analytic epistemologists and philosophers of mind. How do we apprehend particulars? What is the experience of qualia? In what ways might our consciousness of objects be law-governed? Beginning with Chapter 4, however, things are very different.

The topics now center around forms of worldly practice in pursuit of the public satisfaction of desire. What is it to live freely? How might agents achieve recognition? What political institutions, forms of art, and religious conceptions that have been developed historically will help us to live freely and to achieve recognition?

Hegel's argument in moving from Chapter 3 to Chapter 4 is that answering the latter set of questions will settle all the epistemological problems that were raised in the first three chapters, and that nothing else will. But *that* stretch of argument – the treatment of "Force and the Understanding" and then of "life" – is as notoriously obscure and difficult as anything Hegel ever wrote.

So is the absorption of the epistemological by the practical a good idea? Ignoring Hegel's own argument, there are considerations that point both ways, and it is at least possible to understand contemporary analytic philosophy and contemporary Continental philosophy as taking one of these sets of considerations to have decisive force against the other.

In favor of the practical turn, it might be said that our knowing and our epistemological inquiries into the nature of our knowing arise only when we have already managed some cognitive successes and then begun to reflect on the differences between cognitive success and failure. That reflection must involve historical awareness of alternatives, and it must itself be supported by a certain amount of leisure for reflection, over and above a continuous struggle for bare subsistence. Hence knowing and reflection on knowing seem to take place within historical and practical contexts in which people – embodied human agents, with social relations and social interests – are already trying to do something. Much of Continental philosophy since Hegel has been centrally interested in the histories of human cognitive and social practices, taking it for granted that these practices are deeply interrelated. Satisfaction of our aims – including our cognitive aims – if it is to be achieved must be at least in part also a social and practical achievement.

Against the practical turn, it might be said that language, culture, and sociopolitical life – at least in the richly articulated forms in which we humans have them – are all species-specific. Other animals just don't do what we do, linguistically, cognitively, or sociopolitically. If we are the linguistic, cultural, and political animals that we are, this must somehow be because we are the mind/brain endowed animals we are. Surely, further, we have succeeded in knowing some things about our environment by taking in objects in the right way and doing so independently of and often in the face of any political developments. Mathematics and modern scientific knowledge may be evolving and contested, but they are at least more independent of political considerations than are other regions of cultural life. The science and mathematics of China and the United States look a lot more alike than do their paintings or politics or religious rituals. Surely it is reasonable to try to give some culture-independent account of at least our most basic cognitive achievements. Perhaps it is best to leave political philosophy on its own as a set of problems of social organization, without tendentious, quasi-religious essentialisms: political, not metaphysical. Much of contemporary analytic epistemology and philosophy of mind and language has been centrally interested in explaining the roots of culture in given human endowments and in characterizing our cognitive successes by reference to our species-specific powers.

Rough and tendentious though these sketches of argument are, and granting that there are numbers of interesting and important philosophers who are working somehow between them, these two paradigms do map two large and largely divergent routes of current philosophical imagination. For Cavell, by contrast, the argument between these two paradigms is centrally one of those that cannot and must not be won. Our practical and cognitive lives *are* intertwined – it is no accident that one of Cavell's central terms, *acknowledgment*, is a transcription of Hegel's *Anerkennung* – but neither full satisfaction in shared social practices nor full and self-standing absolute knowing of 'the' way things are, free of practical commitment and risk, is possible. In both social and cognitive practice, there are always resistances and remainders, both socially and within oneself. These resistances and remainders will call for and enable departures from what is already done, either cognitively or socially. New regions of interest and ways of pursuing them will emerge out of them, and these will have to be and can (sometimes) be articulated on behalf of a more perfect ordinary. Investigation into how individuals, by drawing on the capacities of the species, manage this feat will always be invited. Yet these regions of interest and ways of pursuing them can establish their sense – for oneself as well as for others – only insofar as they are acknowledged: taken up and lived out, yet also setting up their own resistances and remainders. We live between acknowledgment and avoidance.

To come to discursive consciousness of self in relation to a set of existent and evolving practices, together with their distinctive resistances and remainders, is to participate, in Cavell's formulation, in "a self's judgmental forming of itself, as something to be further possessed *or* to be overcome."[42] One seeks unity with oneself and in relation to others in secure mastery of fully reasonable practice – sometimes through acknowledgment by accepting the ordinary and one's legibility within it; sometimes through departure, daring to say, and gesturing toward an eventual, more perfect ordinary. Yet there is no escape from this seeking into either absolute knowing or absolute freedom.

Hence, in living within this condition – timidly or boldly; gracefully or assertively; cleverly, decently, or badly – "each life is exemplary of all, a parable of each; that is humanity's commonness, which is internal to its endless denials of commonness."[43] To think philosophically about this condition, refusing either its abandonment or its absolute cure, in any region of practice, will be also to participate in it, in one way or another. It will involve aligning one's life and pursuits both with and against other lives and pursuits, as one moves oneself between acknowledgment and avoidance. Central to such alignments will be philosophizing as the work of reading:[44] hence Cavell's endless finding of aspects of himself, and of oppositions to himself, in Plato, Descartes, Emerson, Nietzsche, Luther, Rousseau, Wittgenstein, Poe, Shakespeare, Verdi, Hawks, and Capra. In these thinkers and in their works (and in others, without end), Cavell finds exemplary ways of responding to our "continuing task"[45] of finding and enacting our freedom, of "guiding the soul, or self, [together with its practices] from self-imprisonment toward the light or the instinct of freedom."[46] Such findings and enactments, or such routes of self-creation, imply that in taking them up we both could and "would have to accept responsibility for ourselves, in particular have to consent to our present state as something we desire, or anyway desire more than we desire change,"[47] if we are to find satisfaction within them. This possibility and burden might, Cavell notes, further drive one mad, perhaps into Othello's or Lear's region of avoidance and of the refusal of legibility: anything but to have to consent again, and yet again, to the ordinary as it stands. Or this possibility and burden might, as in the remarryings of the pairs considered in *Pursuits of Happiness*, enable and motivate acknowledgment and a certain consent to one's state, where these might further sustain their own reachievement in a fit enough ordinary, experienced as these paired individuals' daily wit and romance with one another.

When each life is thus seen as a parable of each, whether exemplary or admonitory, there will be no single perfect way of human life, individual or social, even while possibilities of further perfection make themselves available and haunt us. Hence philosophers' "solutions" to "problems" – whether of knowing or of social life – will present themselves not so much or so centrally as "answers" to be accepted or rejected, but as bound up with available styles of response – all of them partial, some of them exemplary or admonitory – to the condition of the human, styles themselves legible as involving both acknowledgment and avoidance. What would it be to deny that human life and mindedness should be so seen? Is such a denial quite coherently possible? Cavell's articulation of the human would imply that it is not. Through the work of reading, carried out in relation to life, this articulation can sustain itself as encompassing, generous, perceptive, nuanced, and deep, as fitly so as any it is possible to imagine. In this it offers a style of philosophical thinking – the reading of each life as a parable of each – that may well stand comparison with the visions of the human of the analytic and Continental traditions, or of any of the other visionaries upon whom Cavell has touched. One will have to read to see.

The contributors to this volume were asked to address Cavell's work in relation to some more or less standard subfields in philosophy and to some not so standard. Taken in order, they are ethics; the theory of action; the philosophy of mind and language; aesthetics and modernism; Romanticism and German Idealism; American philosophy and the idea of America; Shakespeare; and movies, opera, and the problem of voice. As each contributor is at pains to make clear, however, the sense of what the topic or problem at hand *is* is quite often deeply transfigured by Cavell's handling of it, as that handling draws upon his larger vision of the human. Hence readers of this volume will find essays that begin with sketches of more or less standard problems or readings and then go on to show how in Cavell's hands mindedness, performativity, ethics, aesthetics, poetry, drama, citizenship, and movies inform and draw on one another. The pleasures and insights of following these handlings are in the end the best argument – inseparable from reading, from criticism, from exemplification, and from invitation – on behalf of Cavell's account of the human.

Notes

1. Stanley Cavell, "Knowing and Acknowledging," in his *Must We Mean What We Say?* (New York: Charles Scribner's Sons, 1969), p. 240.
2. Stanley Cavell, *This New Yet Unapproachable America: Lectures After Emerson After Wittgenstein* (Albuquerque, NM: Living Batch Press, 1989), p. 55.
3. Stanley Cavell, *A Pitch of Philosophy: Autobiographical Exercises* (Cambridge, MA: Harvard University Press, 1994), p. 22.
4. Cavell, *This New Yet Unapproachable America*, p. 46.
5. Ibid.
6. Ibid., p. 37.

12 RICHARD ELDRIDGE

7. Cavell's sense of the perennial availability and necessity of movements of both departure and return might usefully be compared to Geoffrey Hartman's reading of Romanticism as involving alternating moments of apocalypse (the unbinding of creative imagination) and *akedah* (rebinding to earth and the common). See Geoffrey Hartman, *Wordsworth's Poetry, 1787–1814*, 2nd ed. (New Haven, CT: Yale University Press, 1964, 1971), esp. pp. ix–xx, 225–42. See also Richard Eldridge, "Internal Transcendentalism: Wordsworth and 'A New Condition of Philosophy,'" in his *The Persistence of Romanticism* (Cambridge: Cambridge University Press, 2001), esp. pp. 107–13.

8. Dieter Henrich, "Hölderlin in Jena," trans. Taylor Carman, in his *The Course of Remembrance and Other Essays on Hölderlin*, ed. Eckart Förster (Stanford, CA: Stanford University Press, 1997), p. 112, emphasis added. Eldridge develops a comparison between Hölderlin and Cavell along these lines in "Cavell and Hölderlin on Human Immigrancy," in *The Persistence of Romanticism*, pp. 229–45.

9. Cavell, *The Claim of Reason: Wittgenstein, Skepticism, Morality, and Tragedy* (New York: Oxford University Press, 1979), p. 140.

10. Ibid., p. 83.

11. Ibid., p. 351.

12. Ibid., p. 344.

13. Ibid., p. 93.

14. Stephen Mulhall, *Stanley Cavell: Philosophy's Recounting of the Ordinary* (Oxford: Clarendon Press, 1994), p. 68.

15. See Stanley Cavell, *Conditions Handsome and Unhandsome: The Constitution of Emersonian Perfectionism* (Chicago: University of Chicago Press, 1990), pp. 83, 92.

16. Cavell, *The Claim of Reason*, p. 44.

17. Cavell, *This New Yet Unapproachable America*, p. 57.

18. Cavell, *The Claim of Reason*, p. 207.

19. Stanley Cavell, "Being Odd, Getting Even," in his *In Quest of the Ordinary: Lines of Skepticism and Romanticism* (Chicago: University of Chicago Press, 1988), p. 135.

20. Cavell, "An Interview with Stanley Cavell," conducted by James Conant, in *The Senses of Stanley Cavell*, ed. Richard Fleming and Michael Payne [*Bucknell Review* 32 (1)] (Cranbury, NJ: Associated University Presses, 1989), p. 50.

21. Martin Heidegger, "The Origin of the Work of Art," trans. Albert Hofstadter, in his *Poetry, Language, Thought* (New York: Harper and Row, 1971), p. 54.

22. Cavell, "The Uncanniness of the Ordinary, in *In Quest of the Ordinary*, p. 154.

23. Stanley Cavell, "The Politics of Interpretation (Politics as Opposed to What?), in his *Themes Out of School: Effects and Causes* (San Francisco: North Point Press, 1984), p. 34.

24. Cavell, *A Pitch of Philosophy*, p. 47.

25. Cavell, "Being Odd, Getting Even," p. 114.

26. Ludwig Wittgenstein, *On Certainty*, ed. G. E. M. Anscombe and G. H. Von Wright, trans. Denis Paul and G. E. M. Anscombe (Oxford: Basil Blackwell, 1969), §378, p. 49e.

27. Cavell, "Being Odd, Getting Even," p. 114.

28. Stanley Cavell, *Pursuits of Happiness: The Hollywood Comedy of Remarriage* (Cambridge, MA: Harvard University Press, 1981).

29. See Cavell, "Being Odd, Getting Even," p. 112.

30. Ibid., p. 111.

31. Ibid., p. 119.

32. Cavell, *The Claim of Reason*, p. 125.

33. Immanuel Kant, *The Critique of Judgment*, trans. J. C. Meredith (Oxford: Oxford University Press, 1928), p. 56. Cf. Cavell, "Aesthetic Problems of Modern Philosophy," in *Must We Mean What We Say?*, p. 94; and Richard Eldridge, "Philosophy and the Achievement of Community: Rorty, Cavell, and Criticism," *Metaphilosophy* 14 (April 1983), pp. 107–25, at p. 121 n.13.

34. Wittgenstein, *Philosophical Investigations*, 3d ed. (New York: Macmillan, 1953, 1958), §288, p. 99, my translation.

35. See Richard Eldridge, "The Normal and the Normative: Wittgenstein's Legacy, Kripke, and Cavell," *Philosophy and Phenomenological Research* 46 (June 1986), pp. 555–75, at pp. 570–75; and Richard Eldridge, *Leading a Human Life: Wittgenstein, Intentionality, and Romanticism* (Chicago: University of Chicago Press, 1997), pp. 107–8.

36. Cavell, *The Claim of Reason*, p. 20.

37. Ibid.

38. See Cavell, "Music Discomposed," in *Must We Mean What We Say?*, pp. 188–9: "the dangers of fraudulence, and of trust, are essential to the experience of [modern] art," and "modernism only makes explicit and bare what has always been true of art."

39. Cavell, "Foreward: An Audience for Philosophy," in *Must We Mean What We Say?*, p. xxii.

40. Cavell, "Aesthetic Problems of Modern Philosophy," p. 94.

41. G. W. F. Hegel, *The Phenomology of Spirit*, trans. A. V. Miller (Oxford: Clarendon Press, 1977), para. 177, pp. 110–11.

42. Cavell, *A Pitch of Philosophy*, p. 150; emphasis added. Compare also Stanley Cavell, *The Senses of Walden* (New York: Viking, 1972), pp. 107–8: "Our first resolve should be towards the nextness of the self to the self; it is the capacity not to deny either of its positions or attitudes – that it is the watchman or guardian of itself; and hence demands of itself transparence, settling, clearing, constancy; and that it is the workman, whose eye cannot see to the end of its labours, but whose answerability is endless for the constructions in which it houses itself. The answerability of the self to itself is its possibility of awakening."

43. Cavell, *A Pitch of Philosophy*, p. 11.

44. Cf. Cavell, "The Philosopher in American Life," in *In Quest of the Ordinary*, pp. 14–15; and Timothy Gould, *Hearing Things: Voice and Method in the Writing of Stanley Cavell* (Chicago: University of Chicago Press, 1998), esp. Chapter 4, "The Model of Reading."

45. Cavell, "Being Odd, Getting Even," p. 111; cf. Eldridge, " 'A Continuing Task:' Cavell and the Truth of Skepticism," in *The Persistence of Romanticism*.

46. Cavell, *A Pitch of Philosophy*, p. 4.

47. Cavell, *The Claim of Reason*, p. 465.

2 | Stanley Cavell and Ethics
STANLEY BATES

INTRODUCTION

Academic philosophy in the twentieth century has become comfortable with a compartmentalized conception of philosophy. Most members of philosophy departments in American universities consider themselves to be specialists in, for example, philosophy of language, or philosophy of mind, or philosophy of science or ethics or aesthetics, or in some period of the history of philosophy, and this is, mostly, a good thing. It permits a detailed mastery of a limited, often technical, body of work, to which one might reasonably aspire to make a small contribution in a sophisticated way. Given the proliferation of the philosophical literature in all fields, and given the need in many specialized areas to master some *other* academic field (contemporary physics, neuroscience, computer science, economics, art history), this all makes good sense. This is what Richard Rorty calls the conception of philosophy as a *Fach* – a specialized discipline that masters a particular body of knowledge. No wonder that it has been difficult for academic philosophy to assimilate the work of Stanley Cavell. On the one hand, Cavell is widely read, admired, and honored by the philosophical profession. He has received its highest marks of professional recognition: selection to deliver the Carus Lectures, the presidency of the Eastern Division of the American Philosophical Association, a MacArthur Fellowship. On the other hand, for many academic philosophers he represents a kind of stumbling block. They don't know how to fit him into the standard pictures of twentieth-century analytical and Continental philosophy. Cavell has perhaps been more influential in literary theory, American studies, and film studies than he has been in academic philosophy. In this chapter, I want to undertake a study of the relationship of Stanley Cavell's work to ethics – ethics conceived both as a subdiscipline of academic philosophy and also, more broadly, as philosophical reflection on how to live a human life. I present these senses of "ethics" not just as my terms of analysis of Cavell, but because I believe that much of his writing directly on the

15

academic literature of ethics thematizes the topic of the relation of that literature to ethics more broadly conceived. Before we can begin an account of the relationship of Cavell to ethics, we shall need some preliminary consideration of both terms of the relationship, and it is to this that I now turn.

Stanley Cavell

I shall begin not with an attempted overview of Cavell's work, but rather with a list of some of the works and topics with which such an overview would have to reckon. Cavell's first book, *Must We Mean What We Say?*, published in 1969, bore on its cover the subtitle *Modern Philosophical Essays in Morality, Religion, Drama, Music and Criticism*, a fair enough characterization of the ten essays on such topics as Wittgenstein, Austin, twentieth-century music, Kierkegaard, and the two masterly "critical" essays – on Beckett's *Endgame* and on *King Lear*.

His next book, *The World Viewed: Reflections on the Ontology of Film*, moved into new territory. The title gives an idea of this territory, but it cannot convey the richness of the content of this work. Cavell's method in this, his first philosophical encounter with film was to start from his own lived experience of the movies and then to test some other influential reflections on film by it. This leads not to abstract theorizing about a "medium" but to a new conception of what the medium of an art is, or can be. In this work, that conception requires a consideration of the genres of film, and Cavell develops a notion of "genre-as-medium." (There is a more systematic account of the concept of genre in "The Fact of Television," reprinted in his *Themes Out of School* [1984].) In his two subsequent books on film, *Pursuits of Happiness* (1981) and *Contesting Tears* (1996), Cavell investigated two "adjacent" genres of Hollywood films of the 1930s and 1940s. I shall return in the last part of this chapter to some discussion of the way in which his handling of these genres intersects with the broad topic of ethics as Cavell conceives it.

Cavell's most single-mindedly "philosophical" book, in terms of the analytical tradition's self-conception of philosophy, is *The Claim of Reason*. The first three of its four parts are a revision of his Harvard doctoral thesis, *The Claim to Rationality*, and present his understanding of Wittgenstein's and Austin's philosophical procedures. The central issues are skepticism (one might say, the threat of skepticism as that threat has been perceived to be internal to the tradition of modern philosophy since Descartes) and the relevance of the work of Wittgenstein and Austin to skepticism.[1] Part IV,

"Skepticism and the Problem of Others: Between Acknowledgment and Avoidance," written considerably later than the rest of the book, carries through this investigation in a somewhat changed voice. I shall look rather closely below at Part III, "Knowledge and the Concept of Morality," since this is one of the central places in all of Cavell's writing where he encounters directly the literature of academic analytical ethical theory.

The other, as yet unmentioned, line of Cavell's philosophical work that will be crucial to our inquiry is his reading of Emerson and Thoreau (which is, therefore, his reading of the possibility of philosophy for America). This began with *The Senses of Walden* (1969), which was published a decade before *The Claim of Reason* but which amplifies a conception already crucially present in the early version of that work – the concept of the "ordinary" and its philosophical relevance. He continued these readings in the enlarged edition of *The Senses of Walden* (1981), and in certain portions of *In Quest of the Ordinary* (1988), *This New Yet Unapproachable America* (1989), and *Conditions Handsome and Unhandsome* (1990). My discussion here will focus on the last of these books, which contains Cavell's Carus Lectures, because it is the other central place where Cavell relates his philosophical view to the literature of academic ethical theory.

I have omitted a number of works and topics from this brief list (for example, Shakespeare and opera), but I hope that the list is sufficient to give some idea of the range of topics dealt with by Cavell. One might infer from such a list simply that the author has many different interests; no doubt in some sense that is true. I would like to enter a modification of that claim here. It seems to me that one could say of Cavell, as Nietzsche writes of himself, "[f]or this alone is fitting for a philosopher. We have no right to *isolated* acts of any kind: we may not make isolated errors or hit upon isolated truths."[2] Cavell's works on these various-seeming topics possess a deep unity – one might say the unity of a life. It is precisely because of this unity that the normally compartmentalized areas of academic philosophy are difficult to align with his work. That difficulty is itself a topic of this chapter. I hope to trace a line of thought from early to late in Cavell's work about ethics in both the narrow and broad senses just mentioned.

Finally, I shall have little to say directly about what might be called Cavell's *style* – the remarkable quality of his writing. Certainly its distance from the norms of academic analytical philosophy has played a role in the difficulty "professional" philosophy has had in receiving Cavell.[3] I hope, however, that what I do write, along with the quotations from Cavell, will bear at least indirectly on the inseparability of "style" and "content" (or of "voicing" and "voiced") in Cavell's writing (just as he emphasizes such an inseparability in his own readings of, e.g., Wittgenstein, Austin, and Emerson).

TWENTIETH-CENTURY ANALYTICAL MORAL PHILOSOPHY

It is difficult now, as the twentieth century begins to slide into philosophical history, to convey the situation of academic analytical ethical theory
in the 1950s. In order to reconstruct that situation (in which Cavell wrote
Part III of *The Claim of Reason*), I need to highlight certain stages of early
twentieth-century analytical ethics.[4] The issue that dominated what had,
by that time, been identified as the main stream of the history of moral theory was the dispute between cognitivism and noncognitivism – an issue that
was about the possibility of having *knowledge* of moral statements or moral
facts or moral principles or definitions of moral terms. Simply to state the
issue in this way is to see that this dispute holds moral philosophy hostage
to epistemology (and later in the century, as we shall see, to philosophy of
language). In this way, ethical theory recapitulated the beginning of modern philosophy itself (in, for example, Descartes), in which the traditional
priority of metaphysics gave way to epistemology. It is difficult now to read
the texts that I shall mention here without the sense that ethical theory had
become a stagnant backwater (or, to vary the metaphor, that it had been
shunted onto a sidetrack that rapidly came to a dead end). And yet these
works could seem exciting, even liberating, to some of their early readers.

The crucial early figure is G. E. Moore. It is difficult for a contemporary reader of Moore's ethical philosophy, especially of *Principia Ethica*,[5]
to understand how it could have been so important both within academic
philosophy and in a wider cultural context.[6] Moore's presence as a teacher,
and as a conversational partner, may have been inspiring. Certainly we have
testimony from those who knew him that it was. However, his writing style,
with its attempted precision through the use of qualification, becomes in-
credibly tedious. As mentioned earlier, it is also the case that early analytic
philosophy, with its emphasis on "meaning," was held hostage to whatever
theory of meaning or reference was available – and these theories now seem
both primitive and outdated. Nonetheless, to Moore's contemporaries his
writing was revelatory. Bertrand Russell claimed that talk about *Principia
Ethica* "dominated ... everything else," and John Maynard Keynes said of
that book that it was "better than Plato."[7] The extravagance of these judgments (and one could add further examples from both within and beyond
Bloomsbury) cries out for explanation. One part of the explanation is surely

that Moore seemed to offer a standard of morality that allowed these young intellectuals and free spirits to reject the values (including the sexual values) of their own time and society. Indeed, it was the last chapter of *Principia Ethica*, "The Ideal," that seemed to have the most resonance for them. In that chapter, after having discussed "Good" (which, for Moore, is an intuited non-natural property), Moore undertakes an account of what *is* good, and articulates a kind of credo for Bloomsbury (identifying the greatest goods as "personal affection" and "aesthetic enjoyments"). Moore's philosophical influence on ethical theory, however, is derived from the earlier parts of his text, particularly his critique of what he calls "naturalistic ethics." That critique is based on Moore's claim that there is something that he calls a "naturalistic fallacy" that would vitiate any attempt to define "good" in naturalistic terms (for example, in terms of human welfare or human desires, or in relation to an essential human nature). Indeed, Moore's argument, were it sound, would vitiate any definition of "good" at all. (I won't attempt to criticize Moore's argument here, though I believe it involves a complex nest of fallacies.) Moore's own theory of "good" (i.e., that it designates an intuited simple non-natural property) looks retrospectively like a desperate attempt to save a "cognitive" status for morality. Historically, it had the effect of clearing the ground for a "noncognitive" analysis of putative moral judgments (or of "moral language"). There were, of course, other moral intuitionists in ethical theory at this time, for example, H. A. Prichard and W. D. Ross; their theories illustrated the traditional difficulty of a strong intuitionism – that philosophers' intuitions about morality clashed. When intuitions did clash, no further argument was possible, and one was left with dogmatism.

If one accepted Moore's critique of naturalism, it might seem that the only alternative to his brand of intuitionism would be some kind of noncognitivism. At any rate, this is what happened historically. What came to be called the "emotive theory" of ethics was first hinted at by C. K. Ogden and I. A. Richards in *The Meaning of Meaning*. However, it was first philosophically grounded on the theory of logical positivism; Rudolph Carnap suggested it, based on his misunderstanding of Wittgenstein's *Tractatus*, as a consequence of the verification principle, which defined logical positivism. However, it was left to A. J. Ayer's *Language, Truth and Logic*[8] to present the implications of the verification principle for ethical theory. This he did in the chapter "Critique of Ethics and Theology." Here are a couple of quotations that will help us to recall the bracing crudity of Ayer's formulation: "We find that ethical philosophy consists simply in saying that ethical concepts are pseudo-concepts and therefore unanalysable," and "we have seen that, as ethical judgments are mere expressions of feeling, there can be no way of determining the validity of any ethical system, and, indeed, no sense in asking whether any such system is true."[9] That these would be the consequences of the verification principle of logical positivism would seem to most reflective thinkers to be the reductio ad absurdam of that principle. But this was not the case for the logical positivists themselves – men in the grip of a theory.

The positivists, following Moore's lead, succeeded for a time in converting ethics into metaethics – an imaginary discipline denoted by a barbarous neologism. Its supposed subject was not "first-order" ethical issues (e.g., what is the best life for humans, what would be the nature of a just society, what are the virtues necessary for the fullest realization of a human life). Rather, it was concerned with "second-order" issues (e.g., what is the "meaning" of "moral" terms, can ethical judgments have truth-value). We have already noted Ayer's suggestion that ethical judgments are "mere expressions of feeling." That this claim is startlingly implausible should have been more apparent to Ayer, since he acknowledged that this expression of feeling depended upon a convention unlike "natural" expressions of feelings such as pain, anger, and boredom.[10] It was left to the American philosopher C. L. Stevenson to attempt to reconcile the radical implications of logical positivism with more commonsense views of morality (and of language).[11] Ayer had been willing to accept, as an implication of his view, that we never in fact do have ethical disagreements. Stevenson attempted to provide an account of ethical language that made room for a kind of ethical disagreement different from a disagreement in belief – what he would christen a "disagreement in attitude" or a "disagreement in interest." Ethical terms had, according to him, an "emotive meaning" (distinguishable from their "descriptive meaning") that could be used to express such disagreements. I won't attempt to say more about Stevenson's theory here, since we shall return to Cavell's discussion of it later. However, one should remark that, despite the attempted concessions to common sense, Stevenson's view was, like Ayer's, a radical noncognitivist view of ethics, grounded on a logical positivist theory of meaning.

By the 1950s, a fairly general rejection of logical positivism had occurred. In part, this developed out of the internal critique that the positivists' program had generated; in part, it was based on the later philosophy of Wittgenstein that was beginning to pass into general knowledge, and on the work of Ryle and Austin as well. It took some time for this undermining of the positivist foundation of the emotive theory to have an effect in ethical theory, but it did. While R. M. Hare, in his influential

The Language of Morals, followed a Stevensonian line in his theory, called "prescriptivism," many other authors attempted to go back to the so-called first-order questions of moral theory.[12] There was a return to a kind of renewed naturalism. This was exemplified in a revived interest in utilitarianism, and an exploration of variant forms of utilitarianism. It was also exemplified in the work of such authors as Philippa Foot.[13] Moreover, the work of the single most important moral and political philosopher of the twentieth century in England and America, John Rawls, began to be published during this period. The most salient common characteristic of all of these post-emotivist ethical theories was that they all refused to accept the positivist way of drawing the cognitive/noncognitive distinction. Hence, a new way of thinking about knowledge, and language, and action, and about what constitutes a self would have to be worked out.

My purpose in giving this brief sketch of the development of analytical ethical theory through the first half of the twentieth century has been to try to establish some sense of what confronted Stanley Cavell in his first extended encounter with this literature, when he was writing the first version of what became *The Claim of Reason*.

THE CLAIM OF REASON, PART III, "KNOWLEDGE AND THE CONCEPT OF MORALITY"

The Claim of Reason was first published in 1979, but in the Foreword to the book Cavell traces out the complex history of its writing. It was to have been a revision of his dissertation, *The Claim to Rationality*, which he submitted to Harvard in 1961. However, as he puts it, "it is no more properly speaking a revision than its predecessor was properly speaking a dissertation."[14] His account of why this is so emphasizes (1) the extensive rearrangement (including the removal of some already-published material) and revision of the material of what was the first part of the dissertation into Part I of the book, and (2) the writing of Part IV of the book. This part, "Skepticism and the Problem of Others," was written much later than most of the rest of the book, and will impress the first-time reader as stylistically distinct from the rest of the book. (Cavell responds to the sometimes-made claim that Part IV is really a different book from the rest of *The Claim of Reason* in a Preface to the 1999 paperback edition.)[15] Cavell recounts that, in the early stages of the long journey to this book, his original plans for a dissertation were upset by his encounter with J. L. Austin's procedures and results, and their implications for philosophical issues. Austin had visited Harvard for a term to give the William James Lectures and a course on excuses. Cavell's developing understanding of Austin's procedures not only was reflected in the title essay of his collection *Must We Mean What We Say?*,[16] but also led to his plan for a dissertation "on the implications of Austin's procedures for moral philosophy – implications, let us say, of the sense that the human voice is being returned to moral assessments of itself."[17] It seems that this plan led to his writing, during the late 1950s, of most of the material that appears as Part III of *The Claim of Reason*. That plan for a dissertation was scrapped for a variety of reasons that Cavell mentions, including his beginning a serious study of Wittgenstein's later philosophy. Cavell writes in the Foreword, "These chapters on morality seem to me the most thesis-bound in this book."[18] Clearly they are, though the irony is that they are bound to a thesis that was never written. Nonetheless, Cavell remained committed to this work – when he published *The Claim to Reason* in 1979 and, presumably, when he wrote the Preface to the new paperback edition published in 1999. These chapters represent his earliest foray into commentary on analytical moral theory that he still uses.[19] Moreover, when he wrote the Foreword to the published chapters, around twenty years after they had been written, he added, "Some of those ideas seem to me worth continuing."[20] It will be part of my argument that he did in fact continue them in his later work. What caught the attention of most readers of *The Claim of Reason* was the interpretation of Wittgenstein's philosophy (the discussion of "criteria," the comparison to Austin, the relating of Wittgenstein's thought to skepticism, and the fantasia on Wittgensteinian themes in Part IV). Part III didn't occasion much comment,[21] though Richard Rorty, in a review generally critical of the "older" parts of the book, wrote of it, "Part III, all by itself, is one of the best books on moral philosophy which has appeared in recent years."[22] I want now to look closely at Cavell's argument and conclusions in this work.

First, it might be useful to coordinate two axes of interpretation of the significance of Part III. The first is the context of the history of twentieth-century analytical moral theory up to the 1950s that I have already sketched – the line from Moore to Stevenson. The second is the context of Cavell's general philosophical project in *The Claim of Reason*. Concerning the first, let us recall the "metaethical" impasse that seemed to have been reached. Perhaps it could be better formulated as a kind of antinomy. On the one hand, one had the cognitivist position of Moore and other intuitionists. This seemed to imply that our moral judgments concerning "good" (or some other "moral" term) ought to agree as much as our empirical judgments about "yellow" – but they didn't. On the other hand, one had the noncognitivist position of the logical positivists and Stevenson.

This metaethical position seemed to be inconsistent with the fundamental assumptions of having and practicing a morality at all. (This latter point was, unpersuasively, denied by Stevenson.) One might put this consequence as follows: if the emotive theory were correct, then a person's use of ethical language would be either an act of bad faith or of alienation, depending on whether he or she did believe that theory or did not. As is usual with an "antinomy," an attempted solution would try to show that both sides assume something (in this case, that these two alternatives are exhaustive) that can be denied.

The other axis of interpretation of Part III is its place in the context of Cavell's overall project in *The Claim of Reason: Wittgenstein, Skepticism, Morality and Tragedy*. The four terms of the subtitle correspond, roughly, to the main topics of the four sections of the book.[23] In the first part, Cavell develops an interpretation of the meaning, and function, of "criteria" for Wittgenstein. This interpretation goes against what was at that time the consensus reading of Wittgenstein, which held that "criteria" were offered by him as a *solution* to the traditional epistemological problem of skepticism. In the second part, Cavell extends this reading into a more general account of the setting of, and the motivation for, traditional epistemology. This part includes an excursus on what he calls "Wittgenstein's Vision of Language." Even this brief characterization is sufficient to show that the problematic of knowledge (or the question of how we are able to learn a language in which we are able so much as to formulate the questions that traditional epistemology asks) is at the center of Cavell's enterprise. Hence, it is no surprise that Part III should be titled "Knowledge and the Concept of Morality." After all, the line of analytical moral theory from Moore to Stevenson had been centrally concerned with the possibility of moral "knowledge" and with "moral language." Cavell had, at this point in his book, laid out an interpretation of Wittgenstein (and Austin) about "knowledge" (though it is clearly not a "theory of knowledge," but rather a diagnosis of what prompted the questions of traditional epistemology); he had also laid out an interpretation of Wittgenstein's vision of language (which, again, is not a "theory of language"). It is not surprising that this would put him in a position to diagnose the assumptions and motivations of that line of analytical ethical theory that had been centrally concerned with knowledge and language. However, there is more that explains the centrality of the discussion of morality in *The Claim of Reason* than this suggests. It might seem from what I have written that Cavell had simply developed views about knowledge and language that he then applied to an independent area of philosophy – moral theory. But, of course, those views of knowledge and language themselves had a "moral" component. When Cavell first mentioned that he had planned to write a dissertation "on the implications of Austin's procedures for moral philosophy," he added, "implications, let us say, of the sense that the human voice is being returned to moral assessments of itself."[24] We can perhaps see an aspect of this kind of assessment when, in a discussion of what philosophy has called "the problem of other minds", he writes:

> In making the knowledge of others a metaphysical difficulty, philosophers deny how real the practical difficulty is of coming to know another person, and how little we can reveal of ourselves to another's gaze, or bear of it. Doubtless such denials are part of the motive which sustains metaphysical difficulties.[25]

The question of whether such a remark is itself "moral" is a particular instance of the general problem that is central throughout Part III – namely, what makes a remark or a judgment or the use of a term "moral?"

I want to briefly acknowledge an important topic regarding Cavell's views on morality that I cannot here explore. (This issue would be particularly pertinent to an exploration of the philosophical influences on his views.) That topic is the relationship of Cavell to pragmatism, particularly to Dewey. Certainly at an earlier stage in his philosophical career this influence was important, but it clearly underwent a sea change after the impact of the work of Austin and of Wittgenstein had registered on him. In an article, titled "Logical Empiricism and Pragmatism in Ethics," coauthored with Alexander Sesonske and first published in 1951, Cavell had taken up the issue of the relationship between Dewey's pragmatism in ethics and the emotive theory, especially Stevenson's version of it.[26] This article attempted to negotiate a rapprochement between a Deweyan cognitivist, empiricist view of ethics and emotivism, though the terms of the proposed settlement seem to me distinctly to favor the pragmatist side. It is not surprising that this early piece is not a part of Cavell's work that he still uses – its tone, style, and content did not survive his encounters with Austin and Wittgenstein. Nonetheless, there are some points raised in this article that bear an affinity to his critique of emotivism in *The Claim of Reason*. What he had learned from Austin, however, was to cast a critical eye on the language, examples, and assumptions that the emotivists used to formulate their views. Let us now turn to the argument about morality that Cavell unfolds in Part III of *The Claim of Reason*. Part III consists of four chapters (9–12), about each of which I have something to say.

Knowledge and the Basis of Morality

What I find to be thematic in Chapter 9 is Cavell's effort to expose, and to make problematic, the assumptions about the nature of knowledge, and of rationality, that underlie intuitionism and emotivism. He begins with two issues that have traditionally raised the issue of the place of reason in ethics: first, the problem of (seemingly) irresolvable ethical disagreement, and second, the problem of the relationship of a person's "rational conviction" in the rightness of an act to that person's acting as morality would require. Cavell writes, "Both of these problems will, I think, lead a moral philosopher to question whether, or to what extent, knowledge can provide a basis for morality."[27] In this chapter, Cavell will concentrate on the former issue and the interpretations of its significance, especially those of W. D. Ross and Stevenson. He considers how it is that a philosopher's conception of ordinary examples of "moral" disagreement can shape, reflect, restrict, or betray a concept of morality itself. Hence, he investigates the way in which both Ross and Stevenson claim to begin with "ordinary" moral beliefs, or with specimens of "ordinary" moral disagreements. Cavell's patient exploration of these examples more than justifies his claim:

> One is . . . perplexed to find, in works purporting to begin from our ordinary moral convictions and conduct, maxims which are not merely 'stilted', but which it is hard, if not impossible, to imagine one moral agent ever using to another . . . and examples whose import about the nature of morality is unclear, and indeed whose very relevance to morality is questionable.[28]

The lesson that Stevenson draws from his examples is, of course, that moral arguments are incapable of rational settlement. Cavell challenges what he sees as the underlying assumptions of the drawing of this lesson. The assumptions challenged are that the rationality of an argument depends upon its leading to a conclusion "which all must accept," and that the goal of all moral arguments is "agreement upon some conclusion."[29] Cavell suggests instead the possibility of an argument reaching a conclusion about which there could be *rational disagreement.* The supposed "failure" of some moral argument to enforce rational agreement might not be a failure at all, though, of course, the hope of agreement is what gives point to the argument. The importance of this point seems to me central to an understanding of Cavell's concern with morality in *The Claim of Reason.* We need fully imagined examples of moral discourse in a recognizably human setting. When we have them, we may find that a claim made by a moral theory that morality *cannot* be rational (because it doesn't exemplify certain

features of what is assumed to be paradigmatically representative of rationality – namely, logic or science) may itself depend upon unjustifiable concepts of rationality and morality (and logic and science).[30] Cavell goes on to
show that the examples chosen by Stevenson to represent "disagreement in
belief" and those that represent "disagreement in attitude" have been carefully preselected to support the claim that some party must be irrational
in the former but that no standard of rationality can apply to the latter. In
opposition to this, Cavell suggests that one of the issues that is relevant
to moral arguments or disagreements is the "competence" of the agents
who engage in them. Contra Stevenson, "competence" can be displayed
in moral argument as well as in scientific or factual argument – hence, the
rationality of the one who disagrees may be on trial in a moral disagreement rather than the rationality of morality.[31] He then makes an indirect
reference to Austin's work on excuses that helps us to locate this idea of
competence. Not surprisingly, "competence" – including the competence
to engage in moral argument – is based on the idea that the meaning of what
we say is not a function of our individual "emotions" or "attitudes" (and
emotions and attitudes are quite different from each other), but is based
instead on our mastery of a common language. Moreover, the mastery of a
common language cannot be explained in the positivist terms that underlie
Stevenson's theory. (Typically, the problem of meaning for positivism is the
problem of how we attach linguistic terms to realities independent of
language – whether sense data or physical objects.) Cavell does not here refer to his reading of Wittgenstein's vision of language. Indeed, this chapter
may have been written before he worked out that reading. Nonetheless,
the relevance of Wittgenstein's antipositivist vision of language is clear. (It
is also the case that Cavell's uneasiness with the logical positivists' way of
contrasting morality and science was partly based on his discussions of the
developing view of the philosophy of science of Thomas Kuhn.)[32]

Cavell goes on to contrast the role of appeals to ordinary language in
the criticism of moral theory with the role of such appeals in the criticism
of traditional epistemology. Since I haven't discussed the latter here, I won't
say much about it. However, I do want to say something about his conclusion here, because it is vital for seeing the connection of this early discussion
of morality with his later work. After discussing some appeals to "ordinary"
examples, he writes, "What is at stake in such examples as we've so far noticed is not the validity of morality as a whole, but the nature or quality of
our relationship to one another."[33] This is because in each of the kinds of
cases Stevenson presents, when they are more fully imagined and contextualized, what is at issue in the disagreement becomes specific. Nonetheless,

Cavell goes on, "There are conflicts which can throw morality as a whole into question. . . ." His examples of philosophers who have claimed this are telling. "This is what Kierkegaard meant by the 'teleological suspension of the ethical', and what Nietzsche meant by defining a position 'beyond good and evil'."[34] The crucial claim being made here is that morality can be seen as *limited*. Moral *theory* has usually been understood to claim a universal competence for itself to make a *final* assessment of every action; hence, it could seem that any limitation or inapplicability of moral theory would necessarily mean its overall failure. Cavell, however, asserts the possibility of "[a] position whose excellence we cannot deny, taken by persons we are not willing or able to dismiss, but which, *morally*, would have to be called wrong. And this has provided a major theme of modern literature: the salvation of the self through the repudiation of morality."[35]

The last sentence presents a highly suggestive idea that is not further explored in Part III. I quote it here because I believe that it adumbrates the theme of "moral perfectionism," which Cavell takes up in his later writing and which I shall discuss later. Certainly his citation of Kierkegaard and Nietzsche as proponents of this view of morality as *limited* would be consistent with that reading. Obviously, what one means by "the repudiation of morality" will depend upon what one takes "morality" to be. That is, after all, the theme of Part III for Cavell. One could mean *Moralität* or *Sittlichkeit*. Hegel uses the former term to denote what he believes to be the empty formalism of Kant's categorical imperative; he uses the latter to refer to the concrete actual functioning morality of a particular society over time. (Famously, Hegel analyzes the inherent instability of the stage of Spirit that he calls "Morality" in the *Phenomenology of Spirit*.)[36] Without attempting a reading of Hegel here, one might say that moral *theory* inevitably moves toward *Moralität* in its formulation of general or universal principles that it sees as underlying the particularity of *Sittlichkeit*, but in leaving behind the specific history and the specific social institutions of a society it creates the possibility of being viewed as limited.[37] Of course, moral theory itself becomes a social practice in certain situations, though perhaps one without relevance outside of itself. When Cavell discusses the "moralization of morality" – that is, the tendency of moral theory to claim that it necessarily must be the final judgment on every action – he writes that "[s]uch a conception has done to moral philosophy and to the concept of morality what the events of the modern world have often done to the moral life itself: made it a matter of academic questions."[38]

We are now familiar with a whole group of contemporary moral and political philosophers who have held that "moral theory" is limited in various ways.[39] The situation was quite different in the late 1950s, when Cavell wrote:

> Morality must leave itself open to repudiation; it provides *one* possibility of settling conflict, a way of encompassing conflict which allows the continuance of personal relationships against the hard and apparently inevitable fact of misunderstanding, mutually incompatible wishes, commitments, loyalties, interests and needs. . . . Other ways of settling or encompassing conflict are provided by politics, religion, love and forgiveness, rebellion and withdrawal. . . . We do not have to agree with one another in order to live in the same moral world, but we do have to know and respect one another's differences. And *what* we can respect, and how far and how deeply, are not matters of what 'feeling' a 'reason' 'causes' in us.[40]

The claim that morality is open to repudiation is not the same as the claim that just *anybody* can repudiate morality at *any* time for *any* reason. "The question *'Who is to say* what is and isn't moral?' is not rhetorical, but demands an answer from moral theorists."[41] More specifically, Cavell asks, "What makes a statement of fact a moral reason for an action or a judgment?"[42] Cavell actually uses this question to structure the remainder of Part III (Chapters 10–12). He suggests that, by coming to understand the kind of answers that some moral theorists have given to his question, "we would then have given something in the way of a characterization of morality." Hence, he is interested in what he wants to call the "grammatical" properties of moral reasons in a number of contemporary theories. I shall have some brief comments about Chapter 10 and Chapter 12, but I want to concentrate my attention on Chapter 11 – "Rules and Reasons."

An Absence of Morality

This chapter title expresses Cavell's judgment of Stevenson's claim that his own "metaethical" position gives a neutral analysis of "moral" judgments that is consistent with *any* substantive moral position. Cavell comments:

> This principle of Stevenson's can be put this way: *Any* statement about any matter of fact must be considered *morally relevant*, provided only that it is considered likely to be effective. That seem to me as paradoxical an assertion about morality as one is likely to hit upon with the unaided intellect.[43]

It is an interesting aspect of Cavell's writing career that almost always when he analyzes, explicates, or criticizes another author's work he does so from a position of sympathy – extending himself to understand the deep, underlying motivation that has led an author to a philosophical position that Cavell himself will reject. (This is most obviously so in *The Claim of Reason* in his attempt to come to an understanding of "traditional epistemology" in Part II.) However, Cavell's sympathy reaches its limits in his encounter with Stevenson; I think that this is because, in Cavell's judgment, the "emotive theory" of ethics is not only profoundly mistaken philosophically, but also profoundly pernicious morally. It is a symptom of the denial of commitment and responsibility that has become endemic in modern life, and that attempts to present itself as a form of morality. I cannot resist quoting a footnote from Cavell's article "The Availability of Wittgenstein's Later Philosophy." In this footnote, Cavell makes reference to the examples that certain philosophers give of "moral discussions," and I think there is no doubt that he is thinking of his then-unpublished discussion of Stevenson:

> If we asked, "In what kind of world would decision be unrelated to commitment and responsibility?" we might answer, "In a world in which morality had become politicized." It is no secret that this has been happening to our world, and that we are perhaps incapable of what would make it stop happening. That is a personal misfortune of which we all partake. But the pain is made more exquisitely cruel when philosophers describe relations and conversations between persons as they would occur in a totally political world – a world, that is, in which relationships are no longer personal, nor even contractual – and call what goes on between such persons by the good (or bad) name of morality. That concedes our loss to have been not merely morality, but the very concept of morality as well.[44]

This last sentence contains the essence of Cavell's charge against Stevenson in Chapter 10. It is that Stevenson has not produced a theory about *morality* at all. There must be something that a theory of morality is true to. We may call it "our prereflective concept of morality," or "how we use the word 'moral'," or something else, but however we identify it, it will limit what can count as a moral reason. Since Stevenson thinks that anything that might prod another person to do what I approve (or want) can be a "reason," Cavell says, "that is, in essence, why Stevenson's analysis is not of *moral* judgments, why I am saying that his theory is not about morality."[45] Of course, this critique is worked out within a detailed discussion of what counts as a reason in a variety of contexts. I won't try to give an account of this subtle and penetrating discussion, which is rich in examples that are more fully imagined than any of Stevenson's. What it shows is that Stevenson, in his theory and in his examples, has abandoned both the *context* in which something might be said, and any full-bodied notion of the *persons* who are speaking or being addressed (who constitute a part of that context.) Of course, Cavell's argument does not show that any particular version of morality is true or must rationally be accepted (and acted on?) by everyone, nor does it show that the concept of morality must always have application. It shows, rather, what morality would be if it existed, hence what would be illusory if all human interaction were simply attempted manipulation through propaganda (as Stevenson believes).[46] Morality's self-understanding is inconsistent with the emotive theory – hence, the emotive theory, rather than being a "neutral" analysis of morality, would, if generally accepted, bring morality to an end. "One can face the disappearance of justice from the world more easily than an amnesia of the very concept of justice."[47]

Rules and Reasons

This chapter is rather different from the other chapters in Part III of *The Claim of Reason*. It concerns the development of what came to be known as "rule utilitarianism" in the 1950s. This was a part of what I called a renewed naturalism in my earlier sketch of the development of analytic moral philosophy through the 1950s. As such, it represented a return to moral philosophy from the detour of "metaethics," and Cavell shows a great deal of respect for it. Moreover, the work that is the chief object of his commentary and criticism is an early article by John Rawls, "Two Concepts of Rules."[48] (As is now well known, Rawls was never any kind of utilitarian, but in that article he undertook "to defend utilitarianism against those objections which have traditionally been made against it in connection with punishment and the obligation to keep promises," and he claimed that such a defense "strengthens the utilitarian view, regardless of whether that view is completely defensible or not.")[49] Cavell's attitude toward this early work of Rawls is quite different from his attitude toward Stevenson, for example. He writes of it, "I share what I take to be the main motives of this theory, and I find myself in thorough agreement with its drift." However, he immediately adds, "It is because of that that I want to make as clear as I can just where I think it is mistaken."[50] It is precisely because his own view is so *close* to Rawls's view that he needs to clarify his differences from Rawls. (I don't mean by this remark that either of them are utilitarians. The closeness is about the issue of what determines competence in presenting moral *reasons*.)

This discussion of Rawls is particularly relevant to our later consideration of Cavell's discussion of Moral Perfectionism, for a couple of reasons. First, it is Rawls's *A Theory of Justice* that is the exemplar of moral theory to which Cavell relates his view in *Conditions: Handsome and Unhandsome*. There, as in *The Claim of Reason*, Cavell indicates his deep respect for, and substantial agreement with, Rawls, while at the same time attempting to articulate his differences from him. Second, as we shall see later, Cavell in his reflections on "Two Concepts of Rules" articulates his thoughts on "practices" and "rules" in a way that is almost preparatory for his view of Moral Perfectionism (though, of course, when he wrote these chapters he had not yet developed that view).

In "Two Concepts of Rules," Rawls undertook to explain the logical basis and "importance of the distinction between justifying a practice and justifying a particular action falling under it."[51] He believed that this distinction, properly understood, could provide utilitarianism with a defense against certain standard arguments used to oppose it. These arguments proceed by attempting to show that there are certain actions that seem to be justified on utilitarian grounds but that "we" have strong intuitive convictions are morally wrong. Hence, our moral intuitions about these examples provide a ground for rejecting utilitarianism. (Of course, there is an alternative response by some utilitarians, which is to accept that our moral intuitions sometimes clash with the principle of utility but to attempt to give up those intuitions in favor of the principle.) The examples that Rawls discusses are cases of promising and punishment. It might seem that the principle of utility would imply that there is always a morally acceptable reason to break a promise when breaking it would yield some utilitarian gain. Similarly, it might seem that there could be cases in which it is morally justifiable, on utilitarian grounds, to punish an innocent person. Rawls's strategy, of course, is to deploy the distinction between justifying a practice and justifying a particular act that falls under the practice in order to reject these putative counterexamples to utilitarianism. He argues that both promising and punishment are "practices." ("Practice," as he uses it, is a technical term "meaning any form of activity specified by a system of rules which defines offices, roles, moves, penalties, defenses, and so on, and which gives the activity its structure. As examples one may think of games and rituals, trials and parliaments.")[52] Further, he maintains that these practices could themselves have a utilitarian justification, while at the same time being *constituted* by rules that (1) would not permit a "merely" utilitarian justification for breaking a promise, and (2) would not permit the punishment of the innocent. Such rules (which he calls "practice rules") are to be distinguished from "summary" rules, which tally up what experience has shown about the probable utilitarian consequences of certain kinds of actions. The latter are what Mill called "secondary principles."[53] In the course of drawing this distinction, Rawls illustrates it by discussing its application in games, specifically in the game of baseball.[54] All of this is well known about this famous article. What is not so well known is Cavell's critique of it.

Cavell writes, "I shall argue, against the view under consideration, that promising is not sensibly characterized as an institution at all...."[55] He does not, of course, deny that promising is a public, linguistic act. That fact implies that no individual promise could (grammatically) be made in the absence of a language that is, in a sense, a social practice. It is Rawls's technical sense of "practice" (quoted earlier) that Cavell denies is applicable to promising. Remember that that sense of "practice" crucially involves the specification of the nature of the practice by rules – and it is these rules that define the offices, roles, defenses, and so forth, of the practice. Here we come to the crux of Cavell's dissatisfaction with Rawls's analysis. Cavell believes that the way in which rules function in Rawlsian "practices" (e.g., games) is precisely unavailable to morality. "Promising," according to Cavell, is on a par with a whole class of social actions. In learning the language of these actions, in mastering their grammar, we must learn such things as that a merely utilitarian excuse for breaking a promise is unacceptable. (Other examples that Cavell gives of actions whose complex grammar must be mastered, but which do not necessarily involve Rawlsian practices, are warning, accusing, forgiving, and comforting.) Rawlsian practices have alternatives, as do games. Justification may be offered for them, and such justification will usually be given in terms of how well they perform some function that could be performed in some other way. The kinds of actions that Cavell is talking about don't seem to have specific alternatives in the same way. (Of course, there are possible alternative linguistic formulations of the speech acts of promising, warning, and so forth, but the acts themselves, though conventional, are based on features of human social life – "forms of life.")[56] Cavell goes on, "This very inexactness in the analogy between games and morality is critically important." He argues that it is an essential feature of competitive games that what counts as a move is *settled* by the game's rules, and the fact that *this* can be known in advance by the participants is what allows there to be officials who can judge when the rules have been violated. In general, this feature is what makes such games possible. He goes on, "That moral conduct cannot be practiced in *that* way, that you cannot become a moral champion in that way, and that no one can settle a moral conflict in the way umpires settle conflicts, is essential to the form of life we call morality."[57] Cavell believes that the "technical" sense of a practice, with its associated emphasis on rules, is not adequate to capture the moral dimension of social phenomena. In learning a language about our conduct (what the words for our actions are, what our actions are) we also learn a language of explanation, justification, excuse, apology, and so forth (i.e., learn to use what Cavell calls *elaboratives*). Failing to master the language of elaboratives, a language that is to be deployed in the defense of, or justification of, or acknowledgment of, or apology for, our actions is equivalent to having failed to master the concept of the action in question. Promising has been a central topic for moral philosophy because (1) it involves an explicit act by which an individual takes on a (moral?) obligation, and (2) it *seems* to have relatively clear rules. Cavell contests the centrality of promising on both counts. He acknowledges that the explicit nature of promises marks them as important, but writes that to take them as "the golden path to commitment is to take our ordinary, non-explicit commitments too lightly."[58] There are many other ways to make or acquire commitments that impute responsibilities to us. Cavell rejects the second of the aforementioned reasons that promising has been thought to be so central to morality because "it makes promises more like legal contracts than they are."[59] He suggests that what Rawls says about promises in this article really is true of *contracts*, which *can* be understood as a Rawlsian "practice." This difference is the difference between morality and legality. Cavell suggests that Rawls's acknowledgement of the variation in the way that people understand the practice (as he calls it) of promising is not a side issue but rather is central to the understanding of promises. Disputes between persons on such understanding may be resolvable, but they may not be – in which case, Cavell says, these persons may not live in the same moral world.

I won't pursue a detailed analysis of this rich and complex chapter here. Cavell goes on to give a typology of four kinds of rules (acknowledging that Rawls had not claimed that his account of rules was exhaustive). I do want to say a bit more about why Cavell is suspicious of a completely generalized conception of rules as definitive of morality (not that he charges Rawls with having such a conception). In his critical discussion of David Pole's *The Later Philosophy of Wittgenstein*, Cavell had occasion to discuss Wittgenstein's account of rules and of "following a rule." I want to quote some of Cavell's interpretation in order to have it available for thinking about the role of "rules" in morality.

> In the various activities which may be said to proceed according to definite rules, the activity is not (and could not be) "everywhere circumscribed by rules." . . .

The concept of a rule does not exhaust the concepts of correctness or justification ("right" and "wrong") and indeed the former concept would have no meaning unless these latter concepts already had....

There is no one set of characteristics...which everything we call "games" shares, hence no characteristic called "being determined by rules." Language has no essence....

We learn and teach words in certain contexts, and then we are expected, and expect others, to be able to project them into further contexts. Nothing insures that this projection will take place (in particular, not the grasping of universals nor the grasping of books of rules), just as nothing insures that we will make, and understand, the same projections. That on the whole we do is a matter of our sharing routes of interest and feeling, modes of response, senses of humor and of significance and of fulfillment, of what is outrageous, of what is similar to what else, what a rebuke, what forgiveness, of when an utterance is an assertion, when an appeal, when an explanation – all the whirl of organism Wittgenstein calls "forms of life." Human speech and activity, sanity and community, rest upon nothing more, but nothing less, than this. It is a vision as simple as it is difficult, and as difficult as it is (and because it is) terrifying.[60]

I hope that this begins to make clear Cavell's uneasiness with the use that some moral theorists wish to make of the concept of a "rule," or of "following a rule." Explaining, or justifying, our actions by reference to a moral rule will work only to the extent that we understand what a rule is, and what following a rule is. A part of Wittgenstein's critique of certain theories of language (and of mathematics) is that they want to explain, or justify, certain behavior by reference to rules, but that the very idea of a rule is unexplored by them and left a mystery. When Wittgenstein attempts to demystify the concept of a rule, by reference to "forms of life," he recognizes that this will feel unsatisfactory to one who had wished to impute "necessity" or "rationality" to that which was to be grounded on rules. We shall have a description rather than a justification. His point, however, is not to undermine, or deconstruct, the notion of "rule" or "morality" or "necessity," but rather to understand such notions. Hence, in reply to his interlocutor's question, "So you are saying that human agreement decides what is true and what is false?," Wittgenstein writes, "It is what human beings *say* that is true and false; and they agree in the *language* they use. That is not agreement in opinions but in form of life." He goes on immediately to add, "If language is to be a means of communication there must be agreement not only in definitions but also (queer as this may sound) in judgments. This seems to abolish logic, but does not do so...."[61]

The task is to understand why this might seem to abolish logic, and why Wittgenstein thinks that it doesn't. I have no room here to attempt an exposition of Parts I and II of *The Claim of Reason*, in which Cavell develops his interpretation of Wittgenstein. I only want to suggest that if we substitute "morality" (understood as *Moralitat*) for "logic" in the last sentence of the Wittgenstein passage just quoted, we begin to approach the position that Cavell is developing in this chapter about "Rules and Reasons." The reason that language's dependence on agreement in judgments among human beings might seem to abolish logic is that "agreement in judgments" may seem to be merely empirical and contingent, whereas logic claims to be nonempirical and necessary. Presumably, Wittgenstein denies that logic is abolished because he believes that the "necessities" of the kind of creatures we are (our "forms of life") are sufficient to ground logic for us. (This is also not to deny that evolutionary biology might provide an explanation of the necessity of agreements in judgments – although presumably evolutionary biology is itself contingent.) This would associate Wittgenstein with a broadly "pragmatic" view of logic (and Cavell's critique of the fact/value distinction that underlies so much of analytical moral theory clearly bears a resemblance to pragmatist views).[62] Similarly, it might seem that morality would be abolished without there being an appeal to rules or principles, where these are conceived to be determinative of morality. To claim that the absence of such rules does not abolish morality is not to deny that there could be moral rules, but rather to say that actual moral rules could not play the theoretical role that traditional moral theory has wanted them to play. They cannot constitute the ultimate level of explanation because they themselves need to be explained.

The Autonomy of Morals

Cavell amplifies this line of thought in the final chapter of Part III, "The Autonomy of Morals." Despite the richness of this chapter, I shall have very little to say about its discussion of the unclarity of the thesis of the autonomy of morals, or about its criticisms of various versions of that thesis. The one theme that I want to mention is Cavell's continuing exploration of the difference between games and morality. It is precisely the difference between the roles that rules play in games and the roles that they can play in morality that is revealing:

> In games, what the other person is doing, the goal he aims for, his way, is clear; what it is you tell him to do is defined; what alternatives he can take

are fixed; what it would mean to say, the grounds upon which you say, that one course is better than another are part of the game; whether he has done it is settled. In morality none of this is so.[63]

This quote emphasizes the connection, obvious enough no doubt, between what Cavell is saying about morality and a view about the philosophy of action. Within the context of a game, what an action is may be specified by the rules. (Of course, one might use a game action to perform some other [nongame] action whose context is outside of the game proper.) In morality, according to Cavell, this is not so. Our actions can seem to have many alternative descriptions, and perhaps more than one such description may be correct.

> What alternatives we can and must take are not fixed, but chosen; and thereby fix us. What is better than what else is not given but must be created in what we care about. Whether we have done what we have undertaken is a matter of how far we can see our responsibilities and see them through.[64]

Throughout the whole of Part III, Cavell has insisted on the complexity of the contexts within which moral discussions are conducted, moral reasons offered, and moral judgments made. Moreover, he has further insisted that understanding those contexts cannot be achieved with a "theory" that is separate and distinct from the way in which we understand human language and action generally. Given his reading of the revolutionary shift in the understanding of language and action proposed by Wittgenstein, it is not surprising that he found the analytical moral theory of his day to have failed to illuminate actual moral issues, or to have mistaken an understanding of a limited area of moral concern for a general moral theory.

MORAL PERFECTIONISM

The topic of moral perfectionism is explored by Cavell most fully and explicitly in *Conditions Handsome and Unhandsome*, subtitled *The Constitution of Emersonian Perfectionism*, and most of my comments will be directed toward that work. A full account of this topic in his work, however, would have to deal with his reconsideration of Thoreau and Emerson, and his work on film. (Fortunately, in *Conditions*, Cavell himself has traced out, or at least pointed to, some of these connections to his other work.) Cavell's work on Thoreau preceded his involvement with Emerson.[65] However, he has returned to Emerson again and again since his first published work on him. He traces part of his involvement with these American thinkers to his earlier interest in the idea of the *ordinary* as he had found it in the work of Austin and Wittgenstein. In repudiating the fairly common reading that both Austin and Wittgenstein are defenders or accepters of ordinary *beliefs*, Cavell writes, "What the ordinary language philosopher is feeling – but I mean to speak just for myself in this – is that our relation to the world's existence is somehow *closer* than the ideas of believing and knowing are made to convey." A bit further on, he adds:

> While I find that this sense of intimacy with existence, or intimacy lost, is fundamental to the experience of what I understand ordinary language philosophy to be, I am for myself convinced that the thinkers who convey this experience best, most directly and most practically, are not such as Austin and Wittgenstein but such as Emerson and Thoreau.[66]

This issue of intimacy with existence extends to those aspects of existence with which moral perfectionism is concerned.

The situation of what I have called analytical moral theory had significantly changed between the time of the writing of Part III of *The Claim of Reason* and the writing of *Conditions Handsome and Unhandsome*. In the latter work, Cavell acknowledges the work of a number of writers who had rejected what had been the mainstream of analytical moral theory in the 1950s.[67] The themes of some of this work had been adumbrated in Part III. He continues, "In the light of such work, the present lectures seem to me, however unpredictably, something of a continuation of the chapters in moral philosophy that constitute Part 3 of *The Claim of Reason*. Those chapters were part of the origin of the dissertation of which *The Claim of Reason* is the development, and were always meant to be continued...."[68] It would be my contention that, however unpredictable these particular lectures might have been, they can be seen very naturally as continuing and developing many of the themes that we have seen in Part III of *The Claim of Reason*.

We must turn to the explication of what Cavell means by "moral perfectionism" and how this relates to the tradition of moral theory. This is an acutely difficult task for at least two reasons. First, moral perfectionism, as Cavell understands it, is not itself a *theory* that can be summarized in a set of characterizing propositions. Indeed, the core of moral perfectionism, as Cavell construes it, is that there is no ultimate principle or rule that covers the whole of what can be of value in human life. (One is reminded of Zarathustra's " 'This is *my* way: where is yours?' – thus I answered those who asked me 'the way.' For *the* way – that does not exist.")[69] The core of the story that mainstream moral theory has told itself for a long time is that the types of contenders for *the* correct moral theory are deontology (usually represented by Kant) and teleology (usually represented by some form of utilitarianism). The long detour of "metaethics" (sketched earlier in the discussion of Moore, Stevenson, et al.) was a departure from this. We have seen Cavell's criticism of that detour – roughly, that it led to the loss of the concept of morality. However, this thought leads him to a consideration of the limitations of moral theory itself as the total articulation of the moral dimension of human life.

The second reason that giving an account of "moral perfectionism" is a difficult task is itself difficult to articulate. At the beginning of this chapter, I distinguished between two senses of ethics: (1) "a subdivision of academic philosophy" and (2) "philosophical reflection on how to live a human life." I suggested then that Cavell's work thematizes the connection between these two senses. In *Conditions*, Cavell writes:

> A definition of what I mean by perfectionism, Emersonian or otherwise, is not in view in what follows. Not only have I no complete list of necessary and sufficient conditions for using the term, but I have no theory in which a definition of perfectionism would play a useful role.[70]

Rather than proposing a definition, Cavell suggests that we think about the interplay among a large number of texts that he then lists.[71] I won't take the space to list the sixty-six texts he mentions – it includes familiar names (such as Plato, Aristotle, Kant, and Mill) from a conventional canon of Western moral philosophy (though the Mill texts mentioned are *On Liberty* and *On the Subjection of Women*, not *Utilitarianism*). However, it also includes many plays, novels, novellas, essays, works of literary criticism, and films. It is not surprising that explicitly narrative texts are central in this interplay from which Cavell takes his paradigm of moral perfectionism to arise. The perspective of moral perfectionism is individual (though that, of course, does not imply that it need be subjective). M. H. Abrams, in his classic study *Natural Supernaturalism*, classified Hegel's *Phenomenology of Mind* as a *Bildungsroman*, comparing it to other Romantic narratives of the development of the self, such as Wordsworth's *Prelude*.[72] It is precisely narratives of the progress of individual selves, or souls, that we should expect to be relevant to the kind of moral perfectionism that concerns Cavell – what he sometimes calls a "secular" perfectionism.[73] Many of the philosophers who are not necessarily thought of as "moral philosophers" but who are relevant to Cavell's inquiry (I'm thinking of figures such as Kierkegaard, Nietzsche, and Sartre) adapt fictional forms involving narrative structures in order to express their views, as did Plato. The possibility of a relationship between narrative fiction and philosophy was something of an embarrassment to some early twentieth-century critical theorists, including figures as different as Collingwood and the practitioners of the New Criticism. Supposedly, literature particularizes and philosophy generalizes; hence, no account of the relationship of their texts can profitably be theorized. It isn't exactly that Cavell has a *theory* about the relationship of philosophy to literature, but the question of that relationship is central to all of his writing.

It is a striking fact that since the latter part of the nineteenth century, when academic philosophy divided itself into subdivisions and the specialty of moral philosophy was created, almost no one who has practiced that specialty has been a "great" philosopher. Since that same time or a bit earlier, almost all the philosophers who have been most significant in helping general readers to understand how to live their lives would not be classified as "moral philosophers." I think of Hegel, Kierkegaard, Emerson, Thoreau, Marx, Nietzsche, Freud, Dewey, Heidegger, Wittgenstein, and Sartre (and, of course, not all of these would be allowed the name "philosopher" by analytical philosophy). These thinkers tend either to produce narrative structures or to reflect on the narrative structure of human existence, not in order to provide a formula, or a template, of human existence but to deny the possibility of such a formula. (Marx might be thought to be an exception to this generalization, but his general refusal to describe fully developed communism could rather be interpreted as an instance of it.)

Here is how Cavell begins to characterize "moral perfectionism" in the Introduction to *Conditions*:

> Perfectionism, as I think of it, is not a competing theory of moral life, but something like a dimension or tradition of the moral life that spans the course of Western thought and concerns what used to be called the state of one's soul, a dimension that places tremendous burdens on personal relationships and on the possibility or necessity of the transforming of oneself and of one's society....[74]

Thus, the works of the thinkers just mentioned are not supposed to share a theory but to participate in a thematics of perfectionism – to be relevant to thinking about the state of one's "soul" or self. Cavell is particularly concerned to develop an understanding of Emersonian perfectionism that does not fall prey to two of the most usual complaints against Emerson and against perfectionism in general. The first is that it is simply antinomian, and therefore antithetical to morality itself. Emerson's famous essay "Self-Reliance," to which Cavell adverts, has often been read in this way, despite Emerson's efforts to counter this objection in the essay itself. Once again, the two senses of "morality" discussed earlier – morality as *Sittlichkeit* and morality as *Moralität* – might be useful. Emerson is certainly averse to *Sittlichkeit* (though not necessarily to the content of its code) in that essay – indeed, that aversion might be said to be the topic of the essay. (To use Kant's vocabulary, what he attacks is heteronomy.) His attitude toward *Moralität* presents a much more difficult issue. Still, it seems fair to say that what Emerson is concerned with throughout has relatively little to do with what we can call the *content* of morality (in either of these senses) and much to do with relationship of the self (or soul) to that content.

The second of the usual objections to perfectionism in general, and to Emerson in particular, that Cavell wishes to counter is that it is, and must be, an elitist view – and, hence, must be inconsistent with democratic aspiration. If the perspective of perfectionism is that of the individual soul, then mustn't it be the case that all that counts for each individual is her or his individual self, and that we can, at most, make aesthetic judgments about the achievement of selfhood by ourselves or others? If value is to be attributed to the highest exemplars of humanity, then what is the role of social and political justice to be? Cavell acknowledges that there are forms of perfectionism (what he calls "false perfectionism")[75] that may be elitist; however, he claims that Emerson's is not. The relationship between Emersonian perfectionism and justice is then for him a crux. This is why the encounter with John Rawls's *A Theory of Justice* is so crucial for him in *Conditions*. He takes Rawls, I think fairly, to have "established the horizon of moral philosophy for the Anglo-American version or tradition of philosophy" since that book's publication.[76] Moreover, Cavell professes admiration for Rawls's project and achievement, which he characterizes, in part, as "establishing a systematic framework for a criticism of constitutional democracy from within."[77] He continues that his own effort to articulate moral perfectionism "builds from my sense of rightness and relief in Rawls's having articulated a concept of justice accounting for the intuition that a democracy must know itself to maintain a state of (because human, imperfect, but), let me say, good enough justice." However, even given this much of an endorsement of Rawls's view, Cavell wants to push against the treatment of perfectionism by Rawls in *A Theory of Justice*.

Rawls considers and rejects what he calls perfectionism as one candidate for a theory of justice. Since Cavell does not hold perfectionism to provide a principle of justice, it might seem that there need be no quarrel between them, and, ultimately, this may be so. However, the issue between them is worth exploring, because it may help us to locate the place of Cavell's moral perfectionism in relation to mainstream moral theory. There are two versions of perfectionism that Rawls rejects. The strong version he interprets as offering a teleological principle in terms of which we could judge the justice of social organization and institutions – "it is the sole principle of a teleological theory directing society to arrange institutions and to define the duties and obligations of individuals so as to maximize the achievement of human excellence in art, science and culture."[78] The "moderate" version simply asserts that perfectionist concerns are to be weighed against other concerns in an intuitionist judgment of justice.[79] (I won't take up Rawls's discussion of the moderate version, which might perhaps be, or be made, consistent with Cavell's position, although the vocabularies they each use would be quite different.)

In his presentation of, and rejection of, the strong version of perfectionism, Rawls quotes a few lines from Nietzsche that he takes to be a formulation of this position.[80] Cavell writes, "My particular fascination with this dismissal is that the passage from Nietzsche is a virtual transcription of Emersonian passages, so that at a certain juncture of Rawls's book there occurs a continuation of American philosophy's repeated dismissal, I sometimes say repression, of the thought of Emerson."[81] Cavell is not saying that the "principle of perfectionism," formulated by Rawls and quoted earlier, is to be *accepted*. Rather, he is claiming that nothing in the perfectionism of Nietzsche (or Emerson) is captured in that formulation.[82] Emersonian perfectionism does not demand some special share of the resources of a society for an identifiable elite. Neither does it reject a claim that our human lives are inevitably social (hence, political) and that because of that we are subject to social and political claims. Recall the line that I quoted earlier from Cavell, where he characterized moral perfectionism as a dimension of moral life that "places tremendous burdens on personal relationships and on the possibility or necessity of the transforming of oneself and of one's society." Moral perfectionism is not about the denial of the significance of others, personally or politically; it is about the dialectic of the self-understanding of a self about itself and its relation to others.

As Cavell acknowledges, his choice of the term perfectionism to characterize Emerson's and Nietzsche's view can be misleading. The idea of an older perfectionism was that there is an ideal state of the soul or the self (or society) that must be sought (an idea that obviously fits well with a religious framework but that doesn't require such a framework). In Cavell's interpretation of Emerson, he specifically disavows such a view: "I assume no role for the idea of a true (or a false) self."[83] In particular, this implies that the attained state of the self is always limited, always imperfect from its own point of view, always capable of being transcended. Hence, one must be careful in interpreting the phrase from Emerson's "History" that Cavell quotes – the "unattained but attainable self."[84] This is not a designation of some specific state to be reached, but a way of characterizing the internal dialectic of a living self – the point of view of every stage of the self. What perfectionism wants is the possibility of self-transformation according to an ideal that is internal to the self's constitution rather than one that comes from without.[85] However, we need to remember that what is "internal" and what comes "from without" are themselves not fixed and permanent categories. If the transfiguration of any particular state of the self is to be possible, then even these categories will be capable of transformation. Of course, part of every state of my self is how I relate to the society that has helped to form me. Cavell is concerned with what Rawls calls "partial compliance" states of society – states in which fully just institutions are not in existence. If, in fact, every state of every society involves less-than-perfect justice, then a question for every individual must be, how committed am I to my society's arrangements, and how complicit am I in its injustices?

> Perfectionism is the dimension of moral thought directed less to restraining the bad than to releasing the good, as from a despair of good (of good and bad in each of us). If there is a perfectionism not only compatible with democracy but necessary to it, it lies not in excusing democracy for its inevitable failures, or looking to rise above them, but in teaching how to respond to those failures, and to one's compromise by them, otherwise than by excuse or withdrawal. To teach this is an essential task in Rawls's criticism of democracy from within.[86]

Thus, as I interpret Cavell's view of Rawls it is not a rejection of Rawls's theory of justice, but rather an appeal for moral thinking to focus on the very areas that Rawls leaves to "intuition." Rawls in Part III of *A Theory of Justice* develops the notion of "goodness as rationality" and talks about the individual perspective of developing a "rational plan of life." Of course, any such plan, as he recognizes, must ultimately start from the actual state (for example, the actual desires) of a particular individual, though Rawls also recognizes that desires themselves are not fixed but rather transformable. Interestingly, in *Political Liberalism*, he recharacterizes his project.[87] There he explicitly offers his theory of justice (which is unchanged) as a proposal about a political conception of justice, and *not* as a part of a "comprehensive view," which is the term he uses for the kind of larger theory, with its account of goodness and political stability, that he had earlier presented. Cavell is interested in the dimension of moral life that must be lived by an individual within a political setting, a life that a "good enough" state of political justice makes possible, but that is not, and cannot be, determined by rules.

All of this I must leave at this relatively abstract level of description. To grasp Cavell's use of "perfectionism" fully one must engage with his own readings of a variety of narrative texts. His account of Plato's *Republic* as a perfectionist text is a brief masterpiece of insight.[88] His essays on Beckett and Shakespeare, for example, are works of moral philosophy, in the broad sense of "moral" that I have been discussing.[89] Both of his books on film genres – *Pursuits of Happiness*, on what he calls "the Hollywood comedy of remarriage," and *Contesting Tears*, on "the Melodrama of the Unknown Woman" – are not only explorations of artistic genres of a major art, but also explorations of narrative structures that are illuminated by concentration on their perfectionist dimension. These structures do not provide us with rules, or even examples to emulate, but rather with exemplars of wit, courage, cowardice, grace, skepticism, hope, success, and failure. They don't answer our questions about how to live our lives, but they do give us means by which we can think about these issues. Nietzsche modestly entitled his autobiography *Ecce Homo*, and he subtitled it *How One Becomes What One Is*, which captures a central theme in his thought – the relationship of being and becoming. In *The Will to Power*, he wrote, "To impose upon becoming the character of being – that is the supreme will to power."[90] This has long been a project of metaphysics, and, one might say, of moral theory, conceived as a comprehensive and final account of morality. Cavell, in his account of Emersonian perfectionism, like Nietzsche, tries to bring us back to thinking about becoming.

Notes

1. See Stanley Bates, "Skepticism and the Interpretation of Wittgenstein," in Ted Cohen, Paul Guyer, and Hilary Putnam, eds., *Pursuits of Reason* (Lubbock: Texas Tech University Press, 1993).

2. Friedrich Nietzsche, *On the Genealogy of Morals*, Preface, sect. 2, in Walter Kaufmann, ed., *Basic Writings of Nietzsche* (New York: Modern Library, 1968), p. 452.

3. Fortunately, there has recently been published a remarkable book by Timothy Gould – *Hearing Voices* (Chicago: University of Chicago Press, 1998) – which treats this and related issues extremely well.

4. For convenience, I shall use the phrase "ethical theory" henceforth in this chapter as equivalent to "twentieth-century analytical ethical theory." Other philosophical movements will be referred to by appropriate particular names.

5. G. E. Moore, *Principia Ethica* (Cambridge: Cambridge University Press, 1960).

6. See Stanley Bates, "G. E. Moore and Intrinsic Value," *The Personalist* (Spring 1973), pp. 163–70.

7. Both bits of autobiographical reminiscence were quoted on the back cover of the paperback edition (Cambridge: Cambridge University Press, 1960).

8. A. J. Ayer, *Language, Truth and Logic* (London: Victor Gollancz Ltd., 1936).

9. Ibid., p. 168.

10. Ibid., p. 159.

11. Stevenson's version of the emotive theory of ethics was put forward in a series of influential articles that he started to publish in the late 1930s and that are collected in the book *Facts and Values* (New Haven, CT: Yale University Press, 1963) and in his book *Ethics and Language* (New Haven, CT: Yale University Press, 1944). In the latter, he gives his own account of his relationship to Ayer and Carnap, pp. 265–8.

12. R. M. Hare, *The Language of Morals* (Oxford: Oxford University Press, 1952). To get a sense of the emerging consensus view of the history of analytical ethical theory in the first half of the twentieth century, it would be useful to look at Mary Warnock, *Ethics Since 1900* (Oxford: Oxford University Press, 1960) and Geoffrey Warnock, *Contemporary Moral Theory* (New York: St. Martin's Press, 1967).

13. For Foot's critique of emotivism and prescriptivism, and for her developing moral views, see her important articles reprinted in Philippa Foot, *Virtues and Vices* (Los Angeles: University of California Press, 1978). For her own organization of twentieth century analytical ethical theory, see her anthology, Philippa Foot, ed., *Theories of Ethics* (Oxford: Oxford University Press, 1967).

14. Stanley Cavell, *The Claim of Reason* (Oxford: Oxford University Press, 1999) p. xv.

15. Ibid., p. xii.

16. Stanley Cavell, *Must We Mean What We Say?* (Cambridge: Cambridge University Press, 1999).

17. Cavell, *The Claim of Reason*, pp. xv–xvi.

18. Ibid., p. xvi.

19. There will be a reference later to an earlier published work of which Cavell was the coauthor.

20. Ibid., p. xvi.

21. I myself essentially ignored it in Stanley Bates, "Stanley Cavell's *The Claim of Reason*: A Critical Discussion," *Philosophy and Literature* (Fall, 1980), pp. 266–73.

22. Richard Rorty, *Consequences of Pragmatism* (Minneapolis: University of Minnesota Press, 1982), p. 185.

23. The other sections of *The Claim of Reason* will receive more detailed investigation elsewhere in this volume.

24. Cavell, *The Claim of Reason*, p. xvi.

25. Ibid., p. 90.

26. Stanley Cavell and Alexander Sesonske, "Logical Empiricism and Pragmatism in Ethics," *Journal of Philosophy*, 48 (1951), pp. 5–17, reprinted in Amelie Rorty, ed., *Pragmatic Philosophy* (New York: Doubleday, 1966). This is the article to which reference was made in note 17.

27. Cavell, *The Claim of Reason*, p. 248.

28. Ibid., p. 252.

29. Ibid., p. 254.

30. For a related argument against the dominant analytical moral views of this period, but from a quite different point of view, see Alan Gewirth, "Positive 'Ethics' and Normative 'Science'," *Philosophical Review* 69 (1960), pp. 311–30.

31. Cavell, *The Claim of Reason*, p. 263.

32. He refers to Kuhn's *The Structure of Scientific Revolutions* (Chicago: University of Chicago Press, 1962) in passing on page 264, and to his conversations with Kuhn in the Foreword, p. xxiii.

33. Cavell, *The Claim of Reason*, p. 268.

34. Ibid.

35. Ibid., pp. 268–9.

36. G. W. F. Hegel, *Phenomenology of Spirit* (Oxford: Oxford University Press, 1977), sects. 596–671, pp. 364–409.

37. For an excellent discussion of the complexity of reconciling certain central features of Kantian morality with some of Hegel's insights, see Chapter 2, "The Phenomenology of Moral Consciousness: Principle and Context, Kant and Hegel," in Richard Eldridge, *On Moral Personhood* (Chicago: University of Chicago Press, 1989).

38. Cavell, *The Claim of Reason*, p. 269.

39. I'm thinking of such philosophers as Bernard Williams, Alasdair MacIntyre, Martha Nussbaum, the so-called communitarians in political theory, and – in some of his moods – Richard Rorty. I'm not, of course, implying any general agreement among this disparate group about "moral theory." Richard Eldridge's book mentioned in note 36 is also a good place to investigate these issues.

40. Cavell, *The Claim of Reason*, p. 269.

41. Ibid., pp. 269–70.

42. Ibid., p. 270.

43. Ibid., p. 274.

44. Stanley Cavell, *Must We Mean What We Say?* (Cambridge: Cambridge University Press, 1999), p. 54.

45. Cavell, *The Claim of Reason*, p. 283.

46. Compare this to what Kant writes at the end of the second section of the *Grundlegung*, after he has developed the various formulations of the categorical imperative. "Furthermore, we have not here asserted the truth of this proposition, much less professed to have within our power a proof of it. We simply . . . develop[ed] the universally accepted concept of morality. . . . Whoever, then, holds morality to be something real, and not a chimerical idea without any truth,

must also admit the principle here put forward." Immanuel Kant, *Grounding for the Metaphysics of Morals*, 3d ed. (Indianapolis: Hackett, 1993), p. 48.

47. Cavell, *The Claim of Reason*, p. 283.

48. John Rawls, "Two Concepts of Rules," *The Philosophical Review* 64 (1955), pp. 3–32, reprinted in his *Collected Papers* (Cambridge, MA: Harvard University Press, 1999).

49. Rawls, *Collected Papers*, p. 21.

50. Cavell, *The Claim of Reason*, p. 293.

51. Rawls, *Collected Papers*, p. 21.

52. Ibid., p. 20.

53. John Stuart Mill, *Utilitarianism* (Indianapolis: Hackett, 1979), p. 24.

54. Rawls, *Collected Papers*, pp. 37, 38.

55. Cavell, *The Claim of Reason*, p. 293.

56. For a discussion of Cavell's reading of Wittgenstein's idea of "forms of life," see Stanley Bates, "Skepticism and the Interpretation of Wittgenstein," cited in note 1.

57. Cavell, *The Claim of Reason*, p. 296.

58. Ibid., p. 298.

59. Ibid., p. 299.

60. Cavell, *Must We Mean What We Say?*, pp. 49, 50, 52.

61. Ludwig Wittgenstein, *Philosophical Investigations*, 3d ed. (New York: Macmillan, 1969), §§240–41, p. 88e.

62. Of course, this remark depends upon how "broadly" the term 'pragmatism' is construed. If we think of John Dewey as the exemplary pragmatist, the differences between Dewey and Wittgenstein (as Cavell construes him) may be of decisive importance. Cavell gives his own account of what those differences are from his own perspective in *Conditions Handsome and Unhandsome* (Chicago: University of Chicago Press, 1990), pp. 13–16. Thus, to say that the critiques mentioned in the text bear a resemblance is not to say that they are the same.

63. Cavell, *The Claim of Reason*, p. 324.

64. Ibid.

65. In Stanley Cavell, *The Senses of Walden: An Expanded Edition* (San Francisco: North Point Press, 1981), he added two essays on Emerson to the original book. In "Thinking of Emerson," he traces part of his path to his reading of Emerson (including his resistances to Emerson's writing).

66. Cavell, *The Senses of Walden*, pp. 145–6.

67. Cavell, *Conditions*, p. xix.

68. Ibid., p. xx.

69. *Thus Spoke Zarathustra*, third part, "On the Spirit of Gravity," in Walter Kaufmann, ed., *The Portable Nietzsche* (New York: Viking Portable Library, 1976), p. 307.

70. Cavell, *Conditions*, p. 4.

71. Ibid., p. 5. Many of the texts listed there are used by Cavell in a course on perfectionism that he has taught at Harvard.

72. M. L Abrams, *Natural Supernaturalism* (New York: Norton, 1971), passim.

73. Cavell, *Conditions*, p. xix. Hence, Cavell's Emersonian perfectionism differs fundamentally from earlier versions of moral perfectionism, for example, the seventeenth and eighteenth century theories discussed in Part II of J. B. Schneewind's *The Invention of Autonomy* (Cambridge: Cambridge University Press, 1998).

74. Ibid., p. 2.

75. Ibid., pp. 16, 18.

76. Ibid., p. 3.

77. Ibid.

78. John Rawls, *A Theory of Justice* (Cambridge, MA: Harvard University Press, 1971), p. 325.

79. Ibid.

80. Ibid.

81. Cavell, *Conditions*, p. 4.

82. Cavell discusses the Nietzsche passage in question on pp. 48ff. in *Conditions*. The passage comes from section 6 of "Schopenhauer as Educator," the third of the four *Untimely Meditations*. That whole section, or indeed the whole of that meditation, should be read to understand the perfectionist setting of the quote.

83. Ibid., p. xxxiv.

84. Ibid., p. 8.

85. I owe this phrase to Timothy Gould.

86. Cavell, *Conditions*, p. 18.

87. John Rawls, *Political Liberalism* (New York: Columbia University Press, 1993), esp. the Introduction.

88. Cavell, *Conditions*, pp. 6–8.

89. Both are in *Must We Mean What We Say?*

90. Friedrich Nietzsche, *The Will to Power* (New York: Random House, 1967), p. 330.

3 The Names of Action

TIMOTHY GOULD

We take some *very simple action*, like shoving a stone, usually as done by and viewed by oneself, and use *this*, with the features distinguishable in it, as our model in terms of which to talk about other actions: and we continue to do so, scarcely realizing it even when these other actions are pretty remote and perhaps much more interesting in their own right than the acts originally used in constructing the model ever were, and even when the model is really distorting the facts rather than helping us observe them.

J. L. Austin, "A Plea for Excuses"

And thus the native hue of resolution
Is sicklied over with the pale cast of thought,
And enterprises of great pith and moment
With this regard their currents turn awry,
And lose the name of action.

Hamlet, III.i.86–90

Almost anywhere you turn in the work of Stanley Cavell you will encounter some aspect of the problem of human action. What is it for human beings to act? What is it for us to be active rather than, for instance, passive or inactive? From Cavell's early defense of J. L. Austin to his latest remarks about Emerson and Nietzsche, Fred Astaire and Henry James, or *Middlemarch* and *Macbeth*, Cavell's investigations are twined around his interest in our capacity for being the origin of our actions and for bearing up under our vulnerability to accidents and inadvertancies and, indeed in our ability to make something out of these very inadvertancies and happenstances.

Indeed, Cavell is careful to tell us that his interest in the concept of action existed before his encounter with Austin, and his interest surfaces in a wide range of discussions that follow that encounter. We find it at work already in the later chapters of his first book, *Must We Mean What We Say?* – for instance, in the discussion of improvisation and chance in "Music

Discomposed." That essay was written in roughly the same moment as Cavell's essay on Beckett's *Endgame*, which contains a discussion of *Hamlet* and leads directly to his discussion of *King Lear*. From then on, we are never very far from the question of the limits of action in accomplishing what we most desire or in staving off what we most fear or, indeed, in expressing the most active and essential portion of the suffering human being.

Cavell's accounts of the movies are haunted by the beauty of successful human action and the survivability of its failures. From the beginning, there are the figures of Chaplin and Keaton, whose faces and bodies and gestures must bear up under the burden of human expressiveness, and under their perfect absorption in their passion or in their activity. Allowing ourselves to be absorbed in their slipping and sliding around, Cavell's attentions suggest, can teach us something about the philosopher's certainty that the basic question to be answered is what is *the* difference between a full-fledged human action and mere human movements. Cavell asks us to consider whether it is really true that Chaplin's desperate flailings on roller skates, *after* he becomes aware of the second-story abyss that he is barely evading, have less to tell us about the humanness of activity than his perfected glidings prior to that awareness. And on what criteria do we base this conviction of the relative importance of our questions and investigations? The lesson is not so much that we *ought* to be unconscious of the conditions of our action. It is rather, first of all, that consciousness (and intention and purposiveness and the rest) may interfere with our ability to act; and second, that even without the (obvious) success of our intentions and performances, our movements remain recognizable as human activity.

When Cavell turns to figures such as Bogart or Clift or Brando or Belmondo, expressiveness is discerned to depend on our sense that their power of feeling and hence their capacity for motivation is alive, but hidden from our normal view – as Cavell puts it, a sense of "fires banked." This thought can be seen to correspond to something Cavell says about how the movies as such manage to represent skepticism to us: the audience, there in the dark, at a distance from what we are moved by, "feeling unseen." The suggestion is that the preservation of genuine feeling depends on a willingness to be, at least for a time, unknown, unread: further, that this willingness, which may sometimes feel like a kind of passivity, has now become necessary to the power of effective action in the world.

More than a decade would pass before this version of the question of action and passion (and speech and silence) would ripen into Cavell's explorations of the genre he named "the Melodrama of the Unknown Woman."

There the question becomes focused on the woman – especially in *Gaslight* and the *Letter from an Unknown Woman* – and what will permit her to stop haunting her life and become effectively present in the world. These are not the only movies that come to ask when – and how, and with whom, and to what end – a woman can *act* in the world as it stands – a world dominated not only by male power but by the masculine definitions of action and activity. Such questions are also raised pervasively in the pages of *Contested Tears*.

Cavell's interest in human action took another twist when he encountered Thoreau's *Walden*, with its obsessions about the nature of true labor. Thoreau mingles questions about labor – for example, about hammering and hoeing and measuring – with questions about spending certain passages of your life on your projects within the world. Such questions in turn lead Thoreau to the still more poignant questions of how you are to leave your mark on the world and about how it leaves its mark, or its traces, in you. For Cavell, it becomes inevitable to think of the forms and tropes of labor as so many forms and tropes of writing (and reading).[1]

As Cavell follows Thoreau deeper into these issues, this question about leaving your mark points to a question about what writing is, and about whether, for instance, it is primarily active or primarily passive. It also points to a question about what leaving is, about how we are to let go of our projects and to conclude our labors. That to act effectively is also to let go of action is a way of characterizing Thoreau's reading of the Bhagavad Gita. This is certainly a powerful reading of the Gita's interest in the human confusion of the active and the passive.[2] It is difficult to imagine that we must *learn* how our writing can be a form of leaving the world alone. It might prove to be a useful intermediate step if we could understand how, for example, writing philosophy can be a form of leaving the world alone (as in Wittgenstein's remark at *Philosophical Investigations*, §124). But then one would have to have the prior idea that the first impulse in writing was precisely not to leave the world alone, but to interfere with or alter it in various ways.

The movement from the essays "Must We Mean What We Say?" and "The Availability of the Later Wittgenstein" to *The Senses of Walden* is in part a movement from a conception of the requirement that we learn to leave the world alone to a conception of a requirement that we learn to leave it, period. Action, like writing, like philosophizing in Plato's *Phaedo*, is studying how to die. This is not necessarily easier to accept if one says that we are studying separation and the acceptance of loss.

It should be clear from this expanding range of questions and from the form the questions took after Cavell's early defense of Austin that Cavell's ways of thinking about action will be of precisely no interest at all to those involved in the field of philosophy called "the theory of action." From their point of view, this sort of thing is viewed as at best some kind of literature or, more recently, as some kind of inflated autobiography that could have no possible bearing on what they do when they set out to discover what a human action is.

More immediately, and somewhat more surprisingly, it has apparently proved quite difficult for readers sympathetic to Cavell's projects to bring his concern with action into focus. Perhaps the very range of Cavell's discussions has made them less striking. Moreover, unlike the case of skepticism, this range is not undergirded by the existence of a single place (such as *The Claim of Reason*) where the reader can go to find anything like a comprehensive treatment of the topic of action. In fact, the themes of morality and language also persist from the time of his dissertation – the time of his early work on Austin and Wittgenstein – down through their transformation into *The Claim of Reason*. In both cases, there is something like "Cavell's treatment of language" or "Cavell's treatment of morality" to be taken up and mastered.

The absence of anything like an analogous place where the reader can go to investigate the question of "Cavell on the problem of action" is more than a little daunting. The title essay of *Must We Mean What We Say?* is the closest we have to such a text. Its position as what Cavell invariably calls the first piece of work he still uses makes reasonably compelling its status as a source for this investigation. But the involvement of Cavell's essay in defending J. L. Austin on action and excuses – indeed, its *genesis* as such a defense – makes it difficult to expound to readers not familiar with Austin's "A Plea for Excuses." And though I am suggesting that this defense of Austin continues to be at work in Cavell's other treatments of action, this engagement is not always as visible as it might be.

Nevertheless, the early engagement with Austin's work on action cannot be avoided, either in thinking about action, or – as Cavell keeps insisting – in thinking about what gave him a voice in philosophy. Cavell apprehends the region of philosophy that gave you your voice in philosophy as what continues to give you your voice. At least it must exist in a recognizable intimacy with the origins of your voice. You must learn how to turn back to those sources and those paths – those methods – even as you must keep moving forward in your conviction that you have discovered a new path.

Cavell insists that it was nothing other than the material that went into this first essay that represents the voice that Austin's work allowed him to find. As he puts it in *A Pitch of Philosophy*:

> In practice, however, the moment I felt that something in ordinary language philosophy was giving me a voice in philosophy, I knew that the something was the idea of a return of voice to philosophy, that asking myself what I say when, letting that matter, presented itself as a defiance of philosophy's interest in language, as if what philosophy meant by logic demanded, in the name of rationality, the repression of voice. . . .[3]

If I am right that something about what grants the voice in philosophy continues to grant it – or continues one's relation to that first granting of the voice – then we are in a better position to understand why Cavell keeps returning to that first encounter with Austin (or at least the first one he was willing to go public with).

But then we are confronted with the fact that this idea of having a voice in philosophy has generated no end of confusion in Cavell's readers. The confusion encompasses those who are hostile to the very idea of the voice as a source of significance within philosophy and those who look to Cavell's own empirical voice as, all by itself, constituting the return of philosophy's repressed humanity. I have treated these issues at length in *Hearing Things: Voice and Method in the Writing of Stanley Cavell*,[4] but I want to add three further comments.

(1) Looking back on the fifties and sixties, Cavell is evidently willing to say that this is the voice that was called forth or provoked by Austin's work. But he will also come to say that this is also the very voice that the profession of philosophy keeps trying to foreclose and even to repress. Surely this suggests that Cavell does not imagine that the foreclosure of the voice is the same thing as, let us say, the mistreatment of the person who possesses the voice. (No doubt it is a strain to keep these differences separate in one's reaction to one's profession.)

(2) I want to insist further that Cavell's voice was evidently called for by something about Austin's discussion, not only by something that needed defense but also by something that (at least for Cavell) needed no defense. I will just assert that part of what needed defense was the very idea of method. As Cavell says in "The Availability of the Later Wittgenstein," it is the idea that there are methods for knowing the self (what it does and feels, and hides and reveals) that is the real scandal of Wittgenstein's writing – and presumably to a less insistent degree the scandal of Austin's procedures.

(3) It is not surprising, at least in retrospect, that Cavell was to locate the human voice in response to Austin's account of action, since this account relies so completely on what we *say* about actions (and on how we defend or explain or elaborate the actions we are involved in). Whatever we finally say about the emergence of (his) voice, Cavell's first move was evidently toward the problems of action.

In "Where the Action Is: Stanley Cavell and the Skeptic's Activity,"[5] I pointed explicitly to one of the key issues of action in Cavell's work: the problem of action became attached to, or even submerged in, the problematics of skepticism. In particular, skepticism produces and is in part produced by a certain distance from the world, a distance in which we are to be characterized as powerless to alter the world, or in which our alteration of the world would be irrelevant or contrary to our real need. I am still convinced that this connection to the skeptical sense of our distance from the world is a crucial one for understanding Cavell's various treatments of action. And as I also said in that essay, Cavell seems to have displayed no sense that there was a competing philosopher's problematic of action – or no problematic that would be as rewarding to pursue as the problematic of skepticism.

I am not sure he was right about this. But at any rate, Cavell seems to have felt no such sense of limitation in Austin's work on action, comparable to the limitations that he would expressly address in "Other Minds" and in *Sense and Sensibilia*. Despite some issues that he would come to raise about Austin in *A Pitch of Philosophy* (1994), Cavell continued to stand by Austin's dismantling of the philosopher's concept of action. I will say something about the exception to Cavell's acceptance of Austin's work on action, but for the most part this exception proves the rule.

I want to recapitulate Cavell's version of what I call the negative and positive poles of Austin's "A Plea for Excuses." I will then isolate three strands of Cavell's work on action, each of which provides at least a natural bridge between more visible topics. Beyond that, however, I hope that each of these strands will reflect or illuminate an aspect of human action that is visible to other investigators. This latter hope is not merely a pious wish but a kind of methodological necessity that I have placed on my work, especially, but not solely, in relation to Cavell's. It receives its theoretical elaboration – such as it is – in the latter chapters of *Hearing Things*. But already in "The Plight of the Ordinary,"[6] I was refusing the still-prevalent idea of Cavell (and Wittgenstein) as intuitive geniuses, offering us their ineffable perceptions.

Such an idea of Cavell as shunning argument and method in favor of intuition is primarily the property of those who wish not to have to read his work, perhaps because they don't want to hear what he has to say. Sometimes, however, very similar ideas are found among those who don't want to read Cavell with the critical attention he warrants because they *love* what he has to say. What neither camp wants to have to do is the *work* of reading. (In *Hearing Things*, I characterize this work of reading as a work of reversals: of author into listener and of the reader into the one who is being read.) Reading without the work of reversals becomes an act of pious merger with Cavell's sensitivity – his all-but-inimitable sensitivity to words, to shades of meaning, to music, to images. But it is not an act of philosophical criticism. The goal is to become, one might say, a part of Cavell's biography, where that means more or less consciously that your autobiography as a writer becomes an extension of his. The dismissive critic and the uncritical devotee are made in each other's image, each of them formed apart from the act of reading. Elaborating thematic strands of Cavell's investigations is one way to begin the work of reading.

(1) The first strand I will pursue is the tendency of Cavell's investigations of activity and passivity to replace the concern about the single human action and about what makes it an action (rather than, say, a set of bodily movements; or about what makes an action a voluntary action rather than one done under constraint) with a concern about the sources of human activity and passivity. This tendency alone would have taken him away from the founding questions of the "theory of action." For as I shall be suggesting, that field depends on a fixed sense that what the philosopher of action picks out as "*actions*" can be fairly reliably regarded as something like the basic units of human activity – the events in which human activity is expressed in the world. When Cavell's interest in the active and the passive takes him towards Thoreau, Emerson, Nietzsche, and Freud, his philosophical fate is sealed. The last thing any analytic philosopher wants to hear about is the diagnosis of a problem as the expression of a merely human confusion or illusion. The idea that there is a human wish to cover over the various passivities of the human being with a burst of activity or a round of action is bad enough. The idea that philosophers have connived at that wish, or lived off of it, is in my experience essentially unavailable to the practitioners of the theory of action.

(2) The second strand has to do with what I will call the representative-ness of human action, but also with the relation of action to the activity of those we call "artists." I have in mind some issues and aspects that may in fact seem to clash: (a) that a particular action, to be known as an action, must be

in a sense already familiar; it must not only do what such actions do, it must also do it in the way that such actions do it; it must even, in a sense, *look* like the action that it is; and (b) that certain actions, certain particular actions by particular agents, become representative of human action as such, even, surprisingly, of aspects of action that we hadn't noticed, or acknowledged. A third issue (c) is perhaps too difficult to treat at length here: it stems from the fact that certain kinds of representativeness in human action and activity may arise from persons and places that may be, or may be regarded as, "marginal." The issue needs at least to be mentioned, however, because of its more or less obvious connection to the issue of the making of art as a representative action. This marginality is clearly connected to the ways in which the activity of artists is simultaneously presented as worthwhile, but as isolated from the stream of human conduct. Here is an important link between Cavell's work and Dewey's *Art as Experience*. In this region of his work, Cavell pursues aspects of action that other philosophers might relegate to questions of "performance." Again, this can be seen to emerge out of aspects of Austin's work that did not directly engage in the kinds of controversy that philosophers tend to find productive: I have not seen much in the way of commentary on section 10 of "A Plea for Excuses," which is called "The style of performance."[7] Austin here speaks of the difference between eating your soup *after* deliberation, and eating your soup *with* deliberation: "the style of the performance, slow and unhurried, is understandably called 'deliberate' because each movement *has the typical look* of a deliberate act. . . ." Continuing his career-long effort to disrupt any easy polarization – or fetishization – of inner and outer, Austin continues: "it is scarcely being said that each motion *is* a deliberate act or that he is 'literally' deliberating."[8]

(3) The third strand is perhaps the least visible in Cavell's work, until it emerges quite strikingly in *A Pitch of Philosophy*, in what may be Cavell's most explicit criticism and revision of Austin. Having appreciated more than most the sense in which to say something is, in various ways, to do something, and having appreciated how the doing of something is, in various ways, analogous to the saying of something, Cavell begins to appreciate the disanalogies, and to number the differences. Cavell's sense of how actions are expressions of the human and can sometimes be evaluated as human *utterances* still leaves room for his sense that they are not to be absorbed into some unified field of study, encompassing both doing and saying. There is more than a hint in Cavell's work that it is *saying*, not doing, that penetrates to the heart of the matter, to the "possibilities" of the things that most concern us.

The three strands of Cavell's thinking about action that I have been sketching emerge – I have suggested – out of the negative and positive poles of
Austin's thinking about action. Here is how Austin introduces what I am
calling the negative pole.

> The beginning of sense, not to say wisdom, is to realize that 'doing an ac-
> tion', as used in philosophy, is a highly abstract expression – it is a stand-in
> used in place of any (or almost any?) verb, with a personal subject, in the same
> sort of way that "thing" is a stand-in for any (or when we remember, almost
> any) noun-substantive, and "quality" a stand-in for the adjective. Nobody, to
> be sure, relies on such dummies quite implicitly, quite indefinitely. Yet noto-
> riously it is possible to arrive at, or to derive the idea for, an over-simplified
> metaphysics from the obsession with "things" and their "qualities." In a
> similar way, less commonly recognized in these semi-sophisticated times,
> we fall for the myth of the verb. We treat the expression "doing an action"
> no longer as a stand-in for a verb with a personal subject, as which it has no
> doubt some uses, and might have more if the range of verbs were not left
> unspecified, but as a self-explanatory, ground-level, description, one which
> brings adequately into the open the essential features of everything that
> comes, by simple inspection, under it. We scarcely notice even the most
> patent exceptions or difficulties (is to think something, or to say something,
> or to try to do something, to do an action?).[9]

Most philosophers, if they are aware of Austin at all, are aware of him
primarily as a critic, and as a destructive one at that. The particular mode
of criticism I am citing here is hardly remembered as part of what Austin
has to say. What everyone remembers – what Grice and Searle and others
remind us of – is that Austin said that certain claims about actions are
nonsense (e.g., that all actions are either voluntary or involuntary) and that
certain questions could not be asked of certain actions (e.g., "Is that action
voluntary or involuntary?," where there is nothing remarkable about the
action that suggests that the questions *need* asking).

Such passages about what "the natural economy of language" permits or
forbids do, of course, occur slightly later on in "A Plea for Excuses." I have
already argued, both in "Where the Action Is" and in *Hearing Things*, that
these passages were critical for Cavell's development. This is made explicit
in the opening pages of "Must We Mean What We Say?," but it is also
something that Cavell returns to in his later work.

So much misunderstanding has encrusted these pages of Austin that it
remains almost impossible to read them today. So allow me to enter this

swamp of controversy from a different angle, where one is perhaps not blinded by what Austin called the fetishism of the true and the false, and the power of what he called "the descriptive fallacy" – the sense that our conceptual scheme must apply everywhere if it is to be valid, and the sense that our concepts must yield propositions that are either true (or, as Austin joked, at least false) or nonsense.

But what this passage near the beginning of his essay suggests is *not* that Austin thinks the philosopher is speaking nonsense (or making false statements). He is suggesting – indeed, claiming – that the philosopher is getting guidance from an extremely unreliable source. He certainly is not claiming that the philosopher's concept of action is nonsense – or leads to nonsense – on the grounds that it isn't the ordinary concept of action. He mentions such an ordinary concept in a footnote, but says nothing more about it, at least at this stage of the essay. (Indeed, I think part of what he is suggesting is that it is a good thing, not a bad thing, about our ordinary concepts and their ordinary framework that they come to us piecemeal, even in fragments. To master a concept is not to master a segment of a system; it is more like mastering, say, a region of a territory – or perhaps a sector of a map.)

Austin sees philosophers of action, beginning with such unreliable guidance and then proceeding with an almost comical assurance of being guided by *something* (the structure of our concepts? of the world?), as unreliable. It is the sense of guidedness by the abstract that often drives philosophers in the Anglo-American tradition: One may not yet know the nature of things, but at least one knows (no doubt modestly and cautiously) that one is being guided in the right direction, asking the right sort of question, making the right sort of argument. What Austin sees is not that the philosopher is speaking nonsense or issuing falsehoods, but that philosophers are asking less than they think in asking *tout court* what "doing an action" is. What Austin sees is not that the philosopher *is* speaking nonsense or issuing falsehoods, but that the question he or she is trying to ask comes to nothing much. The import of the answer is significantly less than what the questioner thought was at stake – which was something like the key to the differences of action versus nonaction.

Austin does not even say (what nowadays seems much clearer) that philosophers of action tend simply to presuppose or introduce the concept of action that has been found to favor the progress of their philosophical investigations. This introduction then dictates precisely the entities to be investigated as falling under this concept of action and dictates the questions that philosophers have a right – indeed, a duty – to ask. It is perhaps this sense of intellectual duty or necessity that overrides the philosopher's sense of the inane. For again, Austin is not suggesting that there is some automatic supremacy of ordinary language and its concepts. Neither is Cavell. They suggest rather that the philosopher's concept of action *succeeds* in helping the philosopher to ask a particular question – but at the price of emptying the question of any human interest that might conceivably have brought us to ask it. Then both the concept and the question sag under the weight of their pretension to comprehensiveness and their failure to allow for the interest of exceptions that philosophers ought to find interesting on their own terms.

Of course, Austin (and Cavell) could be wrong. And of course no philosopher is obliged to listen to their warnings not to ask questions that have been deprived of the human interest that led us to ask them in the first place. If someone insists on asking questions that ring false or hollow or just empty, there is nothing much you can do except to go on with your own questions or to get interested in the question of how philosophy keeps producing such questioners. Just as there is something odd about the idea of a conscience that tells you that you ought to have a conscience, so there is something odd about appealing to philosophers to hear that they have a tin ear.

I do think Cavell took Austin to be right about the philosopher's concept of action. And I take him to have gotten interested in the question of how philosophers *keep* asking the question that keeps them from knowing what they want to know. This led him in his treatments of skepticism deeper into the question of how the skeptic succeeds, and of how the skeptical progress, once started, is unstoppable. (It is not to be stopped but tracked or traced – like some old crime of the mind against itself.) He does not similarly – so far as I know – track the progress of the philosopher of action, nor for that matter of the "determinist" or the "compatibilist" or of whatever the various counterparts of the skeptic turn out to be.

Certainly it would not have taken Austin to bring Cavell the news that the effort to locate the human capacity to originate its own actions turns out to fail, when it begins with an impoverished view of what the end product ("the action") is meant to be. What is so intriguing about Austin is the interplay between what I am (inadequately) calling the positive and negative poles. This interplay is sometimes a tension and sometimes a harmony, but it is clear that it takes both poles to produce what Austin calls his "cautious, latter-day version of conduct." (This in itself is a remarkable characterization: "latter-day" as opposed to what? And nearly fifty years later, perhaps we are in a better position to ask about the differences between a theory of action and a version of conduct.)

What excited Cavell – so I reconstruct his recognition – about the positive pole of Austin's work was not merely that it was the continuation of the negative pole by other means. The positive pole, the investigation of excuses (and more generally of the mitigations and exacerbations and intensifications of our actions) was meant to provide a new angle on our actions – though one that Austin certainly knew to be as old as Book III, Chapter 1 of the *Nichomachean Ethics*. (I learned about this connection between Austin and Aristotle from the late G. E. L. Owen, in lectures given at Harvard between 1966 and 1973. He cannot be responsible for the use to which I have put these links. But I like to think that it would have given him pleasure to see me continue to try them out.) Evidently there was in Austin's seminars a sense of a kind of continuous access to how human actions take place, in what field of operations, against what obstacles, in what stages, and with what sort of planning and execution. Apart from the writings of Cavell that I cite, he has emphasized this to me in conversation over the last thirty years. Others have written about the spirit of those years, the sense that progress in philosophy was somehow once again possible. Not to be interested in Austin's power of evocation and description surely must have seemed not to be interested in action at all. Who was it then who was changing the subject?

The investigation of excuses is, to put it baldly, an investigation of what it is to have not *done* X fully, or completely, or entirely, or strictly. It is paired with – and opposed to – the idea of justification and its various cognates, where the idea is to claim that it wasn't quite, or merely, X that you did, or that doing X is to be judged against some higher principle, or wider context, or bigger project under which it is to be subsumed. Naturally, the effort to excuse and the effort to justify overlap in many cases – both real and imagined – and many philosophers have a hankering for the projects of justification. These are further reasons why the enterprises of excuse and mitigation have been downplayed or overlooked, despite their having bulked so large in human life. Deeper reasons for the human hankering after justification may include the residues of metaphysics that encumber our efforts to think. Austin sees these residues, in his fashion, as much as Nietzsche did. That is, in this version of the matter, it is not so much that human beings seek a true justification or reason for an action. They seek *some* justification or reason, that is, something outside the action that will make human action more bearable, for instance, granting it a place in the unstable economy of human activity. A reason for acting allows the action to fit into a pattern of reasons, perhaps permitting familiar lines of philosophical analysis. (A cause will do, for certain sensibilities.)

This way of proceeding is not so much to be characterized as the achievement of a God's-eye point of view. That phrase has now become an acceptable way for an analytic philosopher to criticize the metaphysical hankerings of *other* analytic philosophers. What Austin discerns is not merely a seeking after emotional self-sufficiency or semidivine invulnerability. It doesn't require the perfect reason or the final cause. It merely requires something larger than the action itself. (This may be another reason why all but the most schematic actions are passed over by the very philosophers who claim to be in search of what is most truly an action. There is something scary about getting interested in actions, as if such an interest will soon lead you beyond philosophy and beyond the familiar forms and patterns of justification.)

In Austin and, I think, in Cavell, the issue of excuses, of not quite or entirely *doing* the action, is **not** simply a preliminary issue, something to get done with before the main bout begins. The effort to look for "actions" that bear no trace of the accidental, the unintentional, the incidental (or the contingent?) is bound to miss the point about human actions. No doubt there are such things as actions that can be described as the product of wholly, or merely, or purely *doing* X. You could describe this as the simplest case of doing X intentionally. But Austin invites us to ask: What would this add to the idea of, under normal conditions, just doing X? What would it explain? And more to the point: what distortions of description and explanation will it commit you to, somewhere down the line? Surely, such a minimal idea of intentionality will contribute to the idea of an action as an isolated slice of purity, whose intentional armor is meant to keep it beyond all accident and inadvertence.

Why should just such an idea of action lay claim to revealing the structure of the basic human action, pure and simple? I am not saying that this cannot have some kind of answer. I am suggesting that the answers seem to have gone, to say the least, in a direction other than Austin's. Many of these directions still seem to me dominated by the idea that the point of uncovering this "outward" slice of "pure activity" called an action is to uncover it as the outer manifestation of an "inward" slice of "pure activity," where nothing that is unintentional or "not active" is allowed entry.

In Austin's vision, it is part of the concept of a human being's coming to act that he or she be vulnerable precisely to these mitigations of agency, these accidents and inadvertencies. On the one hand, that is why we have excuses. But the point of excuses goes far beyond this. Excuses show us something about failure, and failure has a great deal to teach us about successful action.

To examine excuses is to examine cases where there has been some abnormality or failure: and as so often, the abnormal will throw light on the
normal, will help us to penetrate the blinding veil of ease and obviousness
that hides the mechanisms of the natural successful act. It rapidly becomes
plain that the breakdowns signalized by the various excuses are of radically
different kinds, affecting different parts or stages of the machinery, which
the excuses consequently pick out and sort out for us. Further, it emerges
that not every slip-up occurs in connexion with *every* thing that could be
called an "action," that not every excuse is apt with every verb – far indeed
from it: and this provides us with one means of introducing some classifica-
tion into the vast miscellany. If we classify them according to the particular
selection of breakdowns to which each is liable, this should assign them
their place in some family group or groups of actions, or in some model of
the machinery of action.[10]

Of course, if your only goal is to sort the events into "actions" and
"nonactions," then you are also likely to be quite content with assimilat-
ing all forms of excuse to some form of the unintentional, the involuntary,
or the accidental. (And then these three excuses can be assimilated to one
another.)

Austin, however, clearly thought that, properly treated, the differences
between excuses (e.g., between your accidentally shooting my donkey and
your mistakenly shooting my donkey – let alone your shooting my donkey
under constraint or duress) show us at least as much about the structure
of agency as the purely intentional act, with no trace or hint of accident
or animal habit. Indeed, he thought (and I think that for some time Cavell
thought) that "the philosophical study of conduct [could] get off to a fresh
start."[11]

In the two philosophical generations or so that intervene between Austin
and now, something happened to this possible "fresh start." (Along with
Cavell, Annette Baier is the other figure in my education who most clearly
was responding to this sense of possibility.) Whatever happened, I think
Cavell retained a number of insights and methods from that moment. And
I think it is already visible in that first essay that he was beginning to diagnose the opposition to the investigation of excuses – for example, by
reducing them to peripheral phenomena – as a wish to avoid one facet of
the passivity that surrounds and infiltrates human action.

This issue of activity and passivity is the largest issue where Cavell's
inheritance of Austin parts company from Davidson and those who came
after him. As I suggested earlier, such investigations tend to rely on a kind
of one-to-one correspondence between the idea of agency and the idea of

that which produces actions. If that puts all the weight on "action," and "agency" becomes a dummy word for "that which produces actions," then so far so good. But if "agency" is supposed to be related to some other powers and passions in human beings that we may wish to group under the heading of "activity," then the problem is not so clear.

Late in *The Claim of Reason*, Cavell twists his reflections on active and passive up a notch or two:

> If I say that any action can be done actively or passively, then I should say that an action done through will is done passively. I realize that one's first intuition here, supposing the issue is clear enough to excite intuition, is likely to run the other way. But that would be the will's doing [i.e. to see it from the perspective of our willing]. To act through will is to be commanded by oneself, perhaps driven; it is to be a good soldier.[12]

These reflections will take him back to Kant and forward to Nietzsche. They might have taken him back to the *Republic*, and to the difference between being merely the master of yourself and the just human being's capacity for harmonizing with himself:

> Now the phrase "master of himself" is an absurdity, is it not? For he who is master of himself would also be subject to himself, and he who is subject to himself would be master.[13]

That Cavell could come so close to an old problematic of philosophy's wish for a truer and more authentic activity, but do it in such a way as to make him essentially unintelligible to mainstream philosophers (in the U.S. and England), is certainly one of the ironies of such reflections.

The possibility of actions that are performed out of a kind of passivity – but nevertheless *performed* – has been mostly lost from view in contemporary discussions. This is presumably in part because Socrates' idea is clearly that the "better part" of the mind or soul should rule and that the recognition of this rightful rule by the "worse part" of the soul is what eliminates the clash of the different parts of the soul, making room for the harmony in the life of the just. This recognition is in part a recognition of the rightfulness of a certain kind of activity: the appetitive part doesn't disappear but allows itself to become passive. One recurrent word for this in Plato can be translated, I believe, as "tame."

The modern philosopher of action takes such remarks to be the introduction of something like normativity. Austin has his own criticism of Plato and also of Aristotle: they conflate giving in to temptation with losing control of oneself. This criticism is also related to an idea of normativity. But caution is needed. Again, we see Austin breaking down the effort to make the "outside" – the action that shows us giving in – correspond too neatly to an otherwise unknowable hierarchy of the true self, which is inwardly giving way to something lesser.

Nowadays we have lost the discussion of those actions that can be produced "passively" but are still in some very full-fledged sense "actions." Such passivity therefore is not to be conflated with the passivity of addictions and the kind of compulsions that crop up, predictably, in contemporary discussions. Here one has the sense of how difficult it is for contemporary philosophers even to contemplate the notion that passivity (or a wish for passivity) could express itself in an action (or a series of actions or activities). To conceptualize this sort of passivity, in general, they must conceive of the motive power as overwhelming – as if it were "really" external to the mind, even though it is in another sense "internal." It is as if they were seeking to characterize an inner storm that brooked no resistance. In the currently fashionable metaphor, it is as if the "action" had been hardwired into the system, which can do nothing else but what it was "programmed" to do.

That is, in the image conjured up by "addiction" the passivity is occasioned by something imagined to be something essentially "external" to the agent. Such ideas of externality are produced by the corresponding ideas of passivity – a kind of passive wish that my passivity not really be mine, and hence not express anything of me. (This reads like a parody of Aristotle, composed by those who seem to remember that what is most a part of me is truly "inner" and who end up concluding that what is not really meant to be me had better not be thought of as "inner.") What is precisely left out of this picture is the idea of an action, done passively, yet nevertheless *expressing* me, expressing at the very least my passivity. It is noteworthy that Cavell introduces the issue of the doubleness of active and passive with a distinction from the arts, in particular, the sound of early and later performances by Horowitz. No one would here think of the "passive" performance as other than an expression of the "agent." Indeed, it is the agent's capacity to permit a certain kind of passivity (in the face of the text of the music, for instance) that permits this particular kind of expressiveness. It is significant that Cavell does not privilege the more active mode.

The second theme that I wish to sketch starts out as subordinated to some questions about art and composition. But this "subordination" – while it once again contributes to the difficulty some readers have in treating Cavell as a philosopher – is scarcely irrelevant to his ways of proceeding with such questions, nor to his sense of the significance of art. It is relevant that already in *Must We Mean What We Say?* we pick up this particular trail, in the chapter entitled "Music Discomposed."

Cavell has been suggesting that in music before Beethoven, even in quite complicated pieces of Bach, "one can hear . . . how the composition is *related,* or could grow in familiar ways, from a process of improvisation; as though the parts meted out by the composer were re-enactments or dramatizations, of successes his improvisations has discovered" (200–1). But "somewhere in the development of Beethoven, this ceases to be imaginable."[14] Something about music and something about the world has changed.

Whether or not one shares this perception about improvisation (or whether one even has a clear sense of what experiences one would have to share in order to share Cavell's perception), the use to which Cavell puts this perception is striking.

> But in the late experience of Beethoven, it is as if our freedom to act no longer depends on the possibility of spontaneity; improvising to fit a *given* lack or need is no longer enough. The entire enterprise of action and communication has become problematic.[15]

It takes a little while to see that Cavell is saying something about human action in general – about "*our* freedom to act" – and not just about Beethoven or some composer with a similar urge to fathom the resources of music and of human expression and activity.

Of course, the very idea that a composer – composing, after all, something as specialized as music – is somehow exploring the resources of human action and activity will not be welcome to many philosophers.[16] Moreover, Cavell seems to be basing his perception on something even more specialized, namely, the experience of, for instance, a late Beethoven quartet. Are we supposed to be making an inference from such a small sample, moving from one person's experience of one artist's development to the entire field of human action? Such an inference would seem to invite a squadron of criticisms. What other forms of representative insight do we have at our disposal? This latter is a question as much for aesthetics as it is for the philosophy of action, and this is one version of a question that Cavell's work has been posing since his first book. Matters will get still more extreme. But it will be two decades before Cavell makes explicit that he is attributing the capacity for experience, and indeed knowledge, to the quartet itself. More to the immediate point, Cavell will trace out the grounds of this fantasy of the work of art as possessing knowledge. Since that knowledge is a knowledge of us – anyway of its audiences and auditors – the fantasy is also a fantasy of a kind of transference. We want to hear not just how beautifully expressive the work is; we also want to know what the work knows. Such reflections were certainly beyond what Cavell was prepared to entertain publically when he first broached the issues of "Music Discomposed."

The way the passage continues makes it clear that Cavell takes the conditions under which art is made to tell us something about the conditions under which human beings act:

> The problem is no longer how to do what you want, but to know what would satisfy you. We could also say: Convention as a whole is now looked upon not as a firm inheritance from the past, but as a continuing improvisation in the face of problems we no longer understand.[17]

Cavell is trying to get us to think of the problem of human action – indeed, the problem of *free* human action – as having to do with our capacity to improvise against a background of convention and need. It is not merely musical conventions and needs that he has in mind, but the resources of comprehensibility that allow us to know what, for instance, "swearing a genuine oath" looks like, or "offering charity in a way that does not oppress the recipient." The analogy with the arts – of course it is more than an analogy – is meant to call attention to what Austin called the "look" of the act, as well as to the kind of sense it makes to perform it, here and now.

Freedom in our actions has come to depend on such issues as well as on the more traditional ones. "Free" here means, as it often does, *getting free* of some constraint – for example, a certain rigidity of the past, a certain exhaustion in the traditions that made sense of our actions; or perhaps some blind spot in our circumspection, or an inability to understand not so much one's motives in general but one's motives and one's problems in this particular situation. But here the constraint that blocks our freedom of action is not the general constraint of nature – for example, some sort of determinism or mechanism. It is the inability to see the connection between what you are doing and what, in a given situation, would constitute the satisfaction of your activity.

The specific form of the more general problem that Cavell is defining for human action now reads like this: we are to fit an action – for example, the composition of a musical phrase – into a situation that is defined not only by the resources of musical significance and activity but *at the same time* by the insufficiency of those resources to supply the agent's or composer's requirements. I would be somewhat sympathetic to those who think that Cavell has not completely elaborated the connection between agent and composer, or between agency and composition. I would be more sympathetic if they were able to bear in mind that the Greeks seemed to find it very important to distinguish between *prattein* (to act? to be active?) and *poeien*, which we translate as "to make, to produce" but surely also as "to compose." At a minimum, these passages show Cavell's sense of a certain kind of utterance as compassing both the acts of speech that Austin teaches us to study and the structure of action that Austin teaches us to discern as something more than some bodily motions plus an intention. The "intention" could help to explain the action: "I wasn't really stealing it; I intended to put it back all long." But the intention could no longer explain itself: That is, it could no longer presuppose the full panoply of (for instance) musical media for making one's intentions plain. What Cavell is pursuing is the sense of the work of art as not merely bearing up under these conditions of action but as living with them in a kind of exemplary way. And if our ordinary actions are more like making music than like kicking stones or knocking over the milk, then our requirements both for a free action and for an action that we can explain or that explains itself have suddenly become more exigent.

In the next chapter of *Must We Mean What We Say?*, Cavell describes certain works, called "modernist" works, as laying bare their own conditions of existence at a given historical moment. But that very characterization suggests that not all works of art need to do this in order to be art, and so presumably that not all the human actions that might be mirrored in a work of art need to be mirrored in a modernist work. Cavell suggests that a burden of self-consciousness became inevitable in the production of certain works at certain periods of our cultural history. That burden of self-consciousness, however, points both to the dangers of what Cavell and Michael Fried call theatricality and fraudulence in our art and toward a difficulty in the very enterprise of human action. In this vision, the consciousness that one is acting, trying to have an effect on the world, has already been taken prisoner by the consciousness of the world that one is acting upon. For the idea of "the world" here includes the human inhabitants, who are from time to time part of the object of one's actions, and their human consciousness, which forms part of the audience for one's actions.

Nothing made Cavell's efforts to break down the barriers between philosophy and certain kinds of criticism more unpalatable to the very audience that might otherwise have been sympathetic than his insistence that philosophy allow modernist art, "the art of [its] own generation,"[18] to become a problem for modern philosophy. This meant first of all that philosophers had to make room for what Cavell insisted on calling the experience of fraudulence. The modernist work of art lays bare specifically what is endemic to all art: You have to entrust yourself to the work – to your experience of the work – before it can teach you what it knows. Very shortly, Cavell – once again, along with Michael Fried – will come to say that the work teaches us what it knows by acknowledging the conditions of its existence. Before we get that far, however, Cavell insists that when we think about art, we are to think about how it is possible to "treat certain objects... in ways normally reserved for treating persons."[19]

I suggest that we could try to think of these objects as "works," not just as products, or as the "work" of the work of art as solidified into something called an "opus." Then what we are trying to do is to think of the work of art – both in its production and in its reception – as continuous modes of human activity. What Cavell calls "continuous presentness"[20] might be thought of more generally as a goal of at least some art, after Shakespeare and Beethoven. His insistence on the possibility of significance within the present moment of perception is very far from some sense of the ineffable presence of the work. It is more like the foregoing of aura and of totality – of the reliance on the past expectations of sense and on the hope of some future fulfillment of sense. Hence Cavell's characterization of "continuous presentness" speaks of a kind of erosion of most traditional forms of our reliance on musical and dramatic presence.

At the very least, it insists that we give up the idea of the work as a kind of object, about which we are compelled to wonder why we treat it in ways normally reserved for human beings. If the work is a reservoir of significant activity, it might awaken your powers of attentiveness and reward them accordingly. (Of course, this may not, all by itself, solve the problem of whether you save the Rembrandt or your brother from the burning house, but we can leave this for certain kinds of ethicists and aestheticians.) In general, at least, one problem – the tinge of psychosis that hovers around our treatment of an object as, or as like, a person – has been eliminated, or at any rate simplified. But now that we have eliminated this tinge, the possibility of other risks awakens. Here we approach the problem of art and action from the side of action, and its attendant modes of consciousness and self-consciousness. Michael Fried's work is especially pertinent to this axis of the inquiry, along with Stephen Melville's extension and critique of it.[21] For Fried – as he made clear in later work, and as his citations of Merleau-Ponty made clear at the time – the negations of art that he called "theatrical" were dangers that he took to threaten the very possibility of human action.[22] Or rather, he took the knowledge of those dangers to be embedded in the great art of the French tradition from David to Manet.[23]

All of these issues drew the fire of those who felt that Cavell and Fried were smuggling in the very "value judgments" that had been so painfully excluded a scant generation earlier. Cavell in effect anticipated such objections in a slightly earlier essay, "Ending the Waiting Game: A Reading of Beckett's *Endgame*."[24] Cavell's engagement in theater, theatricality, and the possible emptiness of human action was already at work in this essay. The issue there was not to distinguish the successful modernist work from the fraudulent pretenders: the issue Cavell raised was whether any work of art, or any human action, or any mode of speeech, could release us from the necessary but confining shelters of meaning that we have constructed for ourselves. In Beckett's play, judgment (whether moral, aesthetic, political, or religious) itself is under indictment, along with action and along with our incessant need to analyze our judgments and our actions. The pride of the human being is no longer exactly that it is made in the image of God, but that it is made in the image of human comprehensibility. Now that image is growing cloudy and evasive.

The characters of *Endgame* attempt to empty out their actions by minimizing both the consequences of their actions and the implications of the words that either constitute a kind of action or might elaborate those actions. Here both actions and words can only further the condition they are trying to escape. In his essay, Cavell writes: "Self-consciousness is many kinds of curse." It has always been the strategy of some spirits – not Beckett's, perhaps – to evade this curse by making your actions very small and your words very insignificant. But the first curse of self-consciousness, in relation to action, is that it makes inescapable the fact that you have done something and, indeed, done it with a certain intention.

By the time Cavell had gotten to this stage of thinking, he was ripe for Emerson's work, however long it would take him to find a way of writing about it:

> The nonchalance of boys who are sure of a dinner, and would disdain as much as a lord to do or say aught to conciliate one, is the healthy attitude of human nature. . . . But the man is as it were clapped into jail by his consciousness. As soon as he has once acted or spoken with *éclat* he is a committed person, watched by the sympathy or the hatred of hundreds, whose affections must now enter into his account. There is no Lethe for this. Ah, that he could pass again into his neutrality! . . . He would utter opinions on all passing affairs, which being seen to be not private but necessary, would sink like darts into the ears of men and put them in fear.[25]

The claims about action and the claims about the history of our experience of the arts are not independent. It becomes clear that Cavell is not claiming that the work of art simply reflects the problematic status of human action as vulnerable to self-consciousness. Nor is he saying merely that works of music and art and literature form a particularly good example in which to study the fate of action. It is rather something about the exemplariness of the work that is at stake, something about the way the work reveals and insists on the conditions of consciousness within which it is made.

> Nothing we now have to say, no *personal* utterance has its meaning conveyed in the conventions and formulas we now share. In a time of slogans, sponsored messages, ideologies, psychological warfare, mass projects, where words have lost touch with their sources or objects, and in a phonographic culture where music is for dreaming, or for kissing, or for taking a shower, or for having your teeth drilled, our choices seem to be those of silence, or nihilism (the denial of the value of shared meaning altogether), or statements so personal as to form the possibility of communication without the support of conventions – perhaps to become the source of new convention. And then of course they are most likely to fail even to seem to communicate.[26]

The nature of this exemplariness of a work might have become a normal subject for aesthetics. But we are much less likely to be comfortable with the idea that certain exemplary actions and certain exemplary works could illuminate the conditions under which the work is made or the action is accomplished.

We are far from coming to a close with the issues of activity and passivity or with the issues of the representativeness of the action (and the balance of activity and passivity) contained in the work of art. It may seem as if we have moved a long way from Austin's topics and, of course, in a sense we have. But in another sense, as I have been suggesting, these investigations are punctuated by Cavell's efforts to return to certain moments in Austin's work. It is as if he wishes to measure his own progress – or sometimes as if he is checking to see that he is getting the rhythm or the pitch right. Accordingly, it is appropriate to try to assess more explicitly what I have been suggesting all along about Cavell's development. Happily, Cavell provides us with a touchstone for such an assessment.

Accordingly, I conclude with a word or two about the directions Cavell suggests in *A Pitch of Philosophy*. This book is the place where Cavell presents his most extensive and detailed consideration of Austin's work, and of his relation to that work, since *Must We Mean What We Say?*. The book equally suggests caution about arriving at any final formulation about Cavell's relation to Austin, for there is clearly work in preparation and lines of thought that remain to be explored. (Since then, Cavell has taught several seminars on Austin, and there is a paper on "Passionate Utterance and

Performatives" in circulation.) The problem of action emerges again into a place of considerable importance within Cavell's structuring of philosophy. But the problem is restored to a place that is subordinate to the question of speech and voice.

Cavell certainly makes some extraordinary remarks about excuses and action – sufficient to reopen some old cases and start some new ones:

> Excuses are as essentially implicated in Austin's view of human actions as slips and over-determination are in Freud's. What does it betoken about human actions that the reticulated constellation of predicates of excuse is made for them – that they can be done unintentionally, unwillingly, involuntarily, insincerely, unthinkingly, inadvertently, heedlessly, carelessly, under duress, under the influence, out of contempt, out of pity, by mistake, by accident, and so on. . . . It betokens, we might say, the all but unending vulnerability of human action, its openness to the independence of the world and the preoccupation of the mind. I would like to say that the theme of excuses turns philosophy's attention patiently and thoroughly to something philosophy would love to ignore – the fact that human life is constrained to the life of the human body, to what Emerson calls the giant I always take with me. The law of the body is the law.[27]

This paragraph might make it seem that the vulnerability of action to the independence of the world is essentially the vulnerability of the body to failure and mishap. This vulnerability is no doubt real, as the image of Chaplin skirting the edge of the department store abyss can serve to remind us. But as I have tried to show, the vulnerability of action to the world is equally a vulnerability to being misunderstood, to acting nonsensically or behaving incomprehensibly or inconsequentially and, indeed, to allowing one's actions to be dictated by the consciousness of others, hence to being captured by certain forms of theatricality.

There is a good deal of evidence that Cavell's interest in the mismatch of actions and their significance ("in the world") is still at work in his formulation of this idea and this list of excuses. In any event, a few pages later Cavell turns almost casually to the question of doing something versus saying something. The train of thought is set in motion by Austin's equally casual introduction of a quotation from Greek tragedy. That quotation in turn seems to endorse a certain splitting of the external behavior of the tongue from the internal behavior of the heart. It is Austin's uncharacteristic overlooking of the context that attracts Cavell's further attention. But perhaps it is of equal importance that a generation of literary theorists had been willing to absorb from Austin's text some fairly vague idea that saying something was, after all, a way of doing something.[28]

Whatever the casualness of the context – and whatever kind of seriousness this particular tone is meant to encourage – we should not allow this
somewhat oblique motivation for Cavell's comments to obscure the radi-
calness of the step that Cavell is proposing. The results should still seem
surprising:

> My immediate guess as to what Austin wanted to forget is that the saying
> of words is not excusable the way that the performance of actions is; or in a
> word, that saying something is after all, or before all, on Austinian grounds,
> not exactly or merely or transparently doing something. So Austin's theory
> of excuses cannot after all be incorporated tidily into the theory of per-
> formatives, hence releases its grounding thought – that in certain critical
> instances saying something is doing something – into the open again.[29]

We might attempt to interpret Austin's theory of excuses as a partial expression of his methodical refusal of philosophy's wish to escape the body. This
ancient wish for escape has expressed itself sometimes by "mechanizing"
the body, sometimes by biologizing it, and in times past by demonizing it
or "animalizing" it. Then we might read Cavell as finding room in Austin's
account for what there is about us that does, after all, need to get somewhere
beyond the body, or at least what there is about us that allows us to achieve
some kind of perspective on the body. That "somewhere" can turn out to
be speech or wherever it is exactly that speech takes place. This possibility
of perspective will turn out to have its price. Speech does not leave the body
behind altogether, and yet it does not remain entirely tethered to its origins.

In good Protestant fashion, the price of escaping the sole authority of
the law of the body is a deeper sense of responsibility and a deeper sense of
our words as the source of our authority over ourselves. Of course, Cavell
does not mean to make the fact of doing something less important *tout court*
than the fact of saying something. He is certainly not denying that we can
usefully think of various ways in which we would do well to remember –
as philosophers and as human beings – that saying something is also doing
something. (And not just in the sense that doing something is [very often]
also making some bodily movements.) He is, however, tuning his ear to a
different register than the ones that Austin has been heard in.

What does Cavell hear when he returns to the place where his voice
began, the place that called for his voice, hence the place *before* the voice?
That is one of the meanings of the quotation from Emerson that forms the
epigraph to *The Claim of Reason*: so much nonsense has been spoken about
this epigraph that it has to be made clear once again. A "provocation" is,
among other things, that which calls you out, in particular that which calls
you out to *respond*, hence calls for your voice. Those critics who see a pure

opposition between "instruction" and "provocation" predictably fail to see
the issue of what constitutes an appropriate response to a provocation.
Cavell finds, among other things, that certain methods, certain paths, must
constantly be reopened or they will fall into obscurity and disuse. One
of these paths is opened by the methods of ordinary language itself. And
by now we should be well aware, at least in general, of the difficulty of
seeing the obvious, the familiar, the ordinary. As Wittgenstein said, we do
not see the things that are of most importance to us exactly because they
are the things of the everyday.

But Austin and Cavell both go further than this, at least on the subject
of action and activity. There is a certain peculiarity that attaches to ordinary
human actions, such as buying a newspaper or waving goodbye or signalling
that you are making a turn or announcing your intention to vote against
a candidate for tenure or for president. Are these things, these actions,
ordinary or not? One might want to say: it depends. (And moreover, it
depends on things "outside" of philosophy.)

In "Must We Mean What We Say?," Cavell writes that Ryle's antitheses

> miss exactly those actions about which the question "Voluntary or not" has
> no sense, viz., those ordinary, unremarkable, natural things we do which
> make up most of our conduct and which are neither admirable nor con-
> temptible; which, indeed, could only erroneously be said to go on, in gen-
> eral, in *any* special way.[30]

Here Cavell is arriving in his own fashion at what Austin called the dictates of "the natural economy of language." Austin puts his insight into the
natural economy of language under the heading, "*No modification without
aberration.*"

> When it is said that X did A, there is a temptation to suppose that given
> some, perhaps indeed *any*, expression modifying the verb we shall be en-
> titled to insert either it or its opposite in our statement: that is, we shall
> be entitled to ask, typically, "Did X do A Mly or not-Mly?" (e.g. "Did X
> murder Y voluntarily or involuntarily?"), and to answer one or the other. Or
> at a minimum it is supposed that if X did A there must be at least one mod-
> ifying expression that we could, justifiably and informatively, insert with
> the verb. In the great majority of cases of the use of the great majority of
> verbs . . . ('murder' is perhaps not one of the majority) such presuppositions
> are quite unjustified. The natural economy of language dictates that for the
> standard case covered by any normal verb – not perhaps a verb of omen such
> as murder, but a verb like 'eat' or 'kick' or 'croquet' – no modifying agent is
> required or even permissible. Only if we do the action named in some *special*

way or circumstances, different from those in which such an act is naturally done (and of course both the normal and the abnormal differ according to what verb in particular is in question) is a modifying expression called for, or even in order.[31]

These are among the most controversial claims that Austin and Cavell ever made. Rather than exacerbate the provocation contained in this controversy, I want to pursue several of the paths that lead off from such a moment, or series of moments. In particular, there are differences – some slight, some perhaps not so slight – between the two versions.

Cavell's version can make it seem as if there is some *type* of thing we do – the ordinary, or the unremarkable thing – that we will be inclined to miss (or miss the significance of) if we persist in asking the question "Voluntary or not?" Austin goes so far as to say that the "natural economy of language" renders the adverbial expression *impermissible* – though sometimes he seems to say that the *asking of the question* is what is impermissible. Austin was challenging – more or less explicitly – the model of conceptual analysis that had dominated English philosophy at least since Russell. Here he chips away at – among other things – the idea that if we have a concept, we must be able to ask about every item in the universe whether our concept applies or not. Later he will have more to say about what makes the asking of a question intelligible or not. He will also come to challenge more explicitly the idea that for every concept and every item in the world, there is some statement linking the concept to the item or denying the existence of such a link. Not incidentally, he also challenges the idea that if something purporting to be a statement fails to be either true or false, our only recourse is to label it nonsense.

However much in debt Cavell found himself to such moments, it was not so much to the idea that the natural economy of language prohibits us from saying something or asking something. Cavell inflects Austin's perception toward the idea (still relatively undeveloped in "A Plea for Excuses") that the philosopher's asking of the question would have special consequences for what the philosopher could then go on to see or not see, say or not say, investigate or not investigate.

Above all, I believe that in this work on action (both Austin's and his own) Cavell had caught a glimpse of what he would himself come to call "the ordinary." What Cavell saw was not primarily what Austin sometimes thought of as the practical world, a world or realm he characterizes as the world that lies in part beneath or beyond our supervision. That latter step toward the idea of what lies "beneath supervision" is one that Austin takes toward the end of the essay. He notes that there is no adverb "advertantly" to make a neat dichotomy with "inadvertently." This allows him to suggest the shortcomings of other dichotomies concerning action without prohibiting them, and it provides for a discussion of human action that is independently absorbing.

Neither what lies beneath supervision, nor those unremarkable actions of the everyday that Cavell addresses, can simply be seized head on and studied directly. In the one case, the wrong kind of consciousness would suggest that all we require in order to supervise the unsupervisable is to become aware of it – for instance, by extending our capacities for awareness in the ways that are normally available to us – as if with a little more effort total supervision of the scene of human action would become available to us. This seems to be another way of avoiding the significance of excuses. In the other case, the wrong kind of self-consciousness about the unremarkable things that we are doing will become part of the theatricality of our concepts. (Compare Strawson: he identifies the stage of philosophy as the stage of self-consciousness about our concepts. It takes only a step or two to render this self-consciousness into a kind of theatricality, and then a step or two more to make the theatricality go away or at least become neutralized and more or less invisible. Most philosophers in my experience are pretty good at this.)

I have suggested that there may be more than one reason why these unremarkable actions cannot be made a theme for investigation in any very direct fashion. One set of reasons has to do, as I have said, with the difficulty in seeing the obvious and the unremarkable and in writing about it. Another relates more specifically to the nature of human action, which of course does not always fall within the limits of the unremarkable and the ordinary. More often, it seems, actions may fall at the borders of the ordinary – which is why Austin singles out what he calls verbs of omen (like 'murder,' he says) and a region that I might call "the ominous." I surmise that both of these issues are part of the background that led Cavell to write about the issues of action in the ways that I have traced: (a) in relation to active and passive, (b) in relation to the representativeness of the work in the work of art, and (c) in constant comparison to speech and expressiveness in general.

"The ordinary" is often cited in critical commentary on Cavell's work. In my experience, this orientation of Cavell's later work is more often understood as a sort of definite locale or a situation than as a direction that we have to learn how to take. Since Cavell explicitly takes marriage and its domesticity – as it is under attack in tragedy and film melodrama – to represent the ordinary, it is easy enough to come to the conclusion that the ordinary is just equivalent to what is attacked within such structures. But it isn't. We can learn to think methodically about the ordinary, for instance, by thinking about melodrama and comedy. But we must bear in mind that these structures are providing dramatic lenses for seeing something that, normally, is too familiar for us to see.

Thinking about action helps us to see some related features of the ordinary: What makes an action ordinary is not some statistical fact about the number of times the action is done. Nor does it consist in some particularly low-key way of performing the action, nor (at least not necessarily) because it is dictated by some particularly dominant force of habit. What makes it ordinary is that the action in question belongs to the ordinary world of the one who does the action. Since the ordinary world is the only world I have – at least under ordinary circumstances – I have not said much more than that the action belongs to *my* world. But I have said a little bit more. I have said that even though an action may be extraordinary, heroic – even tragic – it is unlikely to challenge the limits of my world. This idea of limits is admittedly very obscure. I am not denying that action can be extraordinary and even, in a certain sense, change the world. But the action does not thereby change the *limits* of the world. Here I am explicitly thinking of the limits of the world as forming an epoch in the history of the world. When a new epoch of human history emerges, then there also emerge changes in the possibilities of human action and of what counts as an action. These are also changes in (our sense of) the ordinary.

There is a companion path toward the question of action that is also explored by Cavell but much more rarely mentioned. He writes:

> When I am impressed with the necessity of statements like S [i.e., "When we ask whether an action is voluntary, we imply that the action is fishy"] I am tempted to say that they are categorial – about the concept of an action *überhaupt*.[32]

Now Cavell was presumably aware that active and passive are not categories in Kant, and that human action does not, to say the least, play a very large role in the first *Critique*. (More recently, and exactly in his work on Austin and passionate utterances, Cavell has sketched in something of the history of the active and the passive in the philosophical tradition, in order not so much to touch all the bases as to remind us that the bases were always there, waiting for the right touch.)

But what is a necessity that comes to light or becomes audible when the philosopher is impressed with it or absorbed in it? Isn't this just exactly the kind of reliance on intuition that Cavell (and before him, Wittgenstein) is always being rebuked for? Without trying to give an answer to such a question, I note that when such a reading is applied to Austin it does indeed point Cavell in the direction of the *Philosophical Investigations*. It is difficult to bear in mind that the earliest stages of Cavell's work on Austin were accomplished before Cavell had mounted a full-scale reading of Wittgenstein. We need to be careful not to provide him with answers that he did not then possess. To do so would be to miss the actualities of the exploration that would lead to these answers and also the sense of philosophical exposure and risk that accompany such explorations.

When Cavell does arrive at his reading of Wittgenstein, he is better prepared to link a kind of borrowed Kantian notion of necessity with a more Wittgensteinian inflection of the idea of possibility.

> We feel as if we had to penetrate [*durchschauen*] phenomena: our investigation, however is directed not towards phenomena, but, as one might say, towards the "possibilities" of phenomena. We remind ourselves, that is, of the *kind of statement* that we make about phenomena.[33]

One reading of this passage has, I suppose, taken the "kind of statement" in question to reveal the appropriate type of concept to be applied to the phenomenon. Another line has taken the reminder of the "kind" of statement to be in effect a reminder of the only *permissible* kind of thing to say. This is the sense in which Wittgenstein, like Austin, is supposed to have prohibited philosophical statements and restricted us to the ordinary things that we were already saying anyway.

Neither of these alternative interpretations tell us much about why Wittgenstein thought that reminding us of what we do, in fact, say about something would be directing us not toward that thing but toward the *possibility* of that thing. I do not say that Cavell at this stage of his work was ready to give the full-blown answers of *The Claim of Reason* or *Conditions Handsome and Unhandsome*. I do suggest that his work on Austin on action had prepared him to trace out later the moments of transition that pass between the apparently fragile necessities of our speech, thence to arrive at a perspicuous glimpse of the "possibilities" of some phenomena.

But what *do* we say about action, and how shall we remind ourselves, and what are its possibilities? And what happens when the philosopher starts to chime in with his or her own questions? How does the philosopher who seeks access to ordinary actions, and hence to the realm in which those ordinary actions occur, manage to gain this access without distorting that realm?

This is the place to seek answers to the questions both about the possibility of the ordinary and its inhabitants and their doings, and also about the necessities of that realm. The philosopher is poised between the ordinariness of these activities and the necessities we are seeking within the very possibilities of that ordinary world. From the vantage of this precarious perspective Cavell would soon come to see what Wittgenstein had glimpsed: the sturdiness of the world of the everyday, or what Wittgenstein also called its power. But that power has to be accepted in order to be apprehended. And like grace, whether in the Christian's vision or in Chaplin's, it is not attained by the unaided will and its deeds. (The beauty of human action may be a consequence of such grace.) Only with a willingness for passivity – which goes beyond patience and the willingness to take our lumps – will the incessant round of human activity and action make the kind of sense we want it to make. Only then will it be truly a form of human action.

Notes

1. For me, it became equally important to emphasize that it required a kind of *reversal* to get from the writer-as-reader to the reader-as-writer. See Timothy Gould, *Hearing Things: Voice and Method in the Writing of Stanley Cavell* (Chicago: University of Chicago Press, 1998), Chapters 4 and 5.
2. *The Bhagavad Gita*, trans. Winthrop Sargent (Albany: State University of New York Press, 1994), Book IV, stanzas 16–18 and passim.
3. Stanley Cavell, *A Pitch of Philosophy: Autobiographical Exercises* (Cambridge, MA: Harvard University Press, 1994), p. 87.
4. Gould, *Hearing Things.*
5. Timothy Gould, "Where the Action Is: Stanley Cavell and the Skeptic's Activity," in Richard Fleming and Michael Payne, eds., *The Senses of Stanley Cavell* (London and Toronto: Associated University Presses, 1989).
6. Timothy Gould, "Stanley Cavell and the Plight of the Ordinary," in Joseph Smith and William Kerrigan, eds., *Images in Our Souls, Psychiatry and the Humanities*, vol. 10 (Baltimore: Johns Hopkins University Press, 1987).
7. J. L. Austin, "A Plea for Excuses," in his *Philosophical Papers*, 2nd ed., eds. J. O. Urmson and G. J. Warnock (Oxford: Oxford University Press, 1970), pp. 199–200.
8. Ibid., p. 199.
9. Ibid., pp. 178–9.
10. Ibid., p. 180.
11. Ibid.
12. Stanley Cavell, *The Claim of Reason: Wittgenstein, Skepticism, Morality, and Tragedy* (New York: Oxford University Press, 1979), p. 384.
13. Plato, *Republic*, Vol. 1, trans. Paul Shorey (Cambridge, MA: Harvard University Press, 1937), Book IV, 430e–431a, p. 359.
14. Stanley Cavell, "Music Discomposed," in *Must We Mean What We Say?* (New York: Charles Scribner's Sons, 1969), pp. 200–1.

15. Ibid.

16. One philosopher who does welcome this point, however, is William Day. See his "Knowing as Instancing: Jazz Improvisation and Moral Perfectionism," *The Journal of Aesthetics and Art Criticism* 58 (Spring 2000), pp. 99–111, and also his Columbia Ph.D. dissertation.

17. Cavell, "Music Discomposed," p. 201.

18. Ibid., p. 183.

19. Ibid., p. 189.

20. Cavell, "The Avoidance of Love: A Reading of *King Lear*," in *Must We Mean What We Say?*, p. 322 and passim.

21. Melville's juxtaposition of Cavell, Fried, and Greenberg is found first in his essay "Notes on the Reemergence of Allegory, the Forgetting of Modernism, the Necessity of Rhetoric, and the Conditions of Publicity in Art and Criticism," *October* 19 (Winter 1981), pp. 55–92, and then in his *Philosophy Beside Itself: On Deconstruction and Modernism* (Minneapolis: University of Minnesota Press, 1986). Melville lays bare the notion of time, both in relation to the presentness of the work of art and to the idea of action that is present in that presentness.

22. See Michael Fried, "Art and Objecthood," *Artforum* 5 (June 1967), pp. 12–23, most recently reprinted in his *Art and Objecthood: Essays and Reviews* (Chicago: University of Chicago Press, 1998), pp. 148–72. For a brief take on Fried's significance to Cavell's work and, more generally, to our understanding of human action and its representations in painting and poetry, see Gould, "Utterance and Theatricality," in Ted Cohen, Paul Guyer, and Hilary Putnam, eds., *Pursuits of Reason: Essays in Honor of Stanley Cavell* (Lubbock: Texas Tech University Press, 1993), pp. 133–57.

23. See especially Fried's little-studied essay on "Thomas Couture and the Theatricalization of Action in 19th Century French Painting," *Artforum* 8 (June 1970), pp. 36–46.

24. Cavell, "Ending the Waiting Game: A Reading of Beckett's *Endgame*," in *Must We Mean What We Say?*, pp. 115–62.

25. Ralph Waldo Emerson, *Works*, ed. Edward Emerson, vol. 2 (Boston: Houghton Mifflin, 1883), "Self-Reliance," p. 51.

26. Cavell, "Music Discomposed," pp. 201–2.

27. Cavell, *A Pitch of Philosophy: Autobiographical Exercises*, p. 87.

28. See Timothy Gould, "The Unhappy Performative," in Eve Sedgwick and Andrew Parker, eds., *Performativity and Performance: Selected Papers from the English Institute* (London: Routledge, 1995).

29. Cavell, *A Pitch of Philosophy*, pp. 104–5.

30. Cavell, "Must We Mean What We Say?," in *Must We Mean What We Say?*, p. 7.

31. Austin, "A Plea for Excuses," p. 190.

32. Cavell, "Must We Mean What We Say?," p. 13.

33. Ludwig Wittgenstein, *Philosophical Investigations*, 3d. ed., trans. G. E. M. Anscombe (New York: Macmillan, 1958), §90, p. 42e.

4 | Stanley Cavell's Vision of the Normativity of Language: Grammar, Criteria, and Rules

STEPHEN MULHALL

One striking respect in which Stanley Cavell's way of inheriting the philosophical practices of Austin and Wittgenstein differs from that of most who acknowledge their continuing pertinence is evident in his sense that ordinary language philosophy is in constant dialogue with scepticism. According to Cavell, the sceptic's challenge is neither simply to be accepted on its own terms nor simply to be rejected as nonsensical; it must rather be interpreted as an undismissable threat, a shadow that ordinary language cannot avoid casting, and whose presence and nature tell us something fundamental about the presence and nature of that which casts it. And this interpretation of (ordinary language's relation to) scepticism itself depends upon Cavell's distinctive interpretation of what Wittgenstein (like, and unlike, Austin) takes himself to be invoking when he recalls the grammar or the criteria of words – when, in the face of philosophical confusion, he asks himself, and invites us to ask ourselves, 'what we should say when'.

This invitation is, of course, regularly made by more traditional Wittgensteinians; but it is then typically assumed that its acceptance will demonstrate that scepticism is not so much undismissable as inexpressible – a refusal (more or less self-conscious, more or less duplicitous) of the conditions of intelligible speech. By contrast, Cavell takes it that any humanly serious expression of scepticism will not be describable as a simple refusal of this invitation (since, for him, the sceptic's use of words turns out to be a not wholly unnatural projection of our ordinary use, and the sceptic will have some account to give of its less-than-full naturalness); hence he rejects the familiar Wittgensteinian idea that simply to recall criteria will or must silence the sceptic. Indeed, he takes that idea, insofar as it fails to acknowledge that the sceptic is at once exploiting and impressed by fundamental aspects of ordinary language, as itself expressive of the repression of ordinariness of which the sceptic is accused, and hence as itself sceptical. But from what interpretation of criteria might such a radical and controversial conclusion follow?

To see this, we must of course examine in detail Parts I and II of *The Claim of Reason*,[1] in which Cavell unfolds this interpretation, and its critical differences from that of other Wittgenstein commentators and followers. But even before so doing, one aspect of the surface rhetoric of Cavell's invocation of grammar and of criteria may appear (and has recently been made to appear) salient.[2] For where many Wittgensteinians are happy to gloss Wittgenstein's notion of a criterion as a rule of grammar, and hence to gloss his notion of a grammatical investigation as inviting us to recall the rules governing our uses of words, Cavell typically avoids any such gloss, and repeatedly declares that other commentators' invocations of that concept in these contexts amount to a fundamental misunderstanding of Wittgenstein's philosophical method. In an early essay, for example, we are told: 'That everyday language does not, in fact or in essence, depend upon such a structure and conception of rules, and yet that the absence of such a structure in no way impairs its functioning, is what the picture of language drawn in [Wittgenstein's] later philosophy is about'.[3] And in a much later essay, the same note is struck: 'I ... do not share the sense that Wittgenstein attaches salvational importance to rules. ... Indeed, I take Wittgenstein to say fairly explicitly that rules cannot play the fundamental role Kripke takes him to cast them in'.[4]

However, the proper construal of such passages remains unclear. Taken one way (perhaps when mindful that Wittgenstein's notion of 'language-games' implicitly aligns speech with a species of human activity that is typically rule-governed, and that his extended discussion of rule following apparently emerges in response to a question about how we grasp the meanings of words),[5] Cavell can be read as criticising particular employments of the concept of a rule in the work of particular philosophers – ones in which that concept, and hence the concept of a rule of grammar, has been distorted or sublimed. Taken another way, however (perhaps when mindful that every specific treatment Cavell offers of others' attempts to gloss the idea of criteria as rules of grammar is negative, and that he typically avoids invoking any such gloss himself), we might conclude that Cavell's suspicions extend to any use of the concept of a rule to explicate Wittgenstein's notion of grammar and criteria. We might even wonder whether he regards interpretions of criteria in terms of rules as itself an expression of the scepticism it is so often employed to refute – presenting a vision of language that the *Philosophical Investigations* most fundamentally combats as the vision of language it aims to cultivate.

It is worth emphasizing that the issues at stake here are not of significance only to those who have an already-established interest in

Wittgenstein's vision of language. For when Wittgenstein talks of our capacity to grasp or recall the criteria or grammar of words, he is concerned with what philosophers in the analytic tradition would refer to as our mastery of a certain fragment of a natural language; and they would equate that ability aptly to apply words with mastery of the corresponding concepts. So understood, clarifying the nature of our linguistic abilities will cast light on what it is to master concepts, and hence illuminate a question that has been central to philosophical reflection since Plato. Moreover, since analytic philosophers have tended to assume that our mastery of words is a mastery of the rules that govern their use, arguing instead over how best to understand the nature of those rules (as specifiable in a formal semantic theory, or as not wholly formalizable rules laid down in practice?), to question whether Wittgenstein would think of criteria as rules at all amounts to suggesting that Wittgenstein's work – rather than conforming in this fundamental respect to analytic assumptions – in fact aims to place them in question.

What, then, is the real nature of, and the true basis for, Cavell's hostility to certain interpretations of criteria and grammar in terms of the concept of a rule? Must we eschew this traditional way of glossing Wittgenstein's terms if we are properly to acknowledge Cavell's powerful insights into Wittgenstein's vision of language? I cannot hope to canvass all the relevant textual and argumentative evidence here; what follows is better thought of as an attempt to make a start on this project, by examining three texts in which Cavell comes closest to an explicit and detailed treatment of this issue.

GAMES, LANGUAGE-GAMES, AND CALCULI: CAVELL, POLE, AND AUSTIN

The first of my illustrative quotations came from 'The Availability of Wittgenstein's Later Philosophy' – Cavell's early, famous, and famously scathing critique of David Pole's book on Wittgenstein. A corrosive disdain for Pole's account of Wittgenstein's vision of language as essentially rule-governed is certainly central to that critique; but the essay stays so unwaveringly close to Pole's specific formulations of this imputed vision, and its tone is so unrelievedly hostile, that it is far from obvious exactly how far its conclusions are meant to (and might legitimately) be generalized. In my earlier quotation, for example, Cavell talks not about any and every conception of language as a rule-governed structure, but of a structure and conception of linguistic rules such as Pole's. Does Cavell himself think (and give us good reason to think) that Pole's conception of linguistic rules embodies features that must be part of any such conception?

Cavell summarises Pole's conception as follows:

1. The correctness or incorrectness of a use of language is determined by the rules of the language, and 'determined' in two senses:

a) The rules form a complete system, in the sense that for every 'move' within the language it is obvious that a rule does or does not apply.

b) Where a rule does apply, it is obvious whether it has been followed or infringed.

2. Where no existing rules apply, you can always adopt a new rule to cover the case, but then that obviously changes the game. (MWM, 48)

Versions of these ideas about Wittgenstein's view of linguistic rules continue to have currency long after Pole's initial articulation of them; but it is evident to Cavell that what they best describe is a constructed language, a calculus with fixed rules. In other words, they do not even roughly describe what Wittgenstein thinks of as ordinary or natural language, but rather constitute the very conception of language against which he repeatedly and explicitly sets his face in the *Investigations* (as when, in PI, 81, he identifies as his central target the idea that 'if anyone utters a sentence and *means* or *understands* it he is operating a calculus according to definite rules'). Hence, insofar as this conception implicitly determines Pole's view of what Wittgenstein's concepts of grammar and criteria might be, it interprets Wittgenstein's text in terms that that text puts under unremitting criticism.

Accordingly, Cavell has no difficulty in composing authentically Wittgensteinian objections to it. In particular, he emphasizes that Wittgenstein's comparison of moments of speech with moves in a game delivers the following insights: (against 1a) that rule-governed activities are not everywhere circumscribed by rules; (against 1b) that a rule can always be misinterpreted or misapplied in the name of following it; and (against 2) that whether and how we continue to use words in certain ways, to extend those patterns of use in particular directions, and to find new ways of using them is not a matter of how we freely decide or choose to go on but of our manifesting, acknowledging, and responding to the very general facts of nature, including human nature, that Wittgenstein invokes with the idea of 'forms of life'.

These points count definitively against attributing Polean conceptions of linguistic rules to Wittgenstein. However, nothing in Cavell's recounting of them suggests that he wants us to, or that we should, take these Wittgensteinian insights as grounds for rejecting the very idea that language is fundamentally rule-governed, rather than as grounds for rejecting one interpretation of that idea. On the latter reading, Wittgenstein's comparison of moments of speech to moves in a game implies that language is a rule-governed activity, while simultaneously warding off philosophical sublimations of what such a claim might entail by reminding us that everyday rule-following activities such as games are not everywhere circumscribed by rules, that such rules can be misinterpreted, and that our agreement (or lack of it) in applying or extending these rules is a matter of our agreeing (or failing to agree) in forms of life.

Nevertheless, Cavell does appear to imply that he sees a fundamental incompatibility between acknowledging this last point and emphasising the idea of linguistic rules:

> We learn and teach words in certain contexts, and then we are expected, and expect others, to be able to project them into further contexts. Nothing insures that this projection will take place (in particular, not the grasping of universals nor the grasping of books of rules), just as nothing insures that we will make, and understand, the same projections. That on the whole we do is a matter of our sharing routes of interest and feeling, modes of response, senses of humour and of significance and of fulfilment ... – all the whirl of organism Wittgenstein calls 'forms of life'. Human speech and activity, sanity and community, rest upon nothing more, but nothing less, than this. (MWM, 52)

The history of philosophical reflection on language is littered with depictions (à la Carnap) of linguistic rules as constituting complete, codified systems, and with invocations of our rule-following abilities that ward off the recognition that our agreement in projecting words is no more than a matter of fact – in favour, say, of a Platonic phantasm of those projections as locking onto tracks laid out in advance by the rules themselves. It is indeed hard to hold onto Wittgenstein's simple, difficult, and terrifying vision here; hence, even those who claim to be articulating it can themselves succumb to its fascinations. Once again, however, the deep problem Cavell identifies here appears to lie, not in the very idea that criteria might be thought of as rules, but in a particular use to which particular versions of that idea might be put.

For Cavell, however, Wittgenstein's comparison of moments of speech with moves in a game also implies that, in a fundamental sense, rules no more determine what speaking is than they determine what playing a game is.

> One may explain the difference between, say, contract and auction bridge by 'listing the rules'; but one cannot explain what *playing a game* is by 'listing rules'. Playing a game is 'a part of our . . . natural history' (PI, 25), and until one is an initiate of this human form of activity, the human gesture of 'citing a rule' can mean nothing. . . .
>
> For Wittgenstein, 'following a rule' is just as much a 'practice' as 'playing a game' is (PI, 199). Now what are its rules? In the sense in which 'playing chess' has rules, 'obeying a rule' has none (except, perhaps, in a special code or calculus which sets up some order of precedence in the application of various rules); and yet it can be done correctly or incorrectly – which just means it can be done or not done. And whether or not it is done is not a matter of rules (or of opinion or feeling or wishes or intentions). It is a matter of what Wittgenstein, in the *Blue Book*, refers to as 'conventions' (p. 24), and in the *Investigations* describes as 'forms of life' (e.g., PI, 23). That is always the ultimate appeal for Wittgenstein – not rules. . . . (MWM, 49–50)

We will be able to appreciate the full implications of this highly charged and highly condensed pair of passages only by going back (to the earlier essay 'Must We Mean What We Say?') and forward (to the first two parts of *The Claim of Reason*) within the sequence of Cavell's published writings. If, however, we attempt to evaluate the argument as it stands, it is not obvious why those attracted to an interpretation of criteria as rules should feel abashed.

To be sure, explaining the difference between two games is a very different matter from explaining what it is to play a game – since, among other things, understanding what it is to play a game is a precondition for being able to ask for and to benefit from an explanation of a particular game (or a particular aspect of a game). This is the burden of Wittgenstein's discussion of the powers and limits of ostensive definitions:

> One has already to know (or be able to do) something in order to be capable of asking a thing's name. But what does one have to know? . . .
>
> [T]he words: 'This is the king' (or 'this is called "the king"') are a definition only if the learner already 'knows what a piece in a game is'. That is, if he has already played other games, or has watched other people playing 'and understood' – *and similar things*. (PI, 30–1)

We should not, therefore, expect the business of explaining the difference between two language-games to resemble very closely the business of explaining what it is to play a language-game – that is, to say something in particular, to speak. But must we summarise these dissimilarities as a matter of being able to cite rules in the former case and being unable to cite rules in the latter – particularly if we do not conceive of rules as always codifiable in a neat list or calculus? Does Wittgenstein?

A little earlier, Wittgenstein does say:

> This explanation ['This is the king'] . . . only tells him the use of the piece because, as we might say, the place for it was already prepared. . . . And in this case it is so, not because the person to whom we give the explanation already knows rules, but because in another sense he is already master of a game. (PI, 31)

But Wittgenstein also declares that his conclusion applies only 'in this case' – which is one in which 'one can . . . imagine someone's having learnt the game without ever learning or formulating rules' (PI, 31). This already suggests that the 'mastery of a game' under discussion is mastery of a specific game or games, rather than mastery of what it is to play a game. That aside, although it is true *ex hypothesi* that Wittgenstein's inquirer neither acquired nor displays his mastery of the relevant games by explicitly formulating their rules, there is no suggestion that such mastery must always be so acquired or displayed (indeed, Wittgenstein's phrasing rather suggests that it is unusual). Moreover, the games he has learnt to master (first simple, and then increasingly complex, board games) are rule-governed, and our inquirer presumably can and must display his mastery of those rules in other ways (say, by observing them when playing these various games, or by pointing out mistakes made by those whom he observes playing them).

More generally, Cavell's own elaboration of Wittgenstein's claims about what it is to have a mastery of language suggests that normativity is ineliminable. For he implies that saying something (like playing a game, or following a rule) can be done correctly or incorrectly – that is, that certain ways of going on count as, say, making a report or giving an order or asking a question (PI, 199), and that certain other ways do not. If so, however, these forms of human activity must surely be kinds of normative activity, and becoming an initiate of them must surely be a matter of mastering norms. Is this not, after all, the most natural way of taking Wittgenstein's references to 'conventions', understood (as Cavell appears to understand them) as that which determines whether or not we have made a move in a game, or followed a rule, or asked a question? If so, why may we not attempt to capture this sense of the normativity of ordinary language by talking of rules of grammar?

Cavell's unqualified opposition between what Wittgenstein might mean by 'conventions' and what his commentators might mean by 'rules' is particularly puzzling when taken in conjunction with the argument Cavell himself develops in the paper that precedes his critique of Pole, as they are reprinted in his first book, and that he frequently describes as the earliest of his writings that he continues to use (hence, to find philosophically productive) – 'Must We Mean What We Say?'. For there, in defending the cogency of Austin's (and Ryle's) philosophical method of recalling what we say when, Cavell himself repeatedly glosses his frequent references to linguistic conventions in terms of normativity – as when he declares that '[t]he normativeness . . . which is certainly present, does not lie in the ordinary language philosopher's assertions *about* ordinary use; what is normative is exactly ordinary use itself' (MWM, 21).

Central to Cavell's position is his view that saying something is one kind of doing, that is, that when we talk about talking we are talking about a species of action.

> When we say how an action is done (how to act) what we say may report or describe the way we *in fact* do it . . ., but it may also lay out a way of doing or saying something which is to be *followed*. Whether remarks . . . 'about' ordinary language, and equally about ordinary actions . . . are statements or rules depends upon how they are taken: if they are taken to state facts and are supposed to be believed, they are statements; if they are taken as guides and supposed to be followed, they are rules. . . . Statements which describe a language (or a game or an institution) are rules (are binding) if you want to speak that language (play that game, accept that institution); or, rather, *when* you are speaking that language, playing that game, etc. . . .
>
> The most characteristic fact about actions is that they can – in various specific ways – go wrong, that they can be performed incorrectly. . . . Our successful performance of them depends upon our adopting and following the ways in which the action in question is done, upon what is normative for it. (MWM, 15–16, 22)

Here Cavell first broaches the claim he reiterates in his critique of Pole – that linguistic forms of human activity can be done correctly or incorrectly, rightly or wrongly, which just means that they are either done or not done. Here, however, he presents the question of what is normative for any particular act or moment of speech as a matter of what the rules governing that act require. Similarly, after telling us that ordinary language philosophers are interested in what it is to perform a given action at all (as opposed to performing it well), Cavell tells us that '[r]ules tell you what to do when you do the thing at all' (MWM, 28), and that 'the concept of rule does illuminate the concept of *action*, but not that of *justified action*. Where there is a question about what I do and I cite a rule in my favour, what I do is to *explain* my action, make clear what I was doing, not to justify it, say that what I did was well or rightly done' (MWM, 29: fn27). He even suggests that statements such as Austin's reminders of what we say when might be said to formulate 'the rules [as opposed to] the principles of grammar' (MWM, 32). And he offers the following characterization of such philosophical methods:

> [There is a] special sense in which the philosopher who proceeds from ordinary language is 'establishing a norm'.... He is certainly not *instituting* norms, nor is he *ascertaining* norms...; but he may be thought of as *confirming* or *proving* the existence of norms when he reports or describes how we (how to) talk.... (MWM, 32)

If Cavell is happy to talk here of linguistic normativity as a matter of applying and following norms or rules, and of recalling criteria as a way of confirming or proving that fact, why then talk of what appears to be the same phenomenon in his critique of Pole as something articulable in terms of conventions but very definitely not in terms of rules? In effect, his earlier essay makes the very case that he appears to reject in the later, and does so with more sophistication and power than is mobilised in that highly condensed rejection. It might therefore seem that Cavell's position can best be rendered consistent (with itself, with Wittgenstein's treatment of the issue, and with the nature of language) by viewing his hostility to the idea of linguistic rules in the Pole essay as a hostility to certain ways in which such talk of rules might be distorted, misconstrued, or sublimed.

Suppose, however, we recall that 'Must We Mean What We Say?' aims to explicate Austin's philosophical methods, whereas 'The Availability of Wittgenstein's Philosophy' aims to counter an explication of Wittgenstein, and that both essays draw upon (without presenting) a detailed argument about the nature of criteria within which Cavell sharply contrasts Austin's and Wittgenstein's conceptions of criteria to the latter's benefit (at least with respect to comprehending the sceptical impulse in philosophy). We might then be tempted to conclude that Cavell's essay on Pole marks the point at which his conception of the correct philosophical method attains its Wittgensteinian maturity by sloughing off an exclusively Austinian, rule-based conception of criteria and grammar. We cannot, then, draw any definitive conclusions about Cavell's perspective until we engage more extensively with his discussion of criteria, which was first formulated as part of his doctoral thesis but finally appeared (much changed) in *The Claim of Reason*.

CRITERIA, SCEPTICISM, AND PROJECTION

Cavell interprets Wittgenstein's notion of criteria as an inflection or projection of the ordinary notion – as both like and unlike it. The structure common to both he summarizes as follows:

> ... criteria are specifications a given person or group sets up on the basis of which (by means of, in terms of which) to judge (assess, settle) whether something has a particular status or value. Different formulations bring it closer to other regions of Wittgenstein's surface rhetoric: Certain specifications are what a person or group mean by (what they call, count as) a thing's having a certain status; the specifications define the status; the status consists in satisfying those specifications. (CR, 9)

Against this background, three key differences stand out. First, whereas the ordinary notion of a criterion typically presupposes a distinction between criteria and standards, with the latter determining the degree to which the former are satisfied in a given case, Wittgenstein's notion does not. For him, to have criteria is to know whether or not they apply, or to know that we have no decisive criteria for the given case (since we don't have criteria for all eventualities – whatever what might mean). Second, whereas the objects to which criteria apply in ordinary cases obviously require evaluation of some kind (e.g., dogs, dives, and governments), Wittgenstein's candidate objects raise no obvious evaluative question; they are just the ordinary objects and concepts of the world, and we use criteria to learn what kinds of objects they are (not to evaluate an already-known kind of object). Third, in the ordinary case, the authority that establishes and applies the given criteria varies widely from case to case; but for Wittgenstein, criteria are always 'ours' – the authoritative group seems to be the human group as such, and in articulating our criteria, I act as a representative language-speaker, making a claim to community (which might be rebuffed).

For Cavell, then, criteria are criteria of judgement; in using them, a human being counts something under a concept, for example, judging someone to be in pain on the basis of her winces and groans. Such criteria are context-dependent: groaning, for example, is a criterion of pain (a piece of pain-behaviour) only under certain circumstances. If the person groaning is (would correctly be described as) clearing her throat or calling her hamsters, then the groaning is not a criterion of pain because it is not an expression of pain, not a piece of pain-behaviour. This is not equivalent to claiming that pain-behaviour is a criterion of pain only in certain circumstances; that would imply that a piece of behaviour could be expressive of pain and yet not be a criterion of pain. For something to be a criterion of pain just is for it to be pain-behaviour; in so characterizing it, we must already have included the circumstances under which that behaviour is pain-behaviour (as opposed to throat-clearing or hamster-calling behaviour).

This already entails that Cavell's gloss on Wittgenstein's notion of a criterion cannot be used to refute scepticism. For if identifying a piece of behaviour as pain-behaviour is equivalent to identifying the presence of a criterion of pain, then criteria cannot guarantee the presence of real, existing, actual pain. It is perfectly possible for pain-behaviour to be manifest and pain to be absent, hence for the criteria of pain to be satisfied and pain to be absent. We cannot avoid this conclusion by describing such circumstances as ones in which criteria only appear to be satisfied (and in fact are not); for then any doubts about the reality of another's pain that we might attempt to combat by invoking the satisfaction of criteria will be restateable as doubts about whether what appears to be a case of the satisfaction of criteria really is one.

Since Cavell's understanding of the context dependence of criteria is more faithful to Wittgenstein's than that of other commentators (cf. CR, 37–48), it follows that scepticism is not refutable merely by the invocation of criteria – a conclusion that subverts a central assumption of traditional Wittgensteinian philosophizing. But nothing so far would prevent us from interpreting criteria as a species of rule – a norm governing our applications of words. Nor need proponents of that interpretation contest two further points that Cavell makes in unfolding his conception of criteria.

The first involves the way in which criteria tell us what kind of an object anything is. Cavell emphasizes that they do it in part by determining which other concepts can intelligibly be applied in contexts in which the concept of that object has its application; for example, knowing what a toothache is is in part a matter of knowing what counts as having a toothache, what counts as alleviating a toothache, and so on. To know how to use a word is to know how to use it in conjunction with other words, knowing which other words are relevant and which are not, knowing how various relevant words (used in conjunction with words for different kinds of object) require different kinds of contexts for their employment. A further point, which follows from the first, is that, if the criteria for a concept are satisfied and yet the thing itself is absent, this fact can only be accommodated in certain ways. If the person's groan really was a groan (an expression) of pain, then she can nevertheless not be in pain only if certain eventualities obtain – circumstances in which she is (for example) feigning, rehearsing, or hoaxing pain. Invoking such eventualities will satisfy us as explanations of her not being in pain because they retain the concept whose application these criteria determine; it is because the criteria of pain are satisfied that we know that what she is feigning is pain.

> Criteria are 'criteria for something's being so', not in the sense that they tell us of a thing's existence, but of something like its identity, not its *being* so, but of its being *so*. Criteria do not determine the certainty of statements, but the application of the concepts employed in statements. (CR, 45)

This insight certainly controverts traditional Wittgensteinian attempts to refute scepticism; but Cavell's way of motivating it – his sense of concepts fitting into a web of other concepts, and of knowing the criteria of a concept as knowing the grammatical post at which the concept-term is stationed in that web – seems entirely consistent with what traditional commentators mean when talking of the grammatical framework of a language-game, gesturing thereby to their sense of the systematically interweaving normative structure of language. Indeed, Cavell seems to admit as much when, talking of this background of 'pervasively, almost unimaginably *systematic*' 'necessities which others recognize, i.e., obey (consciously or not)' (CR, 29), he notes that 'Wittgenstein sometimes calls them conventions; sometimes rules' (CR, 30). Is this an aspect of Wittgenstein's practice from which he gives us good reason to diverge?

Cavell does emphasize that this agreement is agreement *in*, not agreement *to*. The idea is not that of arriving at an agreement on a given occasion, but of being in agreement throughout, being in harmony or being mutually attuned. We must not, therefore, interpret criteria as contractual, as if every shade of every word's meaning had been the subject of debate and explicit agreement, later codified in a book or calculus; but of course, we need not have any such conception in mind when talking of that agreement as an agreement in normative or rule-governed behaviour.

Cavell also emphasizes that agreement in the language we use is a matter of agreeing in judgements and in definitions. As he points out,

> Criteria were to be the bases (features, marks, specifications) on the basis of which certain judgements could be made . . . ; agreement over criteria was to make possible agreement about judgements. But in Wittgenstein it looks as if our ability to establish criteria depended upon a prior agreement in judgements. (CR, 30)

Cavell dissolves the air of paradox here by reminding us that our agreement in criteria is not meant to explain our agreement in judgement, or to provide a further foundation of agreement when we find ourselves disagreeing in judgement; for the two kinds of agreement are interwoven. To agree in the criteria for a given word just is to agree in how we apply the word in the context of specific judgements; and if we find that we disagree in a specific judgement employing that word, we thereby show that, to that extent, we disagree in our criteria.

> [This idea of mutual attunement] is meant to question whether a philosophical explanation is needed, or wanted, for the fact of agreement in the language human beings use together, an explanation, say, in terms of meanings or conventions or basic terms or propositions which are to provide the foundation of our agreements. For nothing is deeper than the fact, or the extent, of agreement itself. (CR, 32)

There is no denying that many Wittgensteinians miss this critical implication of Wittgenstein's famous remarks about definition and judgement (PI, 242). Even those whose general accounts of language mastery do not present agreement in criteria as providing a foundation for agreement in specific applications of words may find that their philosophical practice – as evinced, for example, in the assumption that a philosopher's divergent application of a word can be simply and definitively corrected by reminding her of its 'agreed' criteria – betrays them. However, Wittgenstein's resistance to such philosophical foundationalism is surely not best thought of as dependent upon resisting the idea that criteria are a species of rule. For the ideas about agreement in language, definition, and judgment that Cavell draws upon in justifying that resistance famously form part of the conclusion of Wittgenstein's extended discussion of rule following in the *Investigations*. Their pertinence therefore appears to presuppose the legitimacy of understanding grammar as a framework of rules.

Something similar applies to Cavell's way of connecting his account of this agreement with Wittgenstein's idea of forms of life. Responding to the sceptical worry that behaviour normally expressive of pain might have some other meaning (this person's screaming might be the way she calls her hamsters; that person might feel in a whipping what we feel in a caress), Cavell accepts this as a real possibility, but argues that its realization would not place our usual notion of what pain-behaviour is under general suspicion; it would rather place the person whose behaviour it is outside our world of pain. And in the face of sufficiently aberrant behaviour, we would conclude not that it is an abnormal expression of or response to something normal, but that it is the behaviour of someone abnormal – we will withhold our concepts of pain from her.

But what grounds our presumption that suffering and pain, or pity and comfort, go together? For Cavell, these form part of a multitude of

> very general facts of *human* nature.... That *that* should express under-standing or boredom or anger (or: that it should be part of the grammar of 'understanding' that *that* should be what we call his 'suddenly under-standing') is not necessary: someone may have to be said to 'understand suddenly' and then always fail to manifest the understanding five minutes later, just as someone *may* be bored by an earthquake or the death of his child..., or... angry at a pin or a cloud or a fish.... That human beings on the whole do not respond in these ways is, therefore, seriously referred to as conventional; but now we are thinking of convention not as the arrange-ments a particular culture has found convenient, in terms of its history or geography, for effecting the necessities of human existence, but as those forms of life which are normal to any group of creatures we call human, any group about which we will say, for example, that they *have* ... a geographical environment which they manipulate or exploit in certain ways for certain humanly comprehensible motives. (CR, 110–11)

We can imagine, or might encounter, human creatures who hope, fear, and question in forms very different from ours; but we can think of them as human only insofar as, for them, hope is grammatically related to satisfac-tion and disappointment, and fear to some object or reason for fear that we can understand, even if we cannot share it. If the pain connoisseur's form of life is such that we can identify such connections in it, then we can treat her behaviour as an (abnormal) part of our world of suffering and pain; if it lacks them, then in this respect we cannot treat her as (and hence she is not) part of our world. And nothing and no one can tell us just how far to go in our attempts to understand her, to make sense of her world before exiling her from our own.

Being in the human world thus appears as a matter of sharing certain facets of human nature; normality involves finding certain things natural, as if the very distinction between normality and abnormality amounts to a distinction betwen the natural and the unnatural. Cavell takes this to be a central moral of Wittgenstein's tale of the deviant pupil (PI, 185 [cf 143]).

> Our ability to communicate with him depends upon his 'natural understand-ing', his 'natural reaction', to our directions and our gestures. It depends upon our mutual attunement in judgements. It is astonishing how far this takes us in understanding one another, but it has its limits.... And when

these limits are reached, when our attunements are dissonant, I cannot get below them to firmer ground.... For not only does he not receive me, because his natural reactions are not mine; but my own understanding is found to go no further than my own natural reactions bear it. I am thrown back upon myself: I as it were turn my palms outward, as if to exhibit the kind of creature I am, and declare my ground occupied, only mine, ceding yours. (CR, 115)

Cavell here portrays our attunement in criteria, in definitions and judgements, as inseparable from an attunement in natural reactions – in what we find normal, utterly obvious, utterly outrageous, and so on; hence when those attunements become dissonant, we have nothing to which to appeal, no source of authority or guidance in determining how to respond to that dissonance – whether to acknowledge a difference, or withdraw a set of concepts, or see my own reactions as peculiar – except ourselves. It follows that citing criteria cannot constitute an objective resolution to a genuine disharmony in judgements (say, in response to a sceptic's anxieties); for if our agreement in criteria runs no further and no deeper than our agreements in judgments and natural reactions, then citing criteria can never impersonally demonstrate the deviance of one party to the disagreement. It rather amounts to an invitation to reconsider that disagreement and what is truly at stake in it, to ask ourselves whether we wish to take a stand upon it and what stand we wish to take.

Such a view of the power (and hence the powerlessness) of appeals to criteria and grammar is certainly not a traditional one, and its proper acknowledgement would radically alter our sense of the power (and powerlessness) of Wittgenstein's philosophical methods. But does that view depend upon rejecting the idea of a grammatical investigation as an exploration of the normativity of language use? Would talk of rules here necessarily imply exactly the kind of impersonal authority, the exclusion of individual responsibility, that Cavell's account wishes to deny? But that denial results from a recounting of Wittgenstein's claims about agreements in definition and in judgement, and about the deviant pupil; in other words, it applies conclusions from Wittgenstein's investigation of rule following to his notion of criteria, and hence implies that criteria are a species of rule. Cavell's argument is thus better cast as emphasising Wittgenstein's demystification of the impersonal authority of normativity, and drawing out its consequences for his conception of his own philosophical method.

I suggested earlier that Cavell's aversion to glossing criteria as rules might reveal his commitment to a Wittgensteinian as opposed to an

Austinian notion of criteria. Does his detailed comparative discussion of these two philosophers support such a reading? Cavell organizes this discussion around a distinction between specific and generic objects, understood not as different kinds of object but as different kinds of problem that might arise about objects. Austin's discussions of knowledge and scepticism invoke examples of objects that pose a specific problem of recognition or identification (is this bird a goldfinch or a bittern?); Wittgenstein's discussions invoke generic objects, objects as such, examples of materiality such as tables, chairs, and houses – about which no problems of recognition arise, but in relation to which our ability to know of the reality or existence of worldly things can be exemplified. The Austinian criteria elicited by questions of knowledge with respect to specific objects are marks or features that require a special training or environment to have mastered; they relate a specific name to a specific type of object. Wittgensteinian criteria, elicited by questions of knowledge with respect to generic objects, have to do with the ability that any language user has to word the world, to count things under concepts; they do not relate a name to an object, but rather various concepts to the concept of that object.

> If you do not know the (non-grammatical) criteria of an Austinian object . . . then you lack a piece of information, a bit of knowledge, and you can be told its name, told what it is, told what it is (officially) called. But if you do not know the grammatical criteria of Wittgensteinian objects, then you lack, as it were, not only a piece of information or knowledge, but the possibility of acquiring any information about such objects *überhaupt*; you cannot be told the name of that object, because there is as yet no *object* of that kind for you to attach a forthcoming name to: the possibility of finding out what it is officially called is not yet open to you. . . . You have to know *certain* things about an object in order to know *anything* (else) about it. . . . (CR, 77)

The echo of Cavell's earlier anti-Pole emphasis on the difference between knowing a move or piece in a game and knowing what it is to play (a game) is evident; but although an emphasis upon Austinian rather than Wittgensteinian examples might well encourage a conception of criteria as codifiable in a rule book, it remains unclear why anyone who follows Cavell's sense of Wittgenstein's distinctiveness might not think of the knowledge that grammatical criteria embody as a grasp of a web of norms or rules. Indeed, Cavell's immediate characterization of such grammatical knowledge as of a 'schematism mark[ing] out the set of criteria on the basis of which the word is applied in all the grammatical contexts into which it fits and will be found to fit' (CR, 77) would seem to invite precisely such a thought.

Perhaps talk of a network or schematism of rules suggests an inappropriate inflexibility or transparency in the ways in which we project words into new contexts. This is certainly something Cavell is concerned to deny in his provocative excursus on Wittgenstein's vision of language in Part II of *The Claim of Reason*. His primary example is the word 'feed': we learn to 'feed the cat' and to 'feed the lions', and then, when someone talks of feeding the meter or feeding our pride, we understand them; we accept this projection of the word. Cavell's view is that tolerating such projections is of the essence of words. We could, of course, have used other words than 'feed' for this new context, either by projecting another established word or inventing a new one. If, however, we talked of 'putting' money in the meter as we do of putting a dial on the meter, we would lose a way of making certain discriminations (between putting a flow of material into a machine and putting a part made of new material on a machine), we would begin to deprive ourselves of certain of our concepts (could we dispense with talk of feeding our pride and still retain our concept of emotions as capable of growth?), and we would in effect be extending the legitimate range of our alternative word in just the manner that we were trying to avoid. If instead we invented a new word, we would lose a way of registering connections between contexts, open up questions about the legitimate projections of this new word, and at the limit deprive all words of meaning (since no word employed in only one context would be a word).

At the same time, our projections of our words are also deeply controlled. We can, for example, feed a lion, but not by placing a bushel of carrots in its cage; and its failure to eat them would not count as a refusal to do so. Such projections of 'feed' and 'refusal' fail because their connections with other words in their normal contexts do not transfer to the new one; one can only refuse something that one might also accept, hence something that one can be offered or invited to accept, and what might count as an offer and an acceptance in the context of a meal is both different from and related to what counts as an offer and acceptance in the context of mating or being guided. These limits are neither arbitrary nor optional; they show how the place of a concept in a schematism of concepts determines its grammar, and thus the respects in which a new context for a word must invite or allow its projection.

In short:

[A]ny form of life and every concept integral to it has an indefinite number of instances and directions of projection; and . . . this variation is not arbitary. *Both* the 'outer' variance and the 'inner' constancy are necessary if a concept is to accomplish its tasks – of meaning, understanding, communicating etc., and in general, guiding us through the world, and relating thought and action and feeling to the world. (CR, 185)

Is it really possible to imagine that any rule formulation might capture or ground this 'outer' variance? Might there be a rule governing the route of projection that our word 'feed' displays, not to mention the further steps or leaps we might find ourselves taking with it in the future? But can we capture the 'inner' constancy of a concept's projections – as manifest, say, in our responsibility to show how its new context can tolerate the application of the other concepts to which our criteria relate it – without adverting to some idea of a systematic web of norms or standards? *Must* any invocation of rules to hit off this constancy block any proper acknowledgement of that variance?[6]

Such an anxiety would be well grounded if all rules were algorithmic, and if behaviour could count as rule-governed only if an explicit formulation of the rules were manifest either in learning it or engaging in it. But Wittgenstein's investigation of the ways in which games (and hence language-games?) are governed by rules explicitly shows that neither of these assumptions is correct. Not all rules are part of a calculus, and an activity can still be said to be normative even in the absence of any explicit role for the citation of rule formulations – if, for example, those engaging in it can correct themselves and others when they go astray, can teach it to others by example, and so on (cf. PI, 31, 54). A little later, Wittgenstein says:

> We can easily imagine people amusing themselves in a field by playing with a ball so as to start various existing games, but playing many without finishing them and in between throwing the ball aimlessly into the air, chasing one another with the ball and bombarding one another for a joke and so on. And now someone says: The whole time they are playing a ball-game and following definite rules at every throw.
>
> And is there not also the case where we play and – make up the rules as we go along? And there is even one where we alter them – as we go along. (PI, 83)

We are plainly meant to balk at saying what Wittgenstein's imagined observer says; but is that because invoking the idea of rules in order to understand any aspect of these people's play is unhelpful, or because the observer invokes the specific idea of definite rules governing every move in a seamless sequence of games? To think instead of these people as variously following, altering, and making up rules as they go along seems rather less forced; and the aimlessness that may resist such a thought in this context is certainly not a salient feature of the examples of flexibly inflexible projections of words that are central to Cavell's discussion.

Cavell takes that discussion to have a further moral:

> [W]hat goes for explaining my words goes for . . . citing rules in a game . . . and for the thousands of things I do in talking. You cannot use words to do what we do with them until you are initiate of the forms of life which give those words the point and shape they have in our lives. . . . When I cite or teach you a rule, I can adduce only exterior facts about rules, e.g., say that it applies only when such-and-such is the case, or that it is inoperative when another rules applies, etc. But I cannot *say* what following rules is *überhaupt*, nor say how to obey a rule in a way which doesn't presuppose that you already know what it is to follow them. (CR, 184)

Is it not, however, equally true that I cannot say what eliciting or acknowledging or applying criteria is *überhaupt*? I can recall certain criteria that I claim we share; but I cannot say something that cuts beneath their actual specific guidance to that which makes them normative, and my recountings cannot have any effect unless you are an initiate of the forms of life that shape and are shaped by them, and so know what it is to be guided by them. But then following a rule and projecting criteria are on all fours; hence these considerations offer no obstacle to thinking of our capacity to become an initiate of the form of life that our criteria inform as a capacity to become an initiate of an essentially normative mode of existence. Once again, such claims about the nature of rule following should be read not as a reason for distinguishing sharply between rules and criteria, but as a way of clarifying what being guided by criteria is really like, and hence the true power (and powerlessness) of the philosophical practice of recalling criteria.

For of course, Cavell's excursus on projecting words is meant to emphasize the irrefutability of scepticism.

> If words and phrases *must* recur (which means . . . that they must be projected into new contexts, which means that new contexts must tolerate or invite that projection); and if there are no rules or universals which *insure* appropriate projection, but only our confirmed capacity to speak to one another; then a new projection [such as that of the sceptic], though not at first obviously appropriate, may be made appropriate by giving relevant explanations of how it is to be taken, *how* the new context *is* an instance of the old concept. If we are to communicate, we mustn't leap too far; but how far

is too far? If two masters of a language disagree about the appropriateness of a projection, then it cannot be obvious who is right. (CR, 192)

Hence, it cannot be obvious that the sceptic's not fully unnatural projection of our knowledge claims is wrong, self-evidently unjustifiable and shown to be so simply by recalling criteria. To think this would be to deny that which makes words words – to utilise criteria in ways that repress the dimension of language that the term is meant to highlight, and that Wittgenstein himself utilises in projecting the ordinary term 'criterion' into its new philosophical context. But we can recognize this sceptical defence of ordinary language as a sceptical phantasm of linguistic rules without thinking that any conception of language as rule-governed must be a sceptical phantasm.

RULES, INCLINATIONS, AND MATHEMATICS: CAVELL AND KRIPKE

The third text in which Cavell confronts the idea of rules of grammar is the 1988 Carus Lecture from which the second of my opening illustrative quotations was taken, concerning Kripke's reading of Wittgenstein on rules and scepticism. Here is how Cavell introduces his discussion of Kripke's hugely influential work:

> In taking rules as fundamental to Wittgenstein's development of scepticism about meaning, Kripke subordinates the role of criteria in the *Investigations*, hence appears from my side of things to underrate drastically, or to beg the question of, the issue of the ordinary, a structure of which is the structure of our criteria and their grammatical relations. In my seeing criteria as forming Wittgenstein's understanding of the possibility of scepticism, I take this to show rules to be subordinate; but since Kripke's interpretation of rules seems, in turn, to undercut the fundamentality of the appeal to the ordinary, my appeal to criteria must appear to beg the question from his side of things. (CHU, 65–6)

Cavell's formulations will certainly appear question-begging to anyone attracted to the traditional idea that criteria are akin to rules. For he puts his point against Kripke in such a way as to occlude the possibility that that traditional idea holds open: that criteria are no more subordinate to rules than rules are to criteria, but that criteria are rather a species of rule – that their articulation displays an aspect of the normativity of language use. The key idea here is not subordination (of one concept to another, as in a codification or calculus) but clarification (of one concept by another, as in a recounting of grammar) – an option foreclosed by Cavell's assumption throughout this passage that rules and criteria are to be contrasted or opposed. To think that rules are fundamental to Wittgenstein's vision of language (hence meaning, and hence scepticism) does not entail thinking that criteria, and hence the ordinary, are subordinate to rules. Such may be Kripke's way of attaching salvational significance to rules; but then Cavell's critique of Kripke will not generalize.

Cavell's most explicit development of his concern comes in response to Kripke's emphasis upon Wittgenstein's rule-following paradox – that no course of action could be determined by a rule, because every course of action can be made to accord with the rule.

I take Wittgenstein to say fairly explicitly that rules cannot play the fundamental role Kripke takes him to cast them in. In the sentence succeeding the one ... in which Wittgenstein names 'our paradox', Wittgenstein writes: 'The answer was: if everything can be made out to accord with the rule, then it can also be made to conflict with it. And so there would be neither accord nor conflict here.' This seems to me equally readable as suggesting not that this paradox is 'central' but that it is no sooner named than its significance is undermined. Wittgenstein's tone is: What our so-called paradox came to was no more than this so-called answer can completely tame. The facts about possible interpretations of a rule are not sufficient to cause scepticism (though they may play into a sceptical hand, one that has already portrayed rules and their role in language in a particular way). . . .

How do I know that what I called Wittgenstein's 'tone' is what I say it is? My claim is based, for example, on taking Wittgenstein's remark at [section] 199, 'This is of course a note on the grammar of the expression "to obey a rule" ' – in response to a question whether obeying a rule could be something only one man can do and only once in his life – to apply to his entire discussion of rules, for example, to questions of what counts as obedience, following, interpretation, regularity . . . , no one of which is less or more fundamental than the concept of a rule, and each of which is to be investigated grammatically (hence by way of eliciting criteria). (CHU, 67–8)

The first of these paragraphs counters Kripke's assumption that the rule-following paradox is 'the fundamental problem of *Philosophical Investigations*'. Cavell points out that Wittgenstein no sooner enunciates the paradox than he dissolves it; what Kripke sees as an elaboration of the paradox's destructive consequences Cavell sees as its immediate dismissal. Cavell might have continued his quotation a few sentences further, where Wittgenstein declares that his articulation of the paradox contains a misunderstanding, since it initiates an argument in which we give one interpretation of the rule after another; and what this shows is that 'there is a way of grasping a rule which is *not* an *interpretation*, but which is exhibited in what we call 'obeying the rule' and 'going against it' from case to case of its application (PI, 201, translation amended). He does not; but he has already done enough to suggest that 'rules cannot play the fundamental role Kripke casts them in'. This is a strong point against Kripke's reading of the *Investigations*; but it does not show (and Cavell doesn't appear to think that it shows) that rules cannot play the fundamental role in the *Investigations* that the traditional gloss on criteria would assign them.

Cavell's second paragraph reminds us that Wittgenstein's rule-following considerations (say, from sections 143–243 and beyond) form part of a grammatical investigation into the concept of a rule, hence involve the eliciting of criteria. Given his previous assumption that rules and criteria are utterly distinct, with its companion assumption that one must be subordinate to the other, his intended conclusion would appear to be that, since Wittgenstein explores the concept of a rule by eliciting our criteria for using the term, then criteria must be more fundamental than (let's say superordinate to) rules in Wittgenstein's philosophical method.

However, pointing out that the concept of a rule has a grammar, and hence that Wittgenstein's discussion of it proceeds by way of eliciting its criteria, simply fails to engage with the traditional suggestion that a criterion can be illuminatingly compared to – perhaps seen as an inflection of the concept of – a rule, and hence that neither is more fundamental than the other. There is nothing paradoxical in the thought that Wittgenstein's concept of a criterion itself has criteria, to be elicited by way of a grammatical investigation of its use (one might indeed think of Part I of *The Claim of Reason* as summarising just such an investigation); so why should there be anything paradoxical in the thought that our criteria for the concept of a rule might themselves be a species of rule? The assumption implicit in Kripke's, and in the traditional, reading of the *Investigations* is that Wittgenstein's notes on the grammar of the expression 'to obey a rule' (and its related expressions) are meant (among other things) to cast light on linguistic rule-following, and hence on what Wittgenstein's grammatical investigations investigate, on what his eliciting of criteria elicit – that they are, in effect, investigations of the grammar of Wittgenstein's conception of grammar, eliciting the criteria for his term 'criteria'. Simply to emphasize that this particular grammatical investigation (like any other) *elicits* criteria gives us no reason to think that it cannot be taken as a grammatical investigation *of* criteria.

Perhaps, however, the detailed critique of Kripke that follows this prologue develops arguments of a more universal scope, directed against the very idea of thinking of criteria as rules of grammar. To be sure, they are keyed to Kripke's particular interpretation of Wittgenstein's rule-following remarks, and of the *Investigations* as a whole. But they suggest that Kripke's interpretation of rules is itself more sceptical than the sceptical paradox it is designed to overcome; so they at least raise the question of whether that conclusion must apply to any understanding of criteria as a species of rule.

Two aspects of Cavell's argument seem particularly relevant here. The first concerns the relationship between Wittgenstein's deviant pupil and his teacher; Cavell tries to bring out the differences between Kripke's and Wittgenstein's conceptions of it by constructing a Kripkean version of the portrait Wittgenstein paints (in PI, 217) of a moment in that relationship, the famous moment in which bedrock is reached. Wittgenstein presents the matter as follows: 'If I have exhausted the justifications I have reached bedrock, and my spade is turned. Then I am inclined to say: "This is simply what I do"'. Weaving together remarks of Kripke's scattered throughout his account, Cavell gives a Kripkean cast to the same exchange as follows: 'If I have exhausted ... [etc.] Then I am licensed to say: "This is simply what I am inclined to do"' (CHU, 70).

Kripke's teacher isn't just inclined to say something, but is licensed to say it; and what he says gives expression to his inclination to do something, not to his simply doing it. Kripke thereby misses the moment of hesitation in Wittgenstein's teacher – the sense that, despite being inclined to say something, he has reasons to refrain: perhaps the knowledge that, at bedrock, the common background against which the 'this' that he does would be intelligible to his pupil is lacking, perhaps a reluctance to say something that might be interpreted as a threat to discontinue his instruction. Kripke's teacher shows no such hesitation; considerations of mutual intelligibility and mutual civility carry no weight, and thus Kripke's teacher's expression of confident inclination 'prepares for the gesture of excluding, or accepting the exclusion, of the child from participation in the community' (CHU, 73); it resolves a crisis of consent by the exercise of coercive power.

Kripke's teacher also implicitly defines what it is right to do in following a rule of the community in terms of the matching of one's inclinations to go on in a certain way. For Cavell, this embodies a conception of the community that is the reverse of inviting.

[W]hat could my inclination, or profound faith, ever have to do with justifying him here (or licensing him, or judging his action to be correct)? Suppose that driving you to work I say 'I'm inclined to run this red light; if you reply 'My inclination agrees with yours', have you licensed me to run the light? You may be encouraging license. If when the light turns green I say, 'I have faith in going now', and you reply, 'My faith agrees with yours', have you made sense of me and I of you? ... If the situation is as Kripke says Wittgenstein says, why ever say more than: 'I agree with you. That is my inclination too'? Paraphrasing a wonder of Wittgenstein's: What gives us so much as the idea that human beings, things, can be right? ... If the matching of inclinations is all Wittgenstein's teaching leaves us with, then I feel like asking: What kind of solution is that to a sceptical problem? Kripke calls it a sceptical solution. Then I can express my perplexity this way: This solution seems to me more sceptical than the problem it is designed to solve. (CHU, 74–5)

Kripke's talk of inclinations, confident or otherwise, induces a loss of the very idea of rightness or justification, say normativity, that he presents himself as wishing to defend from the sceptic. Hence there is a clear sense in which the conception of rules he proffers as a solution to his sceptical paradox is itself an expression of scepticism. But Cavell's way of reaching this conclusion depends so critically upon the precise implications of every key term in Kripke's commentary that it neither offers, nor seems intended to offer, a reason for believing that a similar charge applies to other commentators simply because they give the concept of a rule a central place in their account of Wittgenstein's philosophical designs.

A further step in Cavell's diagnosis of Kripke's scepticism looks different, however. For Cavell also contests Kripke's conception of the relationship between rule following in mathematical and in nonmathematical (say, ordinary) cases – between the cases of addition (and hence quaddition) and of nonmathematical instances of going on with words. Kripke claims that the problems he sees arising with addition can also arise in the latter case: the only difference is that they can be brought out more smoothly with mathematical examples. To illustrate this, he constructs the concept 'tabair', which he tells us applies to anything that is a table not found at the base of the Eiffel tower, or a chair found there; and he imagines a sceptic asking us how we know that we do not mean tabair by 'table'.

Cavell contests Kripke's sense of similarity: he points out that the sceptic's imputation that the inside and outside of the tower might be included in the function of a concept amounts to an invitation to imagine an interweaving of our criteria for furniture with a geographical singularity, but without actually imagining any recognisably human interest to which it might give expression. As Cavell puts it, 'in explaining the concept tabair this sceptic dissociates criteria from the realm of what Wittgenstein calls our 'natural reactions'. I suppose one could say that my natural reactions change in the face of the Eiffel Tower, but would this not owe an account of why this has happened just to me and in such a way as to produce this concept?' (CHU, 88) And whatever conviction such an account might elicit, it could not produce that sense of the meanings of our words receding generally from our grasp, of the revelation of a universal truth, that Cavell takes as the touchstone of a genuinely sceptical anxiety.

Cavell's further implication is that we do not intuitively sense such an inexplicable complication in our criteria in the case of quaddition; there, one might say, we have no more (although also, of course, no less) sense of puzzlement at the idea that the function of a concept parallel to our concepts of addition might diverge at numbers above 57 (or above 1000) than at any other point in the series they generate. One might say: the relevance or purchase of human interests and concerns upon mathematical functions is not such as to incite demands for an explanation as to why there should be such a parallel function, or why it should 'deviate' precisely as and when it does; to understand it just is to understand the series it generates, and hence the derivability of every step within it. Cavell develops this intuition at length:

> I suppose that something that makes a mathematical rule mathematical – anyway, that makes adding adding – is that what counts as an instance of it ... is, intuitively, settled in advance, that it tells what its first instance is, and what the interval is to successive instances, and what the order of instances is. The rule for addition extends to all its possible applications. (As does the rule for quaddition – otherwise it would not rhyme with addition, I mean it would not be known to us as a mathematical function.) But our ordinary concepts – for instance that of a table – are not thus mathematical in their application: we do not, intuitively ... know in advance ... a right first instance, or the correct order of instances, or the set interval of their succession. And sometimes we will not know whether to say an instance counts as falling under a concept, or to say that it does not count....
>
> To say that concepts of ordinary language do not determine the first, or the succession, or the interval of their instances is perhaps to say that the instances falling under a concept do not form a series. (CHU, 89–90)

For Kripke to think that the sceptical problem he develops so smoothly from the example of addition can be equally well (if less smoothly) developed from nonmathematical examples amounts, therefore, to a failure to appreciate the specificity of mathematical concepts and their associated functions; more precisely, it amounts to assuming that ordinary, nonmathematical concepts have associated functions, that they are or can be presented as having an essentially mathematical structure. This dissociates nonmathematical concepts from their distinctive relationship with our natural reactions and forms of life, and treats mathematical concepts as normative for the nonmathematical – as if the latter would lack something if they failed to manifest those features which, in reality, distinguish mathematical from nonmmathematical concepts within human forms of life.

> Ordinary language will aspire to mathematics as to something sublime; that it can so aspire is specific to its condition. The idea of ordinary language as lacking something in its rules is bound up with – is no more nor less necessary than – this aspiration. This is the place at which Wittgenstein characterizes logic (and I assume the rule for addition is included here) as 'normative', as something to which we compare the use of words (section 81) – to the discredit of words; he takes this further a few sections later in posing the question, 'In what sense is logic something sublime?'(section 89). In this role of the normative, the mathematical is not a special case of a problem that arises for the ordinary; without the mathematical this problem of the ordinary would not arise. (CHU, 92)

Here, Kripke's variant of scepticism meets up with that of Pole, and returns us to Wittgenstein's most fundamental characterization of the sceptical impulse against which he sets his face – the impulse to sublime the logic of ordinary language, to see its grammar either as having the form and nature of a calculus, with its distinctive abstractness, universality, and completeness, or as something to be condemned for failing to do so. And here we can say that Cavell's critique of Kripke has more general implications: for even if most Wittgenstein commentators dissociate themselves from the precise details of Kripke's sceptical problem and solution, they tend not to question the assumption that the example of addition might be a reliable guide to the nature of rule following in general, and hence to the nature of Wittgenstein's conception of grammatical rules. Hence, if Cavell's sense of the distinctiveness of the mathematical is accurate, this assumption might itself justify the charge that those who cleave to it project a sceptical conception of the grammar of language upon Wittgenstein himself.

However, this conclusion would leave us with a problem. For of course, the main reason most Wittgenstein commentators have assumed that the example of addition casts light on the nature of linguistic rules and hence upon grammar is that the text of the *Philosophical Investigations* appears to share that assumption. It takes a mathematical example as normative for the whole of its discussion of rule following, and that discussion appears to be designed to give Wittgenstein's own account of linguistic meaning. Hence, if Cavell's charge of scepticism can be made out against Wittgenstein's commentators, must it not also apply to Wittgenstein himself? Does Cavell's conception of criteria and grammar, then, succeed in avoiding a sceptical inflection from which even the author whose terminology and method Cavell claims to be inheriting could not entirely free himself? Or is the *Investigations* here not so much succumbing to a fantasy as acting one out for therapeutic purposes? Perhaps Wittgenstein deploys his mathematical example with so little overt fuss, and yet so quickly after repeatedly warning us against taking the mathematical as normative for language, so that we might eventually come to see that our previous readings of him have in fact betrayed the insights to which they proclaimed allegiance, and hence to realize the tenacity of the fantasies he opposes, and the real difficulty of properly uprooting them.

CONCLUSION

Philosophy's impulse to regard logic as normative for the normativity of words is emblematic of a broader human impulse to regard such normativity solely as something to which we must impersonally and inflexibly respond rather than as something for which we are also individually and unforeseeably responsible. Given the pervasiveness and depth of that impulse, it should not be surprising that many philosophers' attempts to articulate and deploy Wittgenstein's attempts to overcome it in fact give further expression to it. The impulse might find expression in misrepresentations of Wittgenstein's account of linguistic normativity. Or it might find expression in a failure to allow one's intellectual grasp of that account (with its emphasis upon the intertwining of agreement in definitions with agreement in judgements, and of both with our natural reactions) properly to inform one's deployment of the philosophical method that draws upon that normativity (perhaps by allowing the stability of a word's projectiveness to occlude its tolerance, perhaps by treating one's interlocutor as a deviant pupil rather than as an equal member of the community of speakers). Stanley Cavell's work on and after Wittgenstein is uniquely sensitive to both forms of philosophical confusion, and to the danger (at once intellectual and spiritual) that one's criticisms of others on these grounds might take a self-condemning form. His exemplarity in this respect need not, however, make us write as if the idea of linguistic normativity, in all its ordinariness, is beyond redemption. Given Wittgenstein's own apparent tolerance of the idea that his concepts of grammar and criteria might fruitfully be glossed in terms of rules, and given his sense of the ordinary as what can overcome our bewitchments as well as incite them, it seems far preferable to view him as proposing that we endlessly attempt to recover the everyday idea of linguistic normativity from our ever-renewed impulse to sublime it.

Notes

1. Stanley Cavell, *The Claim of Reason* (Oxford: Oxford University Press, 1979; revised edition 1999). Hereinafter CR.
2. For a powerfully argued elaboration of this impression, see Steven Affeldt, "The Ground of Mutuality: Criteria, Judgment and Intelligibility in Stephen Mulhall and Stanley Cavell," *European Journal of Philosophy* 6 (April 1998), pp. 1–31.
3. Stanley Cavell, *Must We Mean What We Say?* (Cambridge: Cambridge University Press, 1976), p. 48. Hereinafter MWM.
4. Stanley Cavell, *Conditions Handsome and Unhandsome* (Chicago: University of Chicago Press, 1990), p. 67. Hereinafter CHU.
5. Ludwig Wittgenstein, *Philosophical Investigations*, trans. G. E. M. Anscombe (Oxford: Blackwell, 1953), pp. 138–9. Hereinafter PI.
6. For further thoughts on the proper interpretation of this passage, see my "Inner Constancy, Outer Variation," in J. Conant and A. Kern, eds., *Skepticism and Interpretation* (Stanford, CA: Stanford University Press, forthcoming).

5 | Aesthetics, Modernism, Literature: Cavell's Transformations of Philosophy

J. M. BERNSTEIN

From the outset Cavell has proclaimed an intimacy, at times amounting to a virtual identity, between the *logic* of aesthetic claiming (the logic appropriate to our claims, evaluative and interpretive, about works of art and, by extension, the logic of those works, their claiming) and the *logic* peculiar to ordinary language philosophy ("what we say when" and "what we mean when we say it"). Cavell also states that artistic modernism "only makes explicit and bare what has always been true of art" (MD, 189),[1] entailing that now what we think of aesthetics, and so of art, is bound to artistic modernism. Holding onto the first identification of aesthetic claiming and philosophy, this would associate or identify the logical form of modern philosophy – its forms of writing, argument, claiming – as forged paradigmatically in Wittgenstein's late writings, with the logical form of modernist works of art, with their modes of claiming and authenticity. Analogously, at the close of *The Claim of Reason* Cavell is mourning Othello and Desdemona, finding in their fate something that philosophy must be capable of – call it acknowledgment – but that, ever since Plato banned the poets from his ideal republic, philosophy has banned from its precincts. So much is implied both by the analysis itself and by Cavell's explicit statement that "tragedy is the story and study of acknowledgement, of what goes before it and after it – i.e., that the form of tragedy is the public form of the life of skepticism with respect to other minds" (CR, 478). In the light, then, of his demonstration of the entanglement between the philosophical problem of skepticism and the role of acknowledgment,[2] Cavell wonders whether there is space in philosophy for Othello and Desdemona, their fate: "But can philosophy accept them back at the hands of poetry? ... Perhaps it could if it could itself become literature. But can philosophy become literature and still know itself?" (CR, 496) Whether this is meant as a specification of the earlier claims or as an addition is, even in context, difficult to say. At any rate, I presume that these claims of virtual identity between philosophical and aesthetic forms of claiming, between the position of modern philosophy and artistic modernism, and between philosophy and literature, at least at the level of logical form (whatever that means here), are deeply puzzling if not immediately repugnant.

Let me flesh out the puzzle a little, letting the repugnance take care of itself. In making his claims of association or overlap or logical homology or analogy or virtual identity (which is it? is there a difference to be drawn here?) between the logic of philosophical and aesthetic claiming, philosophy and artistic modernism, philosophy and literature, Cavell must be regarding art or literature transcendentally, that is, he must be thinking that art of a certain kind reveals, at least, some necessary conditions for the possibility of there being objective significance, meaning, at all.[3] Hence, the import of art or literature is not given directly by their practice (or the canon that catalogues it), but by what is revealed through it or exemplified by it. So, in a first step, Cavell must believe that there is generally an unrecognized or misinterpreted and suppressed transcendental claim lodged by some artworks that, at least heretofore, has arisen only in relation to them, or has been more perspicuous (surveyable, intense) in them than elsewhere. Some artworks represent a privileged locale or a possibility for the intensification or exhibition or dramatization of a claiming of a certain kind that is, when seen aright, one necessary for the possibility of objective meaningfulness *überhaupt*. But if there is going to be any necessity in philosophy associating itself with art, a second step, then the relevant artworks must be raising more than just any old necessary condition for the possibility of objective meaningfulness – that there be meaning and mattering generally – but one that must be explicitly and self-consciously embodied in philosophy if philosophy is going to be objectively meaningful; the condition can be satisfied only if self-consciously satisfied. It is not enough that philosophy be able to point to the transcendental condition of meaningfulness that art exemplifies; the worth of its own claiming must depend on it too exemplifying that transcendental condition.

A final twist, then, becomes: if philosophy must exemplify the very same transcendental condition that it reveals artworks to exemplify, what becomes of the difference between philosophy and art (literature)? In pointing to the transcendental significance of certain works of art and coming to recognize the generality of the demand that that notion of transcendental significance implies, is there any space left for philosophy beyond flagging its own emptiness and ceding all to art? (Think of this as philosophy's long good-bye.) Or, if philosophy did manage the trick, did manage to attain to the demand to exemplify the condition of meaningfulness it shows to be transcendental, would the product still be recognizable as philosophy? Does this matter? Why? What is the difference between the two final possibilities? I take it that these questions begin to flesh out the open question with which Cavell concludes *The Claim of Reason* – that that and my questions are open because philosophy has not yet attained to the condition that would satisfy the demands on it or completed its long good-bye or become utterly irrelevant. Hence to the extent to which Cavell has meant his writing to satisfy those demands, its sense and worth remain unsettled and the debate over it, exemplary or empty, unresolved. (I take the claims identifying philosophy with aesthetic claiming or literature to be repugnant when heard as courting emptiness, as evacuating precisely the space that philosophy aims to fill. In a more restrained mode, one will find Cavell's claim repugnant just in case he fails in distinguishing philosophy from art. Cavell's general answer to this dilemma is to demand that his philosophizing be responsive to the history of philosophy, and that it be in dialogue with analytic philosophy (contemporary Anglo-American philosophy as dominantly practiced) in ways truly relevant to the latter, hence in ways that analytic philosophy might, ideally, be brought to recognize. That is not a demand that any modernist painter or novelist or poet need feel. That Cavell's kind of philosophy must *recognizably* remain in relation to the tradition and practice from which it is departing makes the conditions for success internal and external: recognition is necessary. It is this issue of recognition, internal and external, that Cavell also had in mind in his closing question.)[4]

While he was composing Part IV of *The Claim of Reason*, Cavell increasingly came to associate the bundle of claims concerning the relation between philosophy and aesthetics/modernism/literature as having its natural home in Romanticism, literary and philosophical.[5] In its critique of scientism, industrialism, and mass culture, Romanticism anticipates modernism; modernism, in turn, certainly extends Romanticism's project for cultural renewal via the renewal or transfiguration of meaning; and it might prove enlightening to compare modernist practices formally with those of German Romanticism, in particular their use of the fragment in exhibiting the reflexive awareness of human finitude and it liabilities (fragments as exemplifying the finitude of thought). All this is to say that there are deep and unexplored affinities between Romanticism and high modernism, that the latter can appear as the severe and self-consciously mortal continuation of the former.[6] Nonetheless, since Cavell's relation to Romanticism is a topic in its own right, I will restrict my observations to those texts most pertinent for unlocking what I take to be the conceptual puzzle involved in the broadening and reforming of philosophy as aesthetical in its claiming, modernist in its condition, almost literature in its particularity, intimacy, and need for self-dramatization. There is an appropriateness in so doing, since, arguably, at the last, the specificity of Cavell's philosophical oeuvre is its demand that philosophy too attain to the modernist condition, that it has done so already in the writings of Wittgenstein, that it recognize that only a modernist philosophy can be an authentic one here and now. Everything else, the Romanticism, the business about American philosophy, and so the role of Emerson and Thoreau in his oeuvre, the particulars of his Shakespeare or movie criticism, are all either inflections of or secondary to or separate countries from the claim for a modernist philosophy. Cavell's aim, sometimes explicitly, more recently only implicitly, has been to bring philosophy within the precincts of modernism, and routinely his own works' mode of claiming is only intelligible if interpreted in modernist terms.[7] I will begin with a précis of "Aesthetic Problems of Modern Philosophy" – the title is the giveaway as to the content – and go on to elaborate Cavell's account of modernism in "Music Discomposed," "A Matter of Meaning It," and *The World Viewed*, Chapters 14–19, before turning to the question of how his philosophy is meant to exemplify what it characterizes as modernism.

AESTHETICS: LOGICS OF MATERIAL MEANING

Let me caricature the philosophy that Cavell means to transform (it does not much matter whether this characterization is accurate or the creation of a straw man, since the opposing burden, what philosophy must become, remains the same). Philosophy is to be an underlaborer to the natural sciences, in the triple sense that it should underwrite the naturalist and materialist vision of the world that, above all, mathematical physics projects (by reforming our everyday understanding of the world accordingly); that it should secure the methodological procedures of natural science as the sole rational procedures for securing knowledge of the world; and that it should in its own practices, therefore, to the degree to which this is appropriate and possible, embody the very methodologies of natural science that it secures. In response to this last charge, modern philosophy, formally, should conceive of its activities as those of problem solving; the problems to be solved and methods of solving them should be impersonal, value-free, hence formally universalist; solutions therefore should be a consequence of logically valid arguments that ideally can be expressed in perfectly deductive form. One can consider this philosophical ideal type as the ghost in the machine of modern philosophical culture, philosophy's self-imposed superego. It is this ideal type that has repressed aesthetic problems.

Aesthetics should not be regarded as essentially about the nature of art
or about our talk about artworks; nor is it about an arty and empty way of
seeing ordinary things (aesthetic perception), nor is it a logic of the beautiful, whatever the beautiful is. It has been understood in all of these ways.
Each of these ways of characterizing aesthetics seems to me a good reason
for ignoring it (unless one so happens to spend time hanging out in art gal-
leries, libraries, musical gatherings, squinting at sunsets, etc.). This is why
I began by expressing the *stakes* of aesthetics, modernism, art/literature in
transcendental terms, that is, in terms of the necessary conditions for cognition, meaning, reason. As a first approximation, let's say that often unknown
to itself (albeit not in Kant or Nietzsche) and in league with the modern
drive to distinguish meaning and cognition from psychology, to undo the
psychologizing of logic and knowledge, aesthetics has been a mode of depsy-
chologizing psychology (AP, 91, 93), indeed the great attempt to do so prior
to Freud. So aesthetics has been a mode of revealing how the apparently
merely subjective aspects of knowing or meaning (say in sensing and feeling)
are not merely so (not merely psychological), but somehow ingredients *in*
objective knowings and public meanings that cannot be fully left behind,
and hence that the familiar drawing of the distinction between appearance
and reality as one between first- and third-person perspectives, how things
stand (look, feel, seem) to me versus how they are for everyone (including
me) which makes psychological life the opposite of logical life and hence its
enemy, what must be overcome or suppressed if logical life is to be achieved –
that duality must be overcome if objectivity is going to be possible at all.
So aesthetics concerns, speaking crudely and indiscriminately, the sensible
conditions of knowing and meaning, which is to say, sensuous or material
meaning, the sensuous element of perceptual claims, and the perceptual
element of objective cognitions, the subjective but not private conditions
for objective knowing, what can be known only in sensing (MD, 191) or
only known in or by feeling (MD, 192). Or, say, aesthetics explores the discursive expression of the logic of experience, the necessities of experience
for meaning, which the making and judging of artworks reveal (because
they crystallize them). At a metaphysical level, aesthetics so understood
entails not only that every universal must be instantiated in some particular (the Aristotelian claim), but also that the particular logically precedes
the universal because universals come to be (the Hegelian claim); and even
further that no universal can be valid unless self-consciously asserted, reflex-
ively embodied and proclaimed (the Kantian/Heideggerian claim).[8] These
are the transcendental claims that aesthetic claiming raises or presupposes
or makes perspicuous. Insofar as modern philosophy takes for granted the

protocols of its ideal type, then they have been repressed; and because repressed then the source of the aesthetic problems of modern philosophy –
aesthetics as the problem for modern philosophy. The fact of aesthetics, if
seen aright, makes the orientation of modern philosophy as specified by its
ideal-type formulation perverse, and because perverse, irrational.[9]

Following the lessons of Kant's *Critique of Judgement*, Cavell approaches
these problems sideways, namely, through an exposition of the peculiar logic
possessed by evaluative judgements concerning works of art. Kant says that
judgements of taste of the form "This is beautiful" are reflective assertions of
the pleasure one takes in particular objects or states of affairs that, without
the mediation of concepts, without being subsumed under a concept –
say, the concept *beauty* – lay claim to intersubjective validity. Reflective
judgments of taste, Kant contends, "demand" or "exact" agreement from
everyone, and everyone "ought" to give the object in question approval and
pronounce it beautiful (e.g., CJ, §7, 213; §19, 237). However, since there
is no fact of the matter (seeing something as beautiful is not like seeing it
as red), and there is no universal principle (seeing something as beautiful is
not demanded in the way that respecting others is demanded by the moral
law), then the aesthetic "ought" is not an ideal prediction of what others will
say, nor a statement of fact to which they must assent on pain of not being
one of us at all, nor a moral obligation deriving from antecedent principle.
Cavell elaborates the oddness of such judgments in terms of patterns of
conflict and argument.

When I judge the gravy too thick and gooey, and you find it just right,
hearty and rich, there is no reason to think our different judgments, reflecting simply what we like or prefer, should not be decisive: what is pleasant
is what we find pleasant.[10] When gravy is at stake, pleasure and its tasty co-
hort remain subjective and psychological. In reflective judgements of taste,
matters are different. I say that I found his playing beautiful. You respond
aghast, urging against me that "there was no line, no structure, no idea
what the music was about. He's simply an impressive colorist" (AP, 91).
How might I respond? I could respond in kind, pointing to aspects of the
playing that I took to express sensitivity to line and structure; or I could
complain that what you call colorist playing I think of as romantic sweep;
as I shall document directly, substantive argument – and not mere rhetorical jostling – is possible. Or I could say, "Well, I liked it," but in so doing I
would be backing off from my original claim – the assertion that the playing
was beautiful, which, so to speak, reflectively raises or lifts my pleasure in
the playing to one fitting or appropriate or deserved by the object and so
demanded of everyone – and retreating to personal taste, as if the playing

were so much gravy. We have a sense of the significance of reflective judgments of taste just in case we do hear in the "Well, I liked it" a retreat, just
in case, that is, the issuing of the statement of mere preference is heard
as a way of withdrawing engagement with either the object or you, and
so a collapsing into subjectivity: walking away.[11] There are costs to such a
retreat. If it is a typical response by me, it may mean my being discounted
by you in all matters musical. But that may be tolerable to me and to you.
It may be a little thing, which is to say that retreat in such matters to mere
preference or liking is not impossible, not something obviously unbearable,
and that it is not obviously so is part of what is logically announced in the
demand's being oughtish without the full force of a moral imperative, factual without the full force of an empirical predication. (In a different mood,
my continuous retreat to preference may make things intolerable between
us – which is also in need of explaining, since whatever is "intolerable" here
it had better be quite other than our wishing to go to different restaurants
on Saturday night.) Here then is the curious pivot of such judgements:
they claim objectivity, they aim to speak with a "universal voice," for everyone, and thus demand that others see things in the same way. Yet there
is no matter of fact or reason (no concept or principle that my judgment
comes under) that grounds any such judgment and thus empirically or logically necessitates that others judge the same. Because there are no ultimate
grounds for judgment, then retreat is possible; because retreat is possible,
the judgments themselves may appear somehow systematically vulnerable,
and because vulnerable then not really objective (rational and cognitive) but
merely psychological. It is not an accidental feature of aesthetic judgments
that they have been misrecognized as being merely psychological in character: their form of universality, in its inability to prove itself, makes them
vulnerable to this form of dismissal. Conversely, Cavell wants to assert that
the import of such judgments is proportional: it is because such claims are
universal but incapable of proof that they have the relevance they do. How
might that be?

Aesthetic arguments are possible. I can give reasons for my claims, offer
evidence, provide analogies from like cases, construct a narrative linking the
work under consideration to what preceded it and so try to make its features
more intelligible. Nor are these structures of support mere auxiliaries to
aesthetic judgements: part of what constitutes them is that they are subject
to distinct patterns of support, refutation, affirmation, and dismissal, and
that without these, without the relevant body of criticism, interpretation,
and history, aesthetic discourse and judgment would be impossible (unrec-
ognizable). The rub here is that apparently valid trains of argument do not

entail or compel the conclusion: this is beautiful. It is this detachment that can make the judgment itself look, at least, logically disconnected from what supports it, and at worst, merely psychological, as if all the arguing were just trying to get the other to feel a certain way. Which is half right; I do want the other to have a certain sensed/sensory/feeling *response* to the object, but that response will matter only if it is, fully and properly, a response to the *object*, a response called down by appropriate sensitivity and/or cognitive alertness to what is there – which is what all the argument, interpretation, and criticism is about.

Let's say: in logic (in empirical inquiry), the goal is for me to surmount my subjective response to what is there in order that there be no gap between valid argument and agreement in conclusion; and learning the logic of empirical inquiry, being inducted into it, internalizing it, is just the way one learns to discount subjective response, letting pattern (of argument and support) and agreement (conclusion) become perfectly aligned. In matters aesthetic, the ambition is otherwise: "The problem of the critic, as of the artist, is not to discount his subjectivity, but to include it; not to overcome it in agreement, but to master it in exemplary ways. Then his work outlasts the fashions and arguments of a particular age. That is the beauty of it." (AP, 94) The reason why there is a dislocation between patterns of support and convergence in a conclusion upon which all can agree in aesthetic matters is that the structure of empirical features constituting the object judged – its being composed of just these sounds, in this order – is *also, at the same time* a structure or order or logic of feeling that demands or calls for a certain (sensuous) response in the hearer. So works of art, in the mastering and including of subjectivity in their construction of an empirical whole, are aligning or meaning to align how things are and how they strike one, how we feel in knowing them and know in feeling them. Because feeling here is neither simply or immediately causally triggered, like the taste of gravy, nor mediated by a concept, like the empirical features of the object, but a feature of the object that – normatively? meaningfully? – calls for a response of a certain kind, then there is the gap, the gap between pattern and agreement, the gap that permits the retreat into mere preference. It is this gap that makes the demand that something arise from me while presuming an intersubjective validity as thoroughgoing as the one attending a simple empirical judgment of a matter of fact that nonetheless can fall into an abyss ("the risk of isolation," AP, 89) without that fact quite obviously impugning the rationality or moral standing of either me or the other. The marker for the gap in aesthetic argument is the moment the critic stops arguing, stops offering discursive support for her claim, and offers *her testimony* as the last ingredient: "don't you see, don't you hear, don't you dig . . . Because if you do not see *something*, without explanation, then there is nothing further to discuss." (AP, 93)

Here Cavell explicitly aligns the situation of the artist and the situation of the critic: both must master and include their subjectivity, and their doing so amounts to the producing of an exemplary object (work of art, piece of criticism). Criticism, as the communication of one's experience of the work of art, "is itself a form of art; the burden of describing it is like the burden of producing it" (MD, 193). Criticism is thus a mechanism for crossing the gap between argument and agreement (without filling it in or obviating it). As Mulhall nicely states the thesis: "What bridges the gap between the imputation of agreement and its realization . . . is the controlled deployment of subjectivity. . . . The good critic . . . by speaking for herself as honestly and accurately as she can . . . discover[s] that she can speak for others."[12] As I shall suggest later, there is very little in what Cavell wants from criticism, philosophy, or for that matter from ethical action conceived of in his Emersonian perfectionist terms, that is not captured by the idea of the mastering and including of subjective response through making it exemplary. One could, I suspect, recover a good deal of what is most structurally challenging in Cavell's thought through the logic of exemplarity.

Thus far I have attempted no more than to make perspicuous the status of reflective aesthetic judgements as Kant and Cavell conceive them, underlining the peculiar gap between support and agreement that makes the demand for agreement, the claim that one is speaking for everyone and so with a universal voice both plausible, even unavoidable, and presumptuous, an inflation of one's own responding as the necessary condition in which a feeling response to an object must be manifest if there is to be about it a meaningful objectivity, which means here there being *also* a solidarity, *as if* we could not speak coherently about the world unless and until we were attuned to how it felt, to what kind of human import or significance it had. It is this side of aesthetic universality – our agreement about meaningfulness, or the conditions of meaningfulness – that is focused, rehearsed, worked through, and dispensed in the making and reception of artworks that can lead my retreat into mere preference to be intolerable; we cannot speak to one another because we cannot trust one another to respond appropriately. The soliciting of convergence between fact and significance is what works of art and criticism do; hence, the precise calibration of the depth, scope, and complexity of that "as if" is what the effort of Cavell's philosophy is about. It is thus no wonder that, having limned the logic of aesthetic reflective judgement, Cavell goes on to urge that with a slight shift of accent, Kant's notion of a universal voice is what we hear recorded in the philosopher's claim about "what we say when," although the philosopher's claim depends on "severer agreement" than is borne by the aesthetic analogue (AP, 94).

MODERNISM

Usages embody the same kind of jointure or convergence of empirical struc-ture and affective significance that artworks do, and they do so because they are a record of our response to such jointures – which is why we say what we do when we do. Hence, the ordinary language philosopher can be a sounding board, so to speak, manifesting the entwinement of how things are and how they mean, as that entwinement is registered in those usages in which our commitments are most staked, which can be just about any word at any time. This can be misinterpreted into a comforting picture, one that imagines the philosopher as the voice of traditional wisdom in a traditional society.[13] Nothing could be easier than knowing what "we think" in a society in which there is no space for dissent, disagreement, collapse. There, what "we think" is all there is to think, and it is the task of parents, elders, priests, the transmitters and voices of traditional author-ity, to police those who would use words out of place. The comforting picture does not imagine the philosopher at all, since in a homogeneous traditional society one presumes that the role of the philosopher is unnec-essary. "What we say when" and "what we mean when we say what we do" can be philosophical matters only when there is no traditional author-ity establishing "what we say when" and hence *only* when there a crisis of authority.

What the analogy between philosophical and aesthetic claiming does not establish by itself is the conditions in which that analogy might come into force, how a culture might need a philosophy like "that." And Cavell's answer is: A culture will need a philosophy that models itself upon the claiming of works of art and the claims appropriate to them at the very moment in which artworks themselves must self-consciously claim that ca-pacity for themselves. Call this the moment of modernism. Modernism is what happens to art under conditions of modernity – after the gods have died off or slinked away or been murdered, thus after traditional authority has withered, and thus after the traditional forms of art have been found to be somehow merely conventional in their authority, merely traditional, and thus have stopped being forms through which we might "depict our conviction and connectedness with the world" (WV, 117); we have discovered that the task of making sense of our standing in the world is somehow wholly up to us. Modernism is the moment in which we no longer have clear criteria for what constitutes a new work of art: neither tradition nor pure reason can determine what a poem or a painting or a sculpture or a musical composition is. But if these things are not known a priori, before we attend to or produce a work, then we also do not know what art is. And not knowing what art is means that the very domain of the aesthetic is not known or knowable a priori, knowable in anticipation of all possible works. The death of God or the collapse of traditional authority or the disappearance of the a priori all amount to the claim that there are no universals that can ground our doings. But if there is none, this is because there never have been any. Modernism is thus not the denial of tradition, but a way of taking up its claims for it.

A modernist work of art is one that can claim validity or authenticity for itself if and only if its claim is transcendentally valid, that is, if *its* claim to validity is at the same time the lodging and sanctioning of a claim as to what art is. Modernist works risk the very idea of being an artwork in order to establish, make possible again, what art is.

> The task of the modernist artist, as of the contemporary critic, is to find what it is his art finally depends upon; it doesn't matter that we haven't a priori criteria for defining a painting, what matters is that we realize that the criteria are something we must discover, discover in the continuity of painting itself. But my point now is that to discover this we need to discover what objects we *accept* as paintings, and why we so accept them. And to "accept something as a painting" is to "accept something as a work of art," i.e., as something carrying the intentions and consequences of art: the nature of the acceptance is altogether crucial. (MM, 219)

Let us say that a modernist work must forge for itself its standing as a work of art by explicitly dispensing with what we thought were the conventions constituting the possibility of that art and somehow carrying on (MD, 201). In carrying on, in somehow managing, if it does, to be a work of sculpture, say, in excess of everything that we thought constituted the possibility of sculpture, it lays bare what sculpture is (and so what art is). So, for example, Cavell says of the sculpture of Anthony Caro:

> I had – I take it everyone had – thought ... that a piece of sculpture was something *worked* (carved, chipped, polished, etc.); but Caro uses steel rods and beams and sheets which he does not work ... but rather, one could

say, *places*. I had thought that a piece of sculpture had the coherence of a natural object, that it was . . . spatially closed or spatially continuous . . . ; but a Caro may be open and discontinuous, one of its parts not an outgrowth from another, not even joined or connected with another so much as it is juxtaposed to it, or an inflection from it. I had thought a piece of sculpture stood on a base (or crouched in a pediment, etc.) and rose, but a Caro rests on the raw ground and some do not so much rise as spread or reach or open. . . . Caro paints his pieces . . .; the experience I recall is perhaps hit off by saying that Caro is not using colored beams, rods, and sheets, but beams and rods and sheets of color. It is almost as though the color helps dematerialize its supporting object. . . . [They seem therefore] neither light nor heavy, resistant to the concept of weight altogether – as they are resistant to the concept of size. . . . They are no longer *things*. (MM, 216–17)

One quick way of underlining Cavell's concluding thesis might be this: It is natural to think of, regard, sculptures as things in space or that occupy a spatial region. But at least some of Caro's works (*Bennington*, *Deep Body Blue*, and *Prairie*, for example) seem to construct or create space, to spatialize by providing overall orientation or spatial schema that one must take up in order to perceive the work at all. It is as if the work creates the spatial conditions in which it is thence perceived, so that it is both a form of intuition and what is intuited.[14]

The sculpture establishes itself *as* a piece of sculpture, and so a work of art, by defeating the perception of it as a mere thing *in* space, by its disenfranchisement of given space, by its spatializing as what its rods, beams, and sheets of metal do.

It is important to have a case before us, since only in its light will we be able to track what sort of burden it is that the modernist work is taking up. Cavell poses Caro's sculpture as between two extremes: it departs from all the obvious and traditional terms that have constituted what it is for a thing to be a piece of sculpture – "I had thought . . ." (Cavell does not even mention how sculpture was not just carved or chipped or molded but that the goal of the carving, etc., was a mimesis of a natural object, often human) – and nonetheless, despite those departures, despite the fact that Caro is employing things that we cannot help seeing as what they in fact are, namely, steel rods, beams, sheets, what appears is not a thing (in the way that a steel rod, beam, or sheet is a thing). Although it will take some fleshing out, Cavell's thought here is this: because the work departs from everything we had thought constituted the possibility of something being a piece of sculpture, then we know that its being a piece of sculpture, if it convinces us that it is, does not rest on *mere* convention, *mere* say-so, *mere* agreement. On the other hand, although the object flirts with, dares, risks, exposes itself to being a mere object, a thing among things (rods, beams, and sheets of steel), it defeats thinghood; it somehow appears as "more." Hence, it is something beyond what nature could provide, a mere thing, beyond utility or functionality or artifactuality (artworks, although intentional objects, made, are "without purpose"), and beyond what might be the case merely because we *decide* it is the case. (Modernism opposes, to the last inch, any idea that what counts as an art work is what is dubbed an artwork or licensed by experts or museum practice as an artwork, or, in accordance with a regime of discursive practice, can be asserted as an art-work.) The rising up of the modernist work of art is, we might say, the rising up of human significance in general, as if with *this* thing there comes into the world meaning or the possibility of meaning itself. This is what I meant by saying, in my second paragraph, that artworks raise transcendental claims: In saying "here is sculpture," the work also says "here is art"; and in saying that, it says too "here is meaning, significance." "A work of art does not express some particular intention (as statements do), nor achieve particular goals (in the way technological skill and moral action do), but, one may say, celebrates the fact that men can intend their lives at all . . . , and that their actions are coherent and effective at all in the scene of indifferent nature and determined society" (MD, 199). In defeating thinghood, for example, the modernist work defeats skepticism, or at least the way in which the skeptical orientation manifests itself in art. Crucial to that defeat is our "acceptance" or acknowledgment of the modernist work.

It is a noteworthy fact about modernist works that they acknowledge and expose their material conditions of possibility: that paintings are made of pigment on canvas, literature of words, music of sounds, and so forth. I think of this invocation and laying bare of the material basis of art as, in part, a work of disenchanting the art work, of making the work of art a secular thing; but also, in part, an insisting on the fact that human meaningfulness belongs to the natural world and has a material basis. Modernist works make all meaning embodied meaning, the meaning of embodied creatures. Nonetheless, it is, Cavell avers, wrong to conceive of the material basis of an art as its medium; to do so is to suppose that the material conditions of meaningfulness are themselves fully given, a priori facts; or better, to presume the material basis of art as given is to presume a fully dualist ontology, with human meaning and intention on one side and raw matter on the other – the old, crude, form-matter story. Nothing can be counted as the medium of an art independently of the art; so

> wood or stone would not be a medium of sculpture *in the absence of the art of sculpture*. . . . The idea of a medium is not simply that of a physical material, but of a material-in-certain-characteristic-applications. . . . [So] there certainly are things to be called various media of music, namely the various ways in which various sources of sound . . . have characteristically been applied: the media are, for example, plain song, work song, the march, the fugue, the aria, dance forms, sonata form. It is the existence or discovery of such strains of convention that have made possible musical expression. . . . (MM, 221)

This sharpens what the ambition of a modernist art must be: "One might say that the task is no longer to produce another instance of art but a new medium within it" (WV, 103), where it is understood that the "medium is to be discovered, or invented out of itself" (MM, 221).

In *The World Viewed*, Cavell contends that in creating a new medium the modernist artist is creating a new "automatism." By automatism Cavell means both broad genres and forms and "those local events or *topoi* around which a genre precipitates itself" (WV, 104). Automatism is another term for and so a way of avoiding using the term "convention" and its component parts (its lexical units and syntactical resources); automatism is meant to reveal some of the depth or power of convention, to yield the intuition that the conventional can be deep, necessary, all there is in the sense-making that a work of art (and so a human life) is. Cavell suggests three impulses behind his coinage: (1) A medium is an automatism in the sense that, once discovered, it generates new instances; automatisms, thus, falsify both nominalism and realism about universals. (2) The notion of automatism is meant to capture our experience of the work of art as "happening of itself"; as I hear it, automatism is Cavell's term for Kant's idea that works of art appear as if "natural," and thereby not there, again, as a matter of mere will or decision (WV, 115). Traditional art gives to its practitioners the automatisms their art is based on; the modernist artist "has to explore the fact of automatism itself, as if investigating what it is at any time that has provided a given work of art with the power of its art as such" (WV, 107). (3) The notion of automatism is meant to record the idea that when I make a work – if the work works, is authentic – it is freed from me; automatism points to the work's autonomy.

A further noteworthy aspect of Cavell's analysis, and the payoff from the account of medium and automatism, is that modernist works, because of their departure from tradition and their need to engender a new medium, new automatisms, occur in a context in which necessarily there is a danger of fraudulence. A traditional artist could fail in the application and/or extensions of the automatisms bequeathed to her; she could produce bad art, and perhaps even art so bad it barely deserved to be called art. And the modernist artist can fail – I think I can see what Morris Louis was up to, the kind of medium he meant to establish, in his veils, but they strike me as just an opportunity for displaying his gifts as a colorist, and so by his own high standards, standards revealed by the best of his later unfurleds, fail. Fraudulence is not failure but the producing of an art look (sound, appearance, shape) without producing, finally, a work. Fraudulent works avail themselves of the look of an artwork while disavowing the responsibilities of art. Because there really is an art look, and indeed a look that is not remote from authentic art, the separation of authentic from fraudulent is not merely difficult, it is the very critical effort necessary for distinguishing the possibility of art meaning from its utter, if deferred or suppressed, repudiation.

In "Music Discomposed," Cavell systematically attacks the idea of "totally organized" music as sponsored by, among others, Ernst Krenek, showing how composition, chance, and improvisation are transformed almost into their opposites by Krenek's theory (and, by implication, practice, although it is only the theory that is explicitly critiqued). For example, in art chance relates not to ceding control and letting materials make their own music, so to speak (MD, 194), which is at least one aspect of the postmodernist view of chance, but to creating one's dangers and taking one's chances; hence for the modernist chance will relate, via composition, to tensions, problems, shocks, surprise, and the response to or resolution of those in fulfillment, release, vision: "The *way* one escapes or succeeds is, in art, as important as the success itself; indeed, the way constitutes the success ..." (MD, 199). So even if the modernist artist will want to give to objective chance (the only notion of chance that the postmodernist recognizes) a larger role than it had in traditional art, still such chances must finally relate to the composition (the intending of the artist) as a whole. In painting, where the matter is vivid, Pollock showed how each chance event was, precisely, the opportunity to compose a work beyond all imagining (beyond all a priori planning). So Pollock showed how one might, under the most extreme of conditions of uncertainty, chance, nonetheless take full or absolute responsibility for one's doings, how in the midst of pours, tube-squeezed ropes, splatters and flecks and spills one might still compose a *work* that was emphatically and unavoidably one's own. In opposition to the ideology of total composition, Cavell asserts that the first fact of works of art "is that they are meant, meant to be understood" (MM, 227–8).

A more fully elaborated critical analysis of artistic fraudulence is provided by Michael Fried in his "Art and Objecthood" and the essays surrounding it.[15] In those essays the mode of fraudulence Fried means to detect, which is not wholly unlike the fraudulence of "total composition," is the repudiation of composed works (paintings or sculpture), which are necessarily the bearers of human intentions, for works that approach or mean to be merely things among other things – but for the fact that they are artworks. Artistic "minimalism" – or "literalism," as Fried calls it – involves the use of obdurate materials in simple, geometric shapes either by themselves or in structures that themselves appear geometric, that have the feel of being the consequence of a formal procedure, algorithm, or mathematical design. Ideally, such works should give no sign of the human hand (arm or wrist), the whole conceivably produced by a machine, or at least a team of workers following precise instructions, like builders following a blueprint. The prime example of such minimalist art would be Tony Smith's *Die*: a five-foot black painted steel cube. Such works appear as artworks, have an art look, because they are *theatrical*, that is, they include the beholder in their possibility of effect, relieving themselves (the artist) thereby of responsibility for meaningfulness. On Fried's analysis, theater is the form of fraudulence common to our situation, and its defeat requires the defeat of the reduction of the work to thinghood – the very achievement of Caro's sculpture. I note that the kind of arguments used to defend minimalism's (and total composition's) eschewal of modernist art can be seen as systematic variations on the protocols of the analytic ideal-type philosophy in its repudiation of subjectivity. Which is chilling – for art and for philosophy.

MODERNISM AND ACKNOWLEDGMENT

Aesthetic judgements and the claims of the ordinary language philosopher speak with a universal voice that is nonetheless incapable of proof (empirical or logical) because they concern the jointure of orders of fact with orders of feeling, call it an expressive empirical order. Such an order must be seen (heard, experienced) and felt *thus*. Objects designed precisely for the purpose of generating such responses are artworks; the ways in which empirical objects (things, persons, typical states of affairs and events) systematically embed an expressive empirical order is recorded in "what we say when." Modernity yields a state of affairs where the expressive empirical order is hounded from three different and identifiable directions: by the collapse of traditional authority, the growing belief that meaning is a matter of mere convention (because all convention is a matter of agreement, because the meaning of the sign is constituted by nothing other than a system of differences, because nominalism is true, etc.); by the emergence of modern reductive naturalism ("indifferent nature") and its rational corollary – the belief that the only rational authority is that which accords with the logical or formal or procedural or mathematical conception of reason modeled by the natural sciences; and by "determined society," say, the consequences for social existence implied by the first two houndings. Cavell routinely expresses this last with Emerson's phrase "every word they say chagrins us" – because every word they say has stopped being an effective jointure of fact and meaning, the world is no longer an expressive empirical order.

Modernism takes up the burden of this situation in art; or better, art is the *necessary* site of this problem because art traditionally was the cultural space in which we collectively rehearsed the experience of society as an expressive empirical order in its force and fragility. So the condition in which the expressive empirical order is hounded generates the *aesthetic problems of modern society,* of which the aesthetic problems of modern philosophy are but the reflective articulation. It is because the problem of modern society can be designated as an aesthetic one that artistic practices become a site of transcendental reflection; that is, art, which used to rehearse (and so reproduce and reaffirm) society's expressive empirical order, must, in the teeth of the triple hounding of that order, show that such an order is possible in general. That is why modernism has the developmental dialectic it does: under the triple hounding, any achievement of art, the establishing of a new medium, new automatisms, and so the very idea of an (new) expressive empirical order become or threatens to become a part of the dead past of convention. What keeps past art alive, including past modernist art, is only present art in its escape from skeptical collapse. But this is to say, and it is this that Cavell's remarks on fraudulence were meant to show, that modernist art is the kind of art that, even for itself, is shadowed by skeptical doubt. Skepticism is the reflective (i.e., philosophical) comprehension of the meaning of the triple hounding,[16] which makes any modern critical discourse, any modern philosophy, that might hope to respond to the predicament of modernity one whose inaugural moment must be framed by the problem of skepticism. Hence, Cavell's recurring claim that for us philosophical problems have the form of: we have lost our way. And it is for this reason that Cavell refuses to think of art or philosophy in directly political terms: "To speak now of modernism as the activity of an avant-garde is as empty as it is in thinking about modern politics or war, and as comforting: it implies a conflict between a coherent culture and a declared and massed enemy; when in fact the case is more like an effort, along blocked paths and hysterical turnings, to hang on to a thread that leads from a lost center to a world lost" (WV, 110).[17] The *stakes* of art are not less than those of politics or war once the easy assumption of a coherent culture on one side and a massed enemy on the other is dropped; for now, at least, the stakes are the possibility of there being a (meaningful) world, the worldhood of the world.

I have been moving slowly over this terrain in the hope of adequately preparing and motivating the final two steps in Cavell's account of modernism, the ones that will come most fully to inform his modernist philosophizing: (1) it is the particular and distinct demand of modernist art that it take the form of *acknowledgment* (acceptance), and that so doing is nondetachable from, say, (2) my voicing my acknowledgment, so from regarding work and criticism as exemplary individual performances. This entails that philosophy must become a performance of the philosopher if it is going to state what is necessary. Said another way: only from the perspective of modernism can the role of acknowledgment for knowledge be articulated fully and so become central; but if the role of acknowledgment in knowledge is the pivot of Cavell's philosophy, then his philosophy can effect itself only as a modernist transformation of the practice of philosophy – which is what I promised to show.

Modernist works of art are exemplary joinings of fact and meaning. Being bereft of traditional backing, such works can appear as nearly the same as a fraudulent impostor. For Cavell, this entails that for modern art the experiences of fraudulence and trust are essential; hence a full answer to the question "What is art?" will, in part, "be an answer which explains why it is we treat certain objects, or how we can treat certain objects, in ways normally reserved for treating persons" (MD, 189). While at first blush this might sound exorbitant, it is the natural extension of the position being outlined. It arises because modernist works are sites of transcendental claiming: they are material formations of mastered subjectivity that claim that human activity *can* be meaningful, that we *can* intend our lives, that even in the midst of indifferent nature and determined society meaning and action are *possible*. Because the particular claim of any modernist work is at the same time the claim that "so here is art (again)," and thus "here I am; here is meaning, value (again),"[18] then their approach to us or claim upon us is not unlike the approach or claim of another person. This thought gains purchase once we concede that the best and unavoidable terms of criticism for such works are precisely the ones we use for discussing persons: "We approach such objects not merely because they are interesting in themselves, but because they are felt as made by someone – and so we use such categories as intention, personal style, feeling, dishonesty, authority, inventiveness, profundity, meretriciousness, etc., in speaking of them" (MD, 198). What is thus appalling and terrifying and nihilistic about total composition and minimalist art is that they would, if they could, and they mean to, do away with such a vocabulary; they aim to put works of art beyond the forms of critical response for meaningful doings. Instead, such fraudulent art practices instrumentalize art making and aesthetics: Either a procedure produces an interesting effect or it does not, and the artist is now the one who makes it more probable that an interesting event or series of events will occur, using "these" pre-given and simple mechanisms. If this oversimplifies the practices in question, and it does, it does not oversimplify the stakes of those practices, what they portend.

Every modernist work raises the issue of fraudulence and trust, which is to say now, every modernist work of art raises an equivalent of the problem of other minds: what is it for a material display to be a display of human meaning, that is, the display of a person? In order to see what is involved in answering this question, we need to return to the way in which modernist works pose *themselves* as responses to it. Now I think that the way Cavell runs his account of this, in the "Excursus: Some Modernist Painting" chapter of *The World Viewed*, is unconvincing; this is one place where Michael Fried's critical program leads him in a wrong direction, not over the question of acknowledgment itself in modernist works, but over their way of expressing and demanding it, what Fried calls "presentness".[19] Let's begin, however, with the issue of acknowledgment itself.

Acknowledgment emerges as an informing gesture of modernist works because each must declare itself for its medium as a whole, and each can only accomplish this by claiming it, that is, by laying bare that it is a laying bare of the art it is showing. A modernist painting can only speak for painting as a whole by exposing itself *as painting, as such*: "any painting might teach you what is true of all painting. A modernist painting teaches you this by acknowledgment – which means here that responding to it must itself have the form of accepting it as painting, or rejecting it [as failure or fraud]" (WV, 110). Premised on the Hegelian idea that late, high modernism reveals the stakes and presuppositions of its earlier avatars,[20] Cavell attempts to think through what is involved here in terms of Fried's pantheon of late modernist painters: Pollock, Morris Louis, Kenneth Noland, Jules Olitski, Frank Stella. Cavell thinks that what Pollock reveals and Fried's crowd elaborates is the idea of "total thereness" – Cavell's term for presentness: "The quality or condition I wish to emphasize here comes out of my speaking of total thereness as an event of the wholly open, and of the declaration of simultaneity ... [which] might be expressed as openness achieved through instantaneousness – which is a way of characterizing the *candid*" (WV, 111). It is not too difficult to see how a painting's candidness, so conceived, might be thought to be a mode of acknowledging itself as painting for painting – a kind of way of saying "Here I am, all of me!": "For example, a painting may acknowledge its frontedness, or its finitude, or its specific thereness – that is, its presentness; and your accepting it will accordingly mean acknowledging *your* frontedness, or directionality, or verticality towards its world, or any world – or your presentness, in its aspect of absolute hereness and of nowness" (WV, 110). I confess I find both almost all of the paintings being here championed (apart from Pollock's, which can be characterized quite differently) and the critical gesture of acknowledgement being offered for them – total thereness – mawkish and meretricious.[21] That is a worry; what lies behind the worry, however, is the concern that if acceptance is linked to presentness, then it is unclear how acceptance can be connected to the *truth of skepticism*: the continuing discovery that the orders of knowledge and reason are not self-moving or, therefore, self-sufficient. I take the truth of skepticism – think of it as the intimate or personal way in which we experience the lack of a metaphysical absolute (an ultimate fact of the matter) and the finitude of human knowledge – as the place where modernism reveals itself as the self-reflection of modernity. But, then, modernism ought to be what connects the truth of skepticism to acceptance and acknowledgement, and what in so doing reveals how the very idea of an expressive empirical order connects to the problem of other minds. What one may feel is the speed or sentimentality of the idea of total thereness – all that candidness and sincerity – derives, I am suggesting, from its failing to connect acceptance to the truth of skepticism.[22] The correct way to make this persuasive is aesthetically.

Rather than directly contesting Fried's canon, let me simply recall my characterization of Caro – a sculptor about whose accomplishment Cavell, Fried, and I agree. I suggested earlier that a singular feature of some of Caro's best work is that it does not presuppose three-dimensional space as a given within which a work appears, but that rather the works spatialize, create space for themselves, give space dimension and orientation, construct the very space they inhabit, and that in so doing they demonstrate how lived spaced itself is not a given container that we appear in. A Caro is the (fictive) transcendental bracketing (*epoche*) and reconstitution of space. In *Prairie*, for example, suspended just twenty-one inches off the ground is a flat sheet of corrugated metal with four grooves or channels in it (you can imagine water running through them); the effect of the low suspension and grooving is the feeling that the sheet is running away from you. In fact, the sheet is resting, inconspicuously, on two V's, each with a short nearly vertical leg that does the supporting, and a long wing of sheet metal that rises out from either side of the grooved sheet in something under a forty-five-degree angle. Suspended eleven inches above the grooved sheet and running east–west to its north–south are four long poles of aluminum tubing; the poles are evenly spaced and run parallel to one another. Set aside from the main construction is a small rectangular wall of sheet metal. All the pieces of the sculpture are painted in a color that is somewhere between a mustard yellow and ripe wheat tan.[23]

In a work like *Prairie* our being upright and forward-looking, which can be taken as given, is revealed as an orientation through its absence or strangeness (I mean the strangeness of the vertical rectangle that is set apart). The space projected by *Prairie* both invites us and, in the radicality of its horizontal orientation (the sense of its spreading and opening), excludes us, in the same way that the one vertical sheet is disconnected or at least held at a distance from the emphatically low horizontal, horizon-forming, stretching or stretching-out structures themselves (in the way that prairies invite and exclude us: human and inhuman at once, the way nature is).[24]

In order to accomplish this end of spatializing, space making, for all its apparent simplicity, Caro's work possesses a (ongoing) *performative* depth and complexity that, apart from particular exclusions of uprightness and frontedness, makes it, beyond that, simply not available to immediate in-spection. *Prairie* first brackets space as a container (say, by its disorienting low, horizontal orientation), and then determines space as spatiality, giv-ing or having space, spacing or pacing, space as *placed* here by its three, crossed formations of horizonality (the poles, the grooved sheet, and the flanking "wings"). And, as always with Caro, space is internally related to, an inflection of, the very objects it would contain.

One cannot take in a Caro all at once because it is a gesture and a per-formance, because one thus has to find one's way into it (move around it in order to "enter" it, assume it; and some ways are blocked), because, better, what it requires of one in terms of spatial orientation, what is involved in appreciating and sustaining its trumping or dismissing of given space, and of making space all over again, is not itself given but an accomplishment of critical perception (what transpires through or in consequence of one's fol-lowing, and so acknowledging, the work). If this work of critical perception could be finished, if the work could be finally and simply there, then it would lose its critical relation to given space, and hence our experience of it would lose its character of being an experience (a continuous and therefore incomplete aspect-dawning), a transformation of our space, a standing invitation or seduction to inhabit spaces-and-things differently. And only because the work *remains* invitation and critique does it remain a work of art distinct from, an interruption of our ordinary empirical experience of, the world.

Learning this kind of Caro is like learning the gestures of a new tribe: what counts as pointing or bowing or turning away or being relaxed or indifferent or straight or crooked needs interpreting and getting used to, and that work is never done.[25] Of course, these are sculptures and not a new tribe, even if the anthropological analogy is apt. But what makes it apt, I now want to say, is that they frankly and radically avow and display their material conditions of possibility, the fact that they are nothing other than metal rods, beams, and sheets.[26]

Cavell's reasonable thesis about the media of art, viz., that they only count as media once worked, does not, as I think he supposes, obviate the necessity of modernist works declaring their material conditions of possibility, indeed twice over. On the one hand, in declaring their materiality they open the possibility of not being seen as works of art at all, of being just metal rods, beams, and sheets. To *declare* this moment is to declare the truth of skepticism: the sheer facts of the case will not yield meaning, and no telling of the facts will make meaning compelling. It is because authentic works do *announce* their less-than-aesthetic facticity that minimalist works, which austerely pose themselves as interesting in their very facticity, can acquire an art look (minimalist works as, so to speak, the skeptical moment within authentic works freed from them). On the other hand, the work also means to say that meaning is nothing other than an arrangement of material stuff, such stuff intended in some way. Such radical exposure is the disenchantment of meaning (and natural beauty); it is the way art accomplishes the disenchantment of meaning. This is the real candidness or openness of such works; it is not their art that is open to view, there, but that such art is made of nothing other than material stuff ordered *thus*; the yield of such ordering, the work, is both present and absent in the same way that people are present and absent, never fully there.

It is from here that we can understand the necessity and function of acknowledgment in modernism. Modernist works take up the burden of modernity by, in virtue of their acknowledging of their material conditions of possibility, declaring the truth of skepticism, as well as accomplishing the continuing disenchantment of knowing through their disenchantment of art-beauty. The material conditions represent both the skeptical denial of meaning, the thought that here there is just stuff, and the achievement once again that from just this stuff art is possible, so meaning is possible, so the world is possible – again. Cavell formulates the situation with respect to painting in this way:

> Painting, being art, is revelation: it is revelation because it is acknowledgement; being acknowledgement, it is knowledge, of itself and of its world. Modernism did not invent this situation; it merely lives on nothing else. In reasserting that acknowledgement is the home of knowledge, it recalls what the remainder of culture is at pains to forget. (WV, 110)

So my contention is that what Cavell calls the truth of skepticism, what can be healed by acknowledgment and not further knowledge, is itself *necessitated* by modernist works only in their declaration of their material basis and means; this declaration encapsulates the triple hounding of meaning and so the skeptical dilemma that each work confronts: both its loss of traditional authority and the threat to meaning posed by logical reason, determined society, and lawlike nature. In confronting such works we confront our skeptical predicament and pass beyond it by, in the teeth of their strangeness, the *risk* of all previous mediums (which is what calls into play the anthropology analogy), and their unmissable exposure of their simple material being, being just stuff configured, nonetheless letting them make a claim on us, exposing ourselves to their claim, so acknowledging them as, in being art (and not mere things), all but one of us. To say that acknowledgment is the home of knowledge is thus to say, first, that I pass beyond the doubt represented by the self-declared strangeness (in relation to past convention) and materiality of the work by exposing myself to the work, letting it perform its work of bracketing and reconstitution, so letting it be a work for me, learning what art is from the work; and thus, second, learning that unless I expose myself to the work, let myself and my possibilities of meaning be tested by it, there is nothing to know and so no meaningful knowledge (art reminds us of what the rest of culture is at pains to forget). That there is something to know, how space *means*, for example, is given through the work's claiming; the necessity configured in the imposingness of its beauty, everything about the work that leads to my wanting to offer my experience of it as objective, demanded of everyone, represents the depth, the human necessity of meaning, that meaning can be deep (necessary), as deep (necessary) as my orientation in space, only in the light of my letting it be so. Depth, significance, necessity are neither metaphysical nor illusory; modernist art reveals how "[c]ustom is our nature" (Pascal), how custom can have the authority of nature.

To say that acknowledgment is knowledge of itself and the world is to say that acknowledgment is a mode of self-consciousness, a mode of how, through the work taking a stand on itself, declaring itself as art, I am forced to take a stand upon myself (as the condition for my perceiving it as a work); only by exposing myself to the other, so only with this acknowledgment, is there a work or a world. If fact and meaning are to be joined, then every look presupposes my looking, my standing on my looking as what makes the look an exposure to meaning and not just a mechanical recording device (as, for example, reliabilist accounts of perception assume).

If modernist works are transcendental sites of meaning, of the joining of fact and meaning in general, of an expressive empirical order as such, that require for themselves and for their observers acknowledgment as a condition of meaningfulness, then there is meaning only if *I* acknowledge it. It is the necessity of acknowledgment for there to be a jointure of material fact and affective significance, the necessity of taking a stand upon my meaning in order for it to mean, that in turn makes the first person noncircumventable in the constitution of meaning. But this is just an inference from the fact of modernism itself: if the possibility of meaning is to be shown through just this work here, and just this work here reveals beyond all previous understanding the possibility of meaningfulness, then there can be meaningfulness at all only if there is some here-and-now. This would make all meaning a matter of conscience: here I stand and I can do no other, that is, if I do not stand here then there is no standing and no I; all falls down.

FRAGMENTS OF PHILOSOPHICAL MODERNISM

My intention so far has been to provide an account of the exigencies and necessities composing modernist art that would entail that any philosophy that would, authentically, inhabit the same world as such art would necessarily be subject to the same demands. One will accept those demands upon philosophy only if one accepts the characterization of modernism; and one can accept the characterization of modernism only if one has already found oneself compelled by, for example, Anthony Caro's sculpture, accepting it as what sculpture can be and so what art can be. Under the conditions that the authenticity of the modernist work projects, the possibility of meaning in general takes the form of there being a communication between two persons unsupported by tradition or convention; all other possibilities of communication having either dissolved or become frozen, reified. Modernist art promises us "not the re-assembly of community, but personal relationship unsponsored by that community; not the overcoming of our isolation, but the sharing of that isolation – not to save the world out of love, but to save love for the world, until it is responsive again" (MM, 229). This is what makes the demandingness of modernist works so odd: they want extreme intimacy (say, because the perfect model of a communication between just two unsupported by convention are the silences exchanged by lovers) and extreme generality (here I am, a work, so here is sculpture and so art and so meaning, again). A philosophy that might bear up to these demands will be as unfamiliar as *Prairie* or *Endgame* or "Sunday Morning," with its unparaphraseable opening in which "she feels the dark / Encroachment of that old catastrophe, / As a calm darkens among water-lights" (see AP, 81). Perhaps it is not, from just these characteristics, obvious how what might characterize a modernist philosophy spells out its becoming literature, or, at least, the sense in which it does so.

The most natural way of thinking about the demand for philosophy to become literature is through the issue of the kind of rational authority that a modernist philosophy can claim for itself. Max Weber claimed that there were three fundamental forms of authority: legal-rational, traditional, and charismatic. These forms should be considered as distinct only analytically, since when they appear in utter isolation from one another the result is perspicuous forms of social irrationality: the mechanical bureaucracy (determined society), the repressive closed society, the delirium of the cult. Philosophy, almost by definition, has been the attempt to show how traditional and charismatic authority must give way to, indeed be totally dissolved into, legal-rational authority. That we might say is the hope expressed in the protocols of the ideal-type analytic philosophy. Modernist philosophy means to show that the Enlightenment either/or of either reason or tradition is a false one. We have already seen how each modernist work is a response to this dilemma: Each shows itself to be more than tradition (by dispensing with tradition) while not deducible from reason; each radically *appears*, and lodges its claim through the very insistence of its appearing. Call the moment of claiming through appearing the work's charismatic authority. Perhaps the oddity of artworks is that their authority can seem as if wholly or purely charismatic. But that is not accurate. Hence, the notion of automatism: a generative convention that in its separation from the artist approaches the authority of nature, natural law, itself. A new medium with its automatisms can reveal itself to be such through the series, for example, Monet's haystacks. The fact of the series reveals that the effectivity of the original, its charismatic authority, is not accidental or arbitrary, that in fact a new medium with its distinct automatisms has been uncovered (WV, 115). Now, of course, in the case of the modernist work of art the charismatic character of the individual work is bound to its being a material object that presents itself to the senses, and to the fact that only through sensuous presentation can the work be grasped at all. Beauty is just a clumsy categorial term for (one form of) charismatic authority.

The most direct way in which modernist philosophy reveals its distance from the ideal type of legal-rational authority has been via its fragmentary form. The fragment defies subordination from first premises; but it is just the structure of subordination (from first premises or from an ideal method or procedure) that constitutes the purely rational authority of the ideal-type analytic philosophy. For Cavell, the paradigm cases of fragmentary philosophical writing are Part I of Wittgenstein's *Investigations* and Emerson's essays, in which each sentence feels like it is nearly self-sufficient but for the fact that its thought is continued or echoed or relayed or commented upon by others surrounding it: "I have taken the familiar experience of Emerson's writing as leaving the individual sentences to shuffle for themselves to suggest that each sentence of a paragraph of his can be taken to be its topic sentence. I welcome the consequent suggestion that his essays are collections of equals rather than hierarchies of dependents."[27] A compelling series of fragments is what is meant by an improvising of convention. Part IV of *The Claim of Reason* is a series of fragments: We gain insight into the *problem* of other minds by seeing it in the context of the treatment of (fragments or journal entries [CR, xix] relating to) slaves and fetuses, monsters and machines, statues and dolls, horror and tragedy, and so forth. These are not just heuristics, but aspects of the depth and pervasiveness of the problem, its cultural and social actuality ("skepticism concerning other minds is not skepticism [the philosopher's conceit] but tragedy" [CR, xix]) as well as its philosophical expression. To recover the fact that the abstract problem is an expression of an actuality, and that actuality itself multifaceted, is to perceive the existential (psychological, social, and historical) figure in the conceptual carpet. One might say that the totality of fragments forms a constellation through which the truth concerning the *problem* of other minds – the truth of skepticism – and its release – the need, demand, and role of acknowledgement – is disclosed. For Cavell, the notion of the philosophical fragment is a general term meant to cover a variety of discontinuous forms of philosophical presentation and writing: aphorism, aside, entry, reading, remark, parenthesis, digression, introduction, sentence, and so on.[28] What all these have in common is their relative autonomy or independence. So, for example, a sentence may show its independence by making its meaning dependent on its *exact* wording (being almost unparaphraseable); exact wording of this kind underlines the writtenness (CR, 5) of the sentence, thus its charismatic authority, which is revealed by its feeling of quotability, hence self-standing, while being, in fact, not easily or directly memorable. Sentences like that approach the status of aphorism. Cavell did not have to await his reading of Emerson to have this ambition for writing; it's there nearly from the beginning.

How, though, does a fragment manage its authority? I take it that Cavell intends a fragment to be the analogue of the modernist work itself, and hence the essay or book the analogue of the series. If so, the puzzle continues, since now we shall want to know what corresponds to the elements of the work (steel beams, rods, sheets)? I think Cavell must say, and does on occasion say, words; it is they that have lost their place, and the work of a modernist philosophy is improvising a sense for them. So Cavell states that Kant's idea that our "understanding of the behavior of the world by understanding the behavior of our concepts of the world, is to be radicalized, so that not just the twelve categories of the understanding are to be deduced, but every word in the language – not as a matter of psychological fact, but as a matter of, say, psychological necessity" (QO, 38). This is a natural enough thought given Cavell's premises, but it cannot be correct as it stands, since there may be different practices that take themselves to be in the business of "deducing" this or that word or concept: Perhaps some political actions deduce the meaning of "free" or "equal" (maybe Martin Luther King's actions did this); perhaps a movie or novel might provide for me a deduction of marriage (showing that all marriage is remarriage). If deduction has the sense of showing how a concept is necessary for the possibility of experience, then while the broadening from a few special concepts, the categories, to potentially all follows upon the denial of the subordination of many to the one consequent upon the discovery that any word *can* become for me what my life is staked upon, it equally must democratize the locales of deduction. If deduction is the singular event as exemplary, then that event need not occur in a philosophical text (although perhaps we still need philosophical texts to nudge us into recognizing that "there" we witnessed a deduction of freedom or tenderness or love or courage or care or gratitude or cruelty or sorrow – philosophy as a form of "concept criticism" analogous to art criticism). Perhaps, for the health of culture, it should not.

It thus becomes natural to assume that only *some* words are the prerogative of philosophy, even in its modernist dispensation. Unsurprisingly, I think, the words that will be philosophy's to engage are just those that have belonged to it, hence just those in which there exists an overwhelming temptation to believe that they possess an atemporal core meaning that can organize and orient everything that comes under them: know, mean, true, good, free, determined, rational, and so forth. But this would seem to suggest that a modernist philosophy cannot proceed as quickly as a modernist art, since philosophy is tied to its past not just as a matter of achievement but substantially. Modernist philosophy must be a critique of its traditional past and rationalist present; modernist philosophy must be explicitly critique. If the philosopher is centrally responsible for the critique and transformation of the tradition, the words and concepts that seek to master and dominate what traditionally did fall under them, then will she not centrally be operating in the very terms she means to displace? Philosophy cannot easily depart from abstract conceptuality if it is to sustain its role as critic of abstract conceptuality. If critique, then how is it going to separate itself formally from what it is criticizing? Whither its particularity, sensuousness, moment of acknowledgment, charismatic authority?

How about if we say that the force of the philosophical fragment derives from the voice or person of the philosopher, where this is understood as the philosopher mastering her subjectivity and making it exemplary? The idea of an exemplary performance certainly responds to the lacunae left by the disappearance of religious charismatic authority. And if there is going to be something corresponding to the sensuousness of the artwork, the singular voice is a plausible candidate. And how better to rebel against the self-righteous impersonality of the analytic ideal type? Let me concede that the idea of an emphatically personal exemplary performance is a modernist one, and that there are locales where it seems unavoidable, the most obvious being ethical action and criticism (of particular works, actions, etc.). But from here the implication is not obviously that philosophy itself should be a matter of exemplary performances in which the person of the philosopher comes to the fore. After all, while in critically responding to an artwork I am aiming to objectify my subjective responses so that they can be seen as what responding to that work involves, and so enabling you to so respond, the artwork itself is not like that. Works may be infused with subjectivity and affect without, for all that, being a matter of a *personal* voice; there is no hint of that kind of individuality in *Prairie*, for example. In theory and practice, Cavell has at times championed the personal voice – his – as a mode or way of bringing philosophy to its modernist state; but there is nothing compelling about that choice for philosophy, no reason why the philosophical fragment should gain its authority and individuation that way. Nor in Cavell at his best is the singular voice the real bearer of authority. Here is a complete Cavell paragraph of great power and beauty:

> I do not make the world that the thing gathers. I do not systematize the language in which the thing differs from all other things in the world. I testify to both, to acknowledge my need of both.[29]

This paragraph occurs in an essay whose explicit or assigned topic is collecting – the way museums or individuals collect things: books, paintings, butterflies, clocks, locks, medals, coins, stamps, skeletons, toys, dolls, inscriptions. In Cavell's hands the problem of collecting quickly turns into: the problem of memory/history/heritage/tradition (collecting the past), the relation between universals and particulars, the individual painting and the series (as a modernist displacement of the universal-particular relation), a person and her experiences, Hume on the self and the contents of its mind, whole and part, a child's loss of or separation from its first object of love and the desire to find it again (so human connectedness and separateness, love and death), Emerson's visit to the Jardin des Plantes, obsession and collection, Heidegger on the thing, and so on. The essay is made up of eighteen numbered fragments/sections, some quite short, a few sentences, some extended, several paragraphs; for the most part each is dedicated to a separate author and/or topic. The essay itself is a collection of curiosities, a thing of things, a series of fragments on the meaning and being of fragments.

At nearly the midpoint of the essay (I do not know what else to call the piece), fragment *X*, there is a long, quiet recounting of, primarily, the first hour of Chantal Akerman's film *Jeanne Dielman / 23 quai du Commerce / 1080 Bruxelles* (1975), a film recording a series of quite ordinary daily activities – potato peeling for the evening soup, coffee making, eating with her son, listening to him read a poem, putting him to bed – methodically done, coolly, distantly observed. ("It is hard to know whether everything, or whether nothing, is being judged.")[30] Cavell's cataloguing of moments in the first hour seeks to mimic the patient detachment of Akerman's camera; the film, covering three days, each explicitly announced, runs three-and-a-half hours. The discreteness of the woman's activities together with a sense of their real-time duration make the film appear as a materialization of the idea of the self as a collection, here of actions rather than impressions and ideas. Cavell recounts how the film shows that on the next day the same routine events occur but slightly awry: a button is missing from her son's shirt, she lets the potatoes burn, she can't make her coffee taste right and has to remake it, and so on. On each day we have seen her enter a room with a man, closing the door behind her, then coming out and being paid. On the third day, we accompany the woman into the room, see her being made love to and, despite her indifference, being brought to orgasm. After finishing making love, Cavell reports, she moves about the room to freshen herself, picks up a pair of scissors that we have seen her use earlier to unwrap a present, walks over to the man still lying on her bed, and "stabs him fatally in the throat, and slides the scissors back into the dressing table as she walks out of the room. In the dining room, without turning on the light, she sits on a chair, still, eyes open, we do not know for how long."[31]

In the course of his recounting and elaboration of the film Cavell mentions how the woman, as she moves from room to room, turns off the light and closes the door, then opens the door and turns on the light in the next room, which sets up, through a circuitous route, a recalling of the link between tragedy and skepticism. Cavell concludes the fragment with the claim that Akerman "has found women to bear undistractibly, however attractively, the marks of supposedly interesting partitions or dissociations. . . . Call this a new discovery of the violence of the ordinary."[32] The film, which had not been cited before its introduction, is not further discussed or even mentioned for the remainder of the essay.

Now I am still on the track of the short paragraph, the opening of fragment *V*, about how I do not (actively) make the world things gather or (actively) systematize the language registering how each thing differs from every other, but rather testify to both, confess my need of both. Here is my hypothesis: The authority of the Cavellian fragment emerges via its exhibition of self-disenfranchisement, its capacity for testimony beyond making and systematizing, which is to say that the Cavellian fragment succeeds when it best approximates the separation of things. This is a delicate operation, since the separation of things from one another is deeply approximate to the violence of separation, as the sublimity of the ordinary is but a hair's breadth from the violence of the ordinary. How are we to distinguish between the patient regard of Akerman's camera, its granting to Jeanne Dielman of every dignity it can (or indignity she suffers?), and Jeanne Dielman's own inability to trust her world, her need for control, order, the careful separating of each activity from every other and the sheer madness of that? How are we to distinguish between Cavell's seeking of literary effect, call it the violence of voice, and his capacity for testimony?

Test the power of the short paragraph now: the first sentence states an obvious truism – I cannot make the world because no one can; we are not gods. The second statement inherits its force from the first sentence: if I am not God and so cannot make the world, then if I try to systematize language then I am pretending to be a god, pretending that I can make it, and so control and dominate things, make them fully and incontrovertibly "mine," say by putting each in a separate room or cabinet or under a universal or natural law or exchange value designed for the purpose of control. The work of the systematic philosopher is not unlike the madness of Jeanne Dielman, all that separation, all those doors opened and closed, lights turned on and off, the unfeelingness of it, the horror of feeling when it occurs, the final violence.[33] In the first sentence, the word "I" is almost redundant: no human can make a world. In the second sentence, the "I" is more individuated because there is a real action eschewed; but the real action eschewed by the real I is eschewed for logical reasons, at least if one allows the relation of analogical inference connecting the first two sentences – that keeps even the second "I" formal, anyone. In the final sentence, the force of the first person is intimate and impersonal at once. Nothing tells us what to do or what conclusions to draw from our humdrum inability to make the world or from our less humdrum inability to systematize the world (if to systematize means to gather things in a final order, divinely). Cavell could have said, "I must offer testimony," but that would displace responsibility, as if the acknowledging of my need of the world were an inference from a rule, or from what is logically demanded by the previous two sentences. Because no inference is given to be drawn, there is no telling what to do; it is up to "I." What we are shown, by the "I" not saying "I (one, we) must" but simply "I testify to both," is that testifying is the recognition of my need, its acknowledgment. To give testimony is to acknowledge need; confessing need is not what must be done; it is what just I do. "I testify to both" is valid if and only if exemplary. Exemplarity is the only kind of validity available to philosophical acts of acknowledgment. Acknowledgment is the exemplary act of self-relinquishment.

How might we be convinced of all this? Everything in Cavell's essay hangs on his letting Chantal Akerman's film, and so the world of Jeanne Dielman, unfold before us. It matters thus that Akerman's film is itself a work of acknowledgment, a film that approaches the status of the fragment in its refusal of explanatory narrative, which is how Cavell tells the film: "I wish to convey in this selected table of events the sense of how little stands out until the concluding violence, and at the same time that there are so many events taking place that a wholly true account of them could never be completed, and if not in this case, in no case.[34]

The Cavellian fragment, its authority, depends on its being itself a form of acknowledgment. It succeeds as a form of acknowledgment when it can make manifest its dependence and need for things; in Cavell, typically, those separate things are works of art or works of philosophy. This is not any old need or dependence; it occurs in the service of a vision in which things are separate yet capable of gathering a world (beyond our power of making or systematizing). The power of the fragment, its authority, is achieved when it releases the thing for that vocation – directly, allegorically, analogically, metaphorically. So philosophy approaches literature only in eschewing the autonomy of reason or concept, their power of gathering through subordination; it does this in Cavell when the individual fragment – sentence, paragraph, aside, parenthetical remark, aphorism – matches the career of the thing in its newly found indigence and beauty.[35] This is not an easy task or one Cavell always manages well, in part because what is demanded is not always clearly in sight. But this is not surprising: philosophy cannot by a force of will alone take on the concreteness, the sensuousness, the dependence on experience that has been the prerogative of art; what created the aesthetic problems of modern philosophy will often leave philosophy beached in abstraction, yearning for a sensuous particularity it cannot quite achieve. And sometimes an odd fragment might manage the difference. After describing Jeanne Dielman's routine of opening and closing doors, Cavell comments:

> The spaces are kept as separate as those in a cabinet of curiosities. (What would happen if they touched? A thought would be ignited.)[36]

Notes

1. Abbreviations used in this chapter are as follows:
   MD = Stanley Cavell, "Music Discomposed," in his *Must We Mean What We Say?* (Cambridge: Cambridge University Press, 1976).
   CR = Stanley Cavell, *The Claim of Reason: Wittgenstein, Skepticism, Morality, and Tragedy* (Oxford: Clarendon Press, 1979).
   AP = Stanley Cavell, "Aesthetic Problems of Modern Philosophy," in his *Must We Mean What We Say?*
   WV = Stanley Cavell, *The World Viewed: Reflections on the Ontology of Film* (Cambridge, MA: Harvard University Press, 1979).
   MM = Stanley Cavell, "A Matter of Meaning It," in his *Must We Mean What We Say?*
   QO = Stanley Cavell, *In Quest of the Ordinary: Lines of Skepticism and Romanticism* (Chicago: University of Chicago Press, 1988).
   CJ = Immanuel Kant, *Critique of Judgment*, trans. Werner S. Pluhar (Indianapolis: Hackett, 1987).
2. It is the failure of acknowledgement, of trust, not of knowledge, that makes Othello's jealous quest death-dealing, making skepticism, its truth, a function of our disappointment in knowledge – from which no knowledge can save us.

3. That for Cavell what I am calling transcendental cannot be pure, in Kant's sense – that is, a pure form knowable a priori – is entailed immediately by the locale of the claim, the domain of the aesthetic. And that will mean that the notion of the transcendental will need to undergo a sea change. Still, the risk or cost of not using it here in trying to fix the correct level of argument seems to be greater than the risk of using it.

4. There is a pathos in the question because it is a plea for recognition there and then, since there and then the two bodies of Othello and Desdemona are lying together before us, an emblem of the truth of skepticism. The becoming has already taken place; so Cavell is asking whether his philosophy, *The Claim of Reason* in its full modernist self-presentation, including its inclusion of Othello and Desdemona, will be recognized as a continuation, fulfillment, and transformation of the debates over skepticism, presented almost decorously in the first three parts of the text.

5. That this occurs at the moment when modernism as the leading edge of high culture is in rapid retreat, leading to its presumed disappearance and replacement by postmodernism, is not without significance. As Cavell was turning to romanticism, Michael Fried, who was his partner in modernist crime, was eschewing art criticism for art history. Dark times for modernism. The premise of this essay is that the cultural eclipse of modernism has not yet made it a thing of the past with which we could be over and done.

6. For a helpful fleshing out of this claim, see Richard Eldridge's Introduction to his *The Persistance of Romanticism* (New York: Cambridge University Press, 2001).

7. This claim is not original with me. For fine and lucid accounts of the topics of this essay, to which I am much indebted, see Stephen Mulhall, *Stanley Cavell: Philosophy's Recounting of the Ordinary* (Oxford: Clarendon Press, 1994), the Forward (pp. vii–xvii), pp. 23–33, 69–74.

8. All this is indiscriminate because it ignores the type of claim at issue. This lack of discrimination echoes an oddity of Cavell's philosophy, namely, his manner of slipping past the exact locale or level of his claims. By speaking about knowledge and skepticism generally, and how these have their human and logical origins in skepticism concerning other minds, and saying that skepticism relates to, baldly, the transcendental facts of human separateness (and so our mortality and isolation) and connectedness, Cavell keeps his interrogations of meaning and knowledge perfectly general, that is, indifferent to the domains of morals or politics or perception or science or. . . . He will alight on each of these at particular moments for particular reasons, but he thinks that his domain of questioning (running from thing to other-person skepticism, and from thence to minimal conditions of intersubjectivity) logically precedes and hence bears on all the traditional areas of philosophy.

9. While I think the antagonism is nearly as grand as I am portraying it, there always have been strains within modern philosophy of an empiricist and pragmatic kind – not to speak of the desire to couple the ideal type with various forms of moral and political individualism – that significantly soften the contrast. In the light of the contrast, Cavell's decision to hold firmly to the line of philosophical reflection

that takes its start from the problem of skepticism becomes comprehensible: The aim of overcoming subjectivity as the path to knowledge is intelligible only as a response to skepticism. Hence, the *problem* of skepticism is the precise place where the antagonists are joined.

10. It may be a terrible thing that I find something pleasant, but that is a different matter entirely. Any claim about "false" pleasures will thus need to contain some account about what is wrong with finding such-and-such pleasant (it is morally corrupting or corrupt; it blocks off the formation of other kinds of – nobler – pleasures, etc.) without in so doing gainsaying what is felt. I leave aside the marginal cases where I say that I find something pleasant because I know that I should find it so, even though I do not, which is awkward because, my self-deception being what it is, I may not know or realize that I do not find pleasurable what I say I do so find. And if I do not know, will never know, then where is the self-deception located, where is the pleasure's falsity?

11. If you do not hear this as a retreat, or find laughable, as Kant remarks, the idea that someone might claim flatly "This is beautiful *for me*," then we shall not be able even to get started. The premise of the argument is the oddness of aesthetic claiming, that we find ourselves irresistibly posing certain types of judgments of taste in curiously objective terms. The philosophical burden is doing something with the grammatical curiosity.

12. Mulhall, *Stanley Cavell*, p. 28. In "Aesthetic Problems of Modern Philosophy," the idea of mastering one's subjectivity and making it exemplary for others, so quickly stated, has to carry a large burden, since it stands in for Kant's deduction of the judgement of taste. But this is just to say that Cavell is shifting the burden of Kant's analysis from our relation to nature as a whole to our relations to one another as a whole. I am here ignoring this lacuna in the argument.

13. Cavell can sometimes present his position as if this is what is being urged; see, for example, CR, p. 29.

14. For essays informing Cavell's and my account of Caro, see Michael Fried, "New Work by Anthony Caro," "Two Sculptures by Anthony Caro," "Caro's Abstractness," and "Anthony Caro," all collected in his *Art and Objecthood* (Chicago: University of Chicago Press, 1998); and Clement Greenberg, "The New Sculpture" and "Modernist Sculpture, Its Pictorial Past," both in his *Art and Culture* (Boston: Beacon Press, 1961).

15. In Fried, *Art and Objecthood*.

16. In posing skepticism in this way, I am agreeing with Steven Affeldt, in "The Ground of Mutuality: Criteria, Judgement and Intelligibility in Stephen Mulhall and Stanley Cavell," *European Journal of Philosophy* 6 (April 1998), p. 21, that for Cavell skepticism depends "upon a fantasy of our language as a framework of rule which itself governs the use and determines the meaning of works and which itself functions to align him with others." Unless it were this fantasy (and the facts of "determined society" that make it something more than a fantasy) that supported skepticism, it would be unclear why Cavell employed an aesthetic logic as its other.

17. I presume this sentence is intended as an interpretation and thus defense of Clement Greenberg's "Avant-Garde and Kitsch," in his *Art and Culture*.

18. "Now I might define the problem of modernism as one in which the question of value comes first as well as last: to classify a modern work as art is already to have staked value, more starkly than the (later) decision concerning its goodness or badness" (MM, 216). "Value" has here the sense of: places a claim upon me, deserves attention, calls for response, and does so intrinsically, as a matter of its configured materials.

19. Fried, *Art and Objecthood*, p. 187.

20. In fact, it is not Hegelian art history informing Fried's theory but Maurice Merleau-Ponty's rendering of Georg Lukács's concept of dialectic in *History and Class Consciousness*.

21. For Cavell's continued allegiance to this idea, see "The World as Things: Collecting Thoughts on Collecting," in the catalogue for the exhibition *Rendezvous: Masterpieces from the Centre Georges Pompidou and the Guggenheim Museums* (New York: Guggenheim Museum Publications, 1998), p. 81. Fried now admits that his reading of Pollock downplayed his paint-on-canvas materialism: "Optical Allusions," *Artforum* 37 (April 1999), pp. 97–101, 143, 146. In making this acknowledgement he acknowledges a certain limit to his reading of Pollock as instantiating the aesthetics of presentness; but all indications are that, despite this, the general view remains intact.

22. Cavell intends the notion of candidness, finally, to connect two separate thoughts: that a work must be done, finished, closed (and thus I have finished with it) and, thereby, that the work can stand apart from me, be an automatism. While these characteristics seem, criterially, fine – they jointly announce my responsibility for the work *and* its separateness from me, where responsibility and separateness are what require acknowledgement – I am not convinced that even they are best thought through the notion of thereness or candidness. For all that, it should be noticed how Cavell's attempt in these pages is to flesh out the antitheatrical ideal implied by Fried in a manner that would demonstrate how the kind of art that avoids theater is equally the kind of art that requires acceptance and acknowledgement. Because some of the art here being championed eschews the sign of hand, wrist, and muscle, then explaining how it nonetheless sustains an ideal of art opposed to the interestingness of minimalism is no easy critical task.

23. For an account and two pictures of *Prairie*, see Fried, "Two Sculptures by Anthony Caro," in *Art and Objecthood*, pp. 181–3, Figure 43 and Plate 14.

24. I am here implying that Fried's account of *Prairie* in *Art and Objecthood*, p. 182–3, goes beyond the critical terms in which it is framed. The "openness," radical horizontality, the "frankly avowed ... physicality" of it, etc., all press toward a sublimity that defeats, and was meant to defeat, presentness. Hence, I am claiming that what we experience in "seeing" *Prairie* is ambiguous between its physical presence and its horizontal orientation, insisting on an ambiguity that Fried tries to resolves in one direction: "*Prairie* compels us to believe what we see rather than what we know, to accept the witness of the senses against the

constructions of the mind" (p. 183). For me, the experience of the piece is the experience of the "against." For ease, brevity, and dialectical advantage I am here accepting Rosalind Krauss's thesis, that with Pollock horizontality becomes a new medium of advanced art, as a way of characterizing at least one feature of Caro's achievement. For a brief restatement of Krauss's position germane to this discussion (there is a footnote on Cavell), see her "The Crisis of the Easel Picture," in Kirk Varnedoe and Pepe Karmel, eds., *Jackson Pollock: New Approaches* (New York: Museum of Modern Art, 1999), especially pp. 168–70. We are not, I think, going to be able to easily separate *Prairie* from Richard Serra's *Cutting Device: Base, Plate, Measure*, pictured on p. 176 of Krauss's essay; the latter is like a scattered version of the former, the vertical now forgotten altogether.

25. Caro's earliest, interesting if unsuccessful work involves the attempt to depict from the outside what human action or gesture feels like from the inside. My suggestion here is that the project remained but its means changed from the quasi-representational to the fully abstract. In their capacity to make the space they inhabit, some of Caro's most abstract works have the sense of being new or unknown gestures or postures that we must grasp as both participants (dialogically, so to speak) and observers (objective field observers excluded from participation). These works, I would claim, are the height of his achievement, what is most unavoidable in his oeuvre. I am using the anthropological analogy not only as a vehicle for the "other minds" aspect of engaging with the work, but also to suggest that the analogy works via a kind of sublimity or interruption.

26. A point Fried acknowledges in *Art and Objecthood*, p. 183.

27. Cavell, "The World as Things," p. 69.

28. A point that Richard Eldridge urged on me – all too rightly.

29. Cavell, "The World as Things," p. 69.

30. Ibid., p. 73.

31. Ibid., p. 74.

32. Ibid., p. 75.

33. It is almost impossible not to perceive *Jeanne Dielman* as the reversed image of Doris Lessing's *The Golden Notebook*.

34. Cavell, "The World as Things," pp. 74–5.

35. For more on the status of the philosophical fragment, see my *Adorno: Disenchantment and Ethics* (New York: Cambridge University Press, 2001), Chapters 6–7.

36. Cavell, "The World as Things," p. 75. My gratitude to Richard Eldridge, who has been the perfect editor, helping me to express better what I have wanted to say, and forcing me to think harder. Alice Crary's reading of the first draft of this essay saved me from a howler or two, and nudged me in the direction I needed to go.

6 | A Second *Primavera*: Cavell, German Philosophy, and Romanticism

WILLIAM DESMOND

ON STYLE OF THOUGHT

Cavell is not one whose thought can be fixed easily with univocal determinacy. This is a thinking always on the move, and it moves more by perplexity and questioning than by arriving at assertoric claims, where finally rest at last offers itself. This is part of Cavell's great attraction and difficulty. *Attraction*: the subtlety of his interrogations lures one toward a moment of truth, less determined in conclusive propositions than in the question that now at last can be put and that, in being put, gives us access to a light that, just in being stayed briefly, also as quickly passes. *Difficulty*: there seems no place to lay one's head, so to say, and one is left to wonder if, in fact, there was that brief access of light, which after all now seems more a new perplexity than any perplexity dissolved or problem solved. To anyone who insists on a more settled univocity in philosophical argumentation, there will be cause enough here for chewing the carpet. And yet there is nothing excessively studied in this, as if it were the *pose* of unsettling us that Cavell struck, rather than in fact offering us access to that place of unsettling where a different thinking might catch fire.

To say more univocally what cannot quite be so said: there is something of art in the philosophical writing of Cavell that draws water from a well whose secret spring still remains underground. This is the clue for my own opening relative to German philosophy and Romanticism. Cavell's concern with the first is, on first glance, less developed than his engagement with the second; and his engagement with both is marked by resistance to any laundry-list summary of themes. The relation of art and philosophy, and more specifically the relation of literature and philosophy, is clearly central to Cavell; and indeed, it is central to German philosophy and to the great cultural movement so familiar to it, called Romanticism. In Cavell's case there is also the ancestor Wittgenstein, who wrote: "philosophy ought really to be written only as a *poetic composition*."[1] Cavell's *The Claim of Reason* ends with the question of whether philosophy, were it to become literature,

143

would still know itself. There is much at stake here, and it is central to the "problematic" given some articulation in classical German philosophy, its seemingly idealistic consummation, and its anti-idealistic dissolution, and not least in Romanticism.

The issue of the style of philosophizing, in particular in relation to autobiography, can also be connected with the Romantic concern with self and with key elements of Cavell's own style of philosophizing. Some of the common reactions to Cavell's alleged idiosyncrasy mirror reactions to Romanticism's so-called irrationalism. I think of Hegel's distaste for Romantic subjectivity, perhaps all the more shrill because of his own proximity to it. Certain reactions to Cavell are quite Hegelian in that regard, and one might equally wonder if they are so out of an anxiety of proximity. One of the dimensions of philosophical naming I find in Cavell relates to what I call the *idiocy of being*: that intimacy of being that cannot be truly rendered in the language of neutral, homogenous generality, for it concerns intimate singularities, which are yet redolent of a fuller, more radiant significance.[2] And yet what cannot be so homogenized in terms of the neutral general is itself more intimately involved in the articulation of language, in the sources of being as communicative: communication is made possible by what cannot be communicated in absolute, determinate terms. The idiocy is not unrelated to the idiom, and the idiosyncratic: philosophy has its idioms, as the philosopher has his idiosyncrasies; and neither finally is a neutral, homogeneous generality. Part of the difficulty of Cavell's philosophical way is also this problem with the autobiographical, the confessional: to communicate oneself, and what is ontologically intimate to being, *without embarrassment*, not only to oneself but to the other who is being offered the confidence.[3]

Philosophers generally do not take this risk of the intimacy of being, which comes across as "too much." They are like anorexics who like the leaner foods of perfections where less seems enough. They shun the "too muchness" of things and decamp to the neutral general. Of course, if they are like such anorexics they have either begun to die, or perhaps something has not been born in them, or allowed to come to be. The later Wittgenstein was a kind of recovering anorexic in that sense: the younger was more under the spell of the austerer perfections of the logical ideal that would recreate or redeem in an ideal language of univocity the contaminating equivocities of the everyday. But it turns out that the contaminating equivocal is the matrix of robust life.

One can see Romanticism as a desire to return to the fragrant world, after the dead purity of the mechanical whole that Newtonianism gives us. But many Romantics were also in the contagion of the anorexia of spirit – hence at times the spectral visitors, the nameless powers, the hidden hindrances of soul that still kept them back from the fragrant world. Sometimes they tried, so to say, to will themselves to wake from the mechanical dream; but they still found themselves in a paralyzed state, even in willing to awaken from such a spell; they would move their legs but they wouldn't move, as if some ominous power had secreted a bewitchment to which they may have more than half succumbed. One cannot just will to awaken from such a bewitchment; for the character of one's willing is implicated in the bewitchment, and hence it too must undergo a *metanoia*; but from where is the saving power to come? The anorexic spirit, in trying to save itself, and with obeisance to what seem like the highest ideals of self-perfection, is in the grip of a spell cast on it, through itself, if not by itself.

This sense of Romanticism is not unconnected with Cavell's engagement of skepticism. Think of a certain kind of skeptic as an anorexic mind: driven by an ideal of perfection, not always fully articulated; seeking a certain power over what initially presents itself as ambiguous and beyond; secretly desirous of its own sovereignty over what always threatens to disappoint it; more and more forced to close the circle of control over that which it believes it subdues; closing down the equivocal, but also closing down the "too muchness" of given life, and indeed its own insurgent energies that still come to surface unbidden; and at the end, binding mastery only over its own "no," as it comes into its kingdom, where it inherits precisely nothing. Such a skeptic is driven to an extremity where a monstrous outcome awaits, like the anorexic who will not accept and live the risk that comes with the ambiguous robustness of the food of life, and the tasting of its gift. Think of the inhumanity to which Cavell believes philosophy can be driven.

How to get our bearings in the muchness of Cavell's writings? The following citation from *In Quest of the Ordinary* might be taken as giving a helpful précis of some central themes to which Cavell gives expression and marking his affinities with major Romantic concerns. He tells us that the purpose of the Romantics was "to redeem genuine poetry from its detractors." This in turn was bound up with

> the preservation or redemption of genuine philosophy, where the preservation of poetry and philosophy by one another presents itself as the necessity of recovering or replacing religion. This contesting of philosophy and poetry and religion (and I guess of politics) with one another, for one another, together with the disreputable sense that the fate of the contest is bound up with one's own writing, and moreover with the conviction that the autobiographical is a method of thought wherein such a contest can find a

useful field, and in which the stakes appear sometimes as the loss or gain of our common human nature, sometimes as the loss or gain of nature itself, as if the world were no more than one's own – some such statement represents the general idea I have of what constitutes serious romanticism's self-appointed mission, the idea with which I seek its figures. (IQO, 43)

In what is to follow I will focus on the concerns here named, forming my remarks around the relations of art, philosophy, and religion (with a bow to Hegel's triad of absolute spirit). I will also touch on central themes such as philosophical migration and inheritance; the death of nature, with some special reference to Coleridge; the displacement of redemption from religion to art; the transcendence of thought and its sanity. But first, the issue of inheritance allows us to offer some more general points of orientation.

INHERITANCES BETWEEN WORLDS

The issue of *philosophical inheritance* is hard to avoid in any consideration of Cavell's relation to German philosophy and Romanticism. We find many references to Kant, to Hegel, to Nietzsche, a few to Heidegger. Perhaps Kant garners most attention in *The Claim of Reason*, given his "enormous prestige" along with Hume in "recent philosophizing" (248), and certainly given Kant's concern with skepticism. Interestingly for our theme, Kant himself speaks of the skeptic as a "species of nomads" of which fortunately (for Kant) there are few. Something of this nomadic spirit clearly has infected Cavell in his own affinities with a variety of skepticisms, and indeed in his skepticism about certain skepticisms. I will return to Kant in relation to Cavell's reading of Coleridge's "Ancient Mariner," but here I want to note certain parallels. In the Anglo-Saxon tradition, Kant was primarily received as an epistemologist in the tradition of classical epistemology, and especially with respect to what was taken as a major outcome of this in Humean skepticism. Of course, there are other faces of Kant. There is the Kant for whom freedom is the heart and soul of the transcendental philosophy, and for whom, arguably, the *Critique of Practical Reason* was decisive, decisive in making a space for human freedom in a world under the iron domination of deterministic mechanism; the power of freedom is from the outset prefigured, haunting in advance the theory of transcendental knowing in the *Critique of Pure Reason*. There is the Kant of the *Critique of Judgment*, the Kant with perhaps the most influence on the Romantic generation. This Kant would, in his own tortured scholastic way, want to bind up the wounds of dualism lacerating the first and second *Critiques*; more than anywhere else in his system, this Kant wanted to think the otherness of nature as not fully figured forth in the mechanism of the Newtonian paradigm. We might see intimations of Romantic and Cavellian themes: bringing nature back to life; bringing the human back to itself in a nature not its dead mechanical opposite but an other to be acknowledged, perhaps in the accordance of beauty, perhaps in the discordance of the sublime. These themes are there in *The Claim of Reason*.

Of course, there is the perceived difficulty with Kant that has some parallel: *transcendental solipsism*. This brings up the problem of the other, central to Cavell's own movement from knowledge to acknowledgment. This is not entirely unlike the problem of recognition that is central to Kant's heirs. Thus Fichte: notoriously transcendental, yet intriguingly obsessed with the other – and perhaps obsessed so, because notorious thus. Thus Hegel too and the place of recognition. Think of the *Phenomenology of Spirit*: the early parts deal, it seems, with very classical problems in epistemology; and then about halfway through the discussion, the human other makes an unceremonious entrance, through desire and the struggle for recognition, and the master–slave dialectic (mentioned in *The Claim of Reason*). The later parts of the *Phenomenology* then offer an obscure dialectical trawl through the seas of history, in search of absolute knowing, or its historical conditions of possibility. The dialectical trawl culminates in philosophical knowing: the point where supposedly knowing no longer needs to go beyond itself. I would say Cavell inverts this: acknowledging is just the point where knowing knows it must go beyond itself. And there is something more involved in acknowledgment than the putative self-certainty of knowing that knows *itself* as the certainty of truth. Cavell is not thus Hegelian.[4] There is a knowing that in acknowledging the other learns of differences, differences it perhaps had already *known from* others. It has perhaps forgotten this "knowing from," though still it is carried by the words of others, words themselves the treasuries of differences carried across time, as if in secret caches. One witnesses something of this treasury of differences being brought to the surface, as one is sometimes stunned to attention and to pause at Cavell's extraordinary wordings of ordinary English.

One of the complications in approaching Cavell's relation to German philosophy and Romanticism is the way Thoreau and Emerson exert a strong influence in the foreground, pushing back the European side into a more recessive shade. The muse must be wooed, and wooed in relation to genius, and genius is not just my genius as this singular thinker or poet or artist, but also the genius of a place or locale, which too is the genius of a people. One is located; and this is a great thing for Cavell, as for Thoreau.

But much of his work is also an attempt to come to terms with a sense of dislocation; where does the dislocation come from? From the very vocation of philosophy itself. But what if this is located in a place that is not always hospitable to the slower leisures of ruminative reflection, indispensable to philosophical thinking? Any ruminative thought must return again and again to what it believed it had digested or exhausted, only to find reserves hidden there still, perhaps reserves that hint finally at an inexhaustibility that will never be done with, that will always haunt all final claims on it. For these reserves claim us, we do not claim them. In some ways America is for Cavell a name for the condition, or perhaps hope, that claims him with this promise of inexhaustibilty, and that never leaves him alone.

Note the stress: rumination returns to what is hidden in the there; while America, mostly, is never quite there, is always on the way, always to come. By contrast, Europe might seem, so to say, more there; and this is perhaps more true of England, relative to the extraordinarily long time of inner stability its ways of life have generally enjoyed. But where is America for Cavell? In many places, but philosophically in the forgotten or repressed. Thus Emerson and Thoreau figure for him as founders of American thought, but founders not now so acknowledged by the regnant caste of contemporary professors of philosophy. To give a local habitation and a name requires a new philosophical imagination: to bring back to life those dead founders.[5]

What has this to do with Romanticism? One might say that a major theme of Romanticism, in its opposition to the allegedly neutral universalism of the Enlightenment, is its concern with a people, in the singularity of its traditions, and in its cultural inheritance (think of Herder). Cavell's relation to Emerson and Thoreau can be seen in this light. So for him, their senses of the "common" serve to underwrite the ordinary language philosophy of Austin, and Wittgenstein (IQO, 4). That Emerson and Thoreau haunted some of the places of Cavell's life (e.g., Harvard) is not insignificant. Their presence lives on in their absence, in the words they can no longer speak, words they need not speak now because they wrote them, and which we must learn perhaps to speak for them, from them.

One might compare Cavell and Heidegger relative to such a Romantic sense of inheritance. Cavell seems intrigued by some things in Heidegger but equally nonplussed or repulsed by other things. The extremity of a certain Romanticism in Heidegger both attracts and repulses Cavell. Heidegger wanted to be the voice of Germany, philosophically, as he claimed that Hölderlin was poetically, and as Hitler then was politically. Cavell is not quite the philosophical voice of America, but one voice seeking to be true to America. Since that voice seeks to be true to a more democratic impulse, there can be no arrogation of voice. Can a voice reach toward its own singularity, if it does not arrogate authority at some point? If not, will it not be like Emerson's scholar (so beloved of citation) who cannot, dare not, say "I think, I am." One might say that this is very close to the predicament of Romanticism: community of source, singularity of voice. The first may be deeper than the second, and yet it is mute without the second, and hence it is a depth lost to itself without the boldness of singulars who say "I am, I say," who have the boldness to arrogate voice. Cavell is working toward this: to speak less to or at the other than for the other, perhaps therein finding that others already have been speaking in him. Hence the claim that Emerson and Thoreau were more true to the common in their seeming uncommonness; perhaps truer to the treasury of differences that is the inheritance of a people, albeit marked by or held together by striking sameness. But one may not hear them, or hear from them, if one only stays at home; for staying at home may not be to be at home; and perhaps one must learn not to be at home in order again to come home.

There are places where Cavell hints at some points of continuity with German idealism, but he hesitates in his commitment to it, especially in regard to something about its philosophy of consciousness: "the concept takes in train a philosophical machinery of self-consciousness, subjectivity, and imagination, of post-Kantianism in general, that for me runs out of control" (IQO, 45). He could not follow. What is a philosophy that comes to be "out of control"? How important is it to be in control (see IQO, 58)? Surely one of the effects of Cavell's writing is to remind us of how much less in control of importances we are than we think we are, and not least in relation to what is tacit in words, in language itself. The poet brings something of this taciturnity to our attention – letting it be tacit while bringing it to speech, respecting the reserve of the true word itself. Resistance to being "out of control" suggests, to some degree, that Cavell is more heir to certain modern notions of self-determining humanity than is always evident. What then of what I call "knowing from," "speaking from"? I mean: the deeper message of Cavell's writing is to show us how little we determine through ourselves alone, not so as to make us powerless, but so as to let us partake of sources of empowerment that are as much other as our own.

Perhaps then it is not that the German idealists were epistemologically "out of control" but rather that they were too much the opposite. They insisted more radically than ever on a knowing that would just be in its own control – absolutely self-determining thought, absolutely autonomous. This is the monster of the self-empowering knower, the self-absolutizing, self-absolving thinker. There will be nothing given to it that (it claims) it does not give to itself. But in fact, we cannot so absolve ourselves of something given. One might say: to be genuinely absolved is to be acknowledged by another, perhaps as the incarnation of forgiveness.

If Emerson and Thoreau are often in the foreground, how do we see beyond this foreground to German philosophy (especially in work after *The Claim of Reason*)?[6] Cavell wants to inherit Emerson and Thoreau and stake a claim to American philosophy; but this means to be in a somewhat sideways attunement to both "England" and the "Continent." One travels to England or the Continent, but one is always drawn back through them, hoping to become drawn back differently to the American scene (Henry James).

One might then say that Cavell's voice begins to find its place somewhere *between* a number of different sources of philosophical inheritance.[7] Being *between worlds* is itself identified by Cavell with the Romantic response to Kant's two worlds. Look here at Cavell's principal non-American forebears. Wittgenstein is different: already in the German world, and in the English; stressed between these two; always perhaps because of stresses both singular and inherited more an outsider than an insider; a onetime professor, seemingly the ne plus ultra of being an insider.[8] Cavell intimates that Wittgenstein's distinctive stress is neither English nor Continental, and yet it has blood that is indebted to both. Between the new world, the old world, and the island of analysis, this stress of "being between" breeds perhaps a new plurivocity: a voice of voices. In some way, it turns out that we are all, in our own way, a voice of voices. Some voices come to mindfulness by entry into the quarrel and persuading of many voices; they speak in this Babel as more than echoes. One voice rises above the din, is heard above it, though it is in the midst of it. Another voice finds itself in a return to being in the midst of other voices, and ceases to claim the prerogative of being above. It does not "sublime," but finds the sublime, as in the blessing of the common: blessing it, being blessed in it, blessed by it.

THE DEATH OF THE WORLD

Suppose we further consider this theme, touched on in the *The Claim of Reason*, central to the Romantic problematic, and also important in *In Quest of the Ordinary*, where we find some of the most important pointers concerning Cavell's relation to German philosophy and Romanticism. In *In Quest of the Ordinary* we are offered an extended discussion of Coleridge and Wordsworth, and some brief discussion of Heidegger. The discussion of Coleridge and Wordsworth is fascinating, taking up themes clearly evident in *The Claim of Reason*, as well as elsewhere, and in a manner that more fully releases them from the terms of more standard epistemological concerns.

It is worth remembering that Coleridge is kind of a double here. Coleridge is the figure from whom American transcendentalism would have learned much about Kant and German philosophy (IQO, 40). In Coleridge's *Biographia Literaria*, Cavell recognizes something of a forerunner of his own interests in linking transcendentalism and ordinary language philosophy (41). We might say that Coleridge instantiates the problem of plural allegiances of intellect, of spirit. In his way, Coleridge was between England and Germany, as he explicitly acknowledges in his *Biographia Literaria*. One sees here also soundings and resoundings, doublings, doublings back, redoublings, of the relation of poetry and philosophy. There is Coleridge's conceded, albeit qualified, debt to Schelling as philosopher, the dark prince of Romanticism, who never received a proper and serious attention in the tradition of English philosophy. How "Hegelian" that reception was in treating his thought as mere Romantic irrationalism! But perhaps Schelling was truer to the familial intimacy of art and philosophy than Hegel: hence his attractiveness for Coleridge and, in his tracks, Coleridge's for Cavell.

I will shortly turn more fully to Cavell on Coleridge, but it is worth pointing out a question that I think Schelling represents for German idealism: Is there any light of self-consciousness without the darkness of what is on the other side of self-consciousness? Does this light come from a darkness that it never completely dispels? This is to touch on the tender Achilles' heel of self-determining knowing. I could put it thus: Is all knowing, finally, *knowing from*: from a source not itself knowing, or perhaps fully knowable? This problem is not outside of consideration of transcendental solipsism. Schelling was more acutely aware of it than Fichte and, to his credit, strongly insisted that nature in its otherness could not be slighted. Transcendental philosophy must be complemented, if not completed, by a new system of the whole in which self and other, human and nature, subject and object are together and known as together. I cannot go into the complications of this system and the influence of Spinoza, among others, but it is worth dwelling a little on nature, as revealing something of the *ethos* within which both transcendental philosophy and *Naturphilosophie* function.

Remember again: modern science, supposedly grounded in its overcoming of skepticism, goes to work with its new mathematical and geometrical tools and produces a world more and more conformed to univocal formulation. But, alas, nature so conceived seems to have little place for the human being who first conceived nature so. Thus, for instance, the difference between the inanimate and animated seems to be undercut by a certain principle of homogeneous intelligibility. If so, the place of the scientist or human who uses the homogeneous principle becomes deeply perplexing. We are not at home in the mathematical machine, nor can we be. Nature as machine, with the extrinsic god of Deism, seems a little like the estranged human dualistically opposed to an other with which it has no inherent rapport. With nature devalued, dedivinized, with any deistic god perpetually on the verge of vanishing, the human being wakes to itself as lost in an immense indifference. The Romantics felt this loss and then sought neither nature as machine, nor God beyond that nature, but nature as an organism, and perhaps the immanent God that Spinoza seemed to promise. Thus in German idealism Spinozism becomes the balancing complement to Kant's transcendental solipsism: substance to subject. Hegel picked up on that, but the issue is very elemental, and the Romantic poets knew this along their pulses. In fact, Spinoza is as much a "mechanist" as an "organicist," but it is the second image that prevails in Novalis's description of him not as an atheist but as the *Gott-vertrunkene Mann*. The generation of Romanticism and transcendental philosophy often saw what they needed and wanted to see, whether in Kant or in Spinoza. Spinoza's God may be a counterfeit double of God, yet the sense of the organic whole here intimated seemed to offer a way to a renewed rapport with the earth.

Different directions open up here. We might go the way of genius: an immanent "inner" pathway of originality prepared by transcendental philosophy. Genius is the favorite of nature through whom nature gives the rule to art, as Kant puts it. Yet here you have something beyond autonomous self-determination, since it arises from a source on the other side of our own self-legislation. The genius is a creative middle, an original medium through whom a more original power comes to articulation: nature beyond the law, which yet brings the law to expression. Kant hesitated here; but he let this genie out of the bottle, and it could not be put back in terms of the education of taste. A source of exceeding otherness even in the innerness of genius, in its intimacy with the secret powers of nature, comes through. This means: no transcendental solipsism in transcendental selfhood itself.

This still leaves the problem of how, even if those immanent powers of self-transcending are released, we are released to nature as other. What will give it back to itself, or how will we be released to its otherness as other, and not as the deadened world that mechanism seems to produce? Coleridge went the first way and realized, with Schelling, that this was not enough. Hence the famous lines: "O lady, we receive but what we give, / And in our life alone does Nature live: / Ours is her wedding garment, ours her shroud!" ("Dejection: An Ode") We are too much there, and the otherness of nature not enough there. The ancient mariner's journey below the line: Is this an entry into the inner otherness, and a transgression in that immanence? Consequence? The world of ice, dead nature: How is the renewed rapport possible? It is renewed in its blessing when he learns to bless – slimy creatures as well as beautiful. But how bless? How be released? It is more a grace than anything we could do; it comes to us, and does not first come from us; and we come to ourselves, and can go from ourselves again toward what is other as other. But these are *religious pathways of redemption*. I will return to this theme.

What here is at issue is hard to map entirely in terms of the inner otherness of self, since this is at stake, in question; nor indeed onto nature in its otherness, for how comes that transformation by which it is restored to its qualitative value? How does it come about that it is seen as blessed, such that we might murmur: It is good? Redemption is assaulted in early modernity: no more witches means no more bewitchment, but it may also mean a world washed of dangers and fragrances, hence a dead place for love, no human place, for there is now nothing to woo, or overcome one.

I could put it in a pedestrian way: in modernity we find a certain objectification of being, itself inseparable from a certain subjectification, and both inseparable from a devaluation, a neutering of being as other to us. As the neuter grows indifferent, we come to hate the indifferent, and hence the neuter grows hateful, for we cannot love it; and when we hate the neutralized world, we do not so much kill it as show rather that it has already been deadened. Have we perhaps deadened it? Are we ourselves perhaps as dead? And is our hatred the spasm of a life that has fallen into a seizure in which the energies of life have incomprehensibly gone astray, even as they frantically or randomly course through our spastic flesh? And so we come to the felt need to restore the world.

Cavell will suggest: now the other must bear the weight previously borne by God.[9] This reminds one of Levinas – but without God. What weight was that, and what weight will that now be, as borne by the other? Can the human other bear that weight? Think but of *Job's lament*: "Oh that my grief were thoroughly weighed, and my calamity laid in the balances together! For now it would be heavier than all the sands of the sea." Who has the measure to weigh such things? Man tries to be the measure of all things, but can he be the measure of Job's outcry? Were one to say yes, would one add to the already far-too-long list of Job's comforters, a vocation of special attraction to many philosophers? Can the human other be the measure? But what if the human other is less a measure than also in the scales, also in the balance? The other whose destiny is in the balance may not be able to give us the balance and ballast suggested by the weight of that other other, God. You still do not like the question? Very well, it is the question of the extremity of loss, or of being at a loss, that the tragic communicates to us: something in excess of the measure of finite recuperation is communicated in tragic loss. If no human can be the source of the recovery, and if all we have is the human, does loss then have the last word? And what becomes of such a loss, if there is nothing at all of finding or being found?

ON CROSSING THE LINE AND COLERIDGE

But let us look a little closer at Cavell's reading of Coleridge in *In Quest of the Ordinary*. A connection is made with Emerson, and Kant, and with Wordsworth's desire to speak of the low and the rustic: the glory of and in the common. We taste the Kantian flavor:

> ... in philosophy the task is associated with the overcoming, say critique of metaphysics, and in literature with the domestication of the fantastic, or the transcendentalizing of the domestic, call these movements the internalizing or subjectivizing, or democratizing of philosophy; and that this communication between philosophy and literature, or the refusal of communication, is something that causes romanticism. (IQO, 27)

We are on now relatively familiar territory: the turn to self characterizing the longer arc of modern philosophy – philosophy as a question to itself. With respect to self-repression and self-liberation, Thoreau and Emerson "first of all teach us that self-liberation is what we require of ourselves"(28). In the more general outlook, how we see Romanticism is a function of how we view the philosophical settlement proposed in Kant's achievement (29). This depends on how we conceive that achievement. Cavell's suggestion: Here we come across an "attacking [of] philosophy in the name of redeeming it." "It is true that philosophy habitually presents itself as redeeming itself, hence struggling for its name, famously in the modern period, since Bacon, Locke and Descartes. But can philosophy be redeemed *this way*, this romantic way?" (30)

In its relations with its others, the "identity" of philosophy and its call are at stake: to make philosophy other by engagement with these others, and so to help it survive its crisis, and perhaps come to itself again with these others. This is a great concern of the Romantics, expressed as a desire for reconstituted harmony in a time of human fragmentation. If a desire to transfigure life brings philosophy into relation with poetry and art, so also does it bring it into relation with the religious. Hegel, for instance, might address this is terms of absolute spirit, but Cavell enacts the issue in the register of the ordinary.

One might ask: Is not Cavell concerned with what one might call a "saving knowing"? Is he a practitioner of a new poverty of philosophy in postsecular form? What might be entailed by a saving knowing, and in connection with Romanticism? Saving knowing – not determinate cognition of new facts or theory; we are saturated with these, their richness is not to be added to; rather a knowing that lets a new light shine on what is granted as there. With certain kinds of knowing, the more we know the more we seem lost, and know we are lost: for instance, Romanticism's sense of being lost in the bright, machine world of Newtonianism. We need a different knowing to save us from being lost, by dwelling with lostness differently. Indeed there might be a losing of oneself differently that is more like a condition of poetry or being religious. Not a new theory or new system, but a release toward what is there and a new rumination. Is this what Cavell suggests in reading redemptively?

Whether redemption, philosophical or otherwise, is a matter of self-redemption is central to the issue, I would say. For self-redemption may not be quite equal to the redemption of self. Cavell gives an economical résumé of Kant by reference to the *Prolegomena*. Kant plots the limits of knowledge, relative to phenomena and the thing itself. Though we must grant the existence of the thing in itself, and though it cannot be known, nevertheless the point is not entirely negative: "In discovering the limitation of reason, reason proves its power to itself, over itself. . . ." It is as if, within the limit Kant claims to determine transcendentally, reason is at home with itself, and in its own way master of itself, and this despite Kant's famously saying the he limited knowing in order to make room for faith. In truth, of course, this faith will be a moral faith in the power of the moral subject to be self-governing or autonomous. Does self-redemption resound with some overtones of "being in control"?

A reoriented questioning of limit, or line, will be central to Romanticism and, with qualifications to which I hope to come, to Cavell himself. For him, Romanticism serves to monitor Kant's philosophical settlement, apparently the most stable in the modern period (IQO, 31). Nevertheless, the line between nature and freedom, the appearance and the thing itself, is hard to keep entirely unmoving, not least because the human being, as having to do with both sides, also seems to be a power moving *between* the two. Cavell considers the Romantic relation to Kant's notion of the two worlds, or two ways of seeing. This is to witness to the human being's dissatisfaction with itself, but also to an appreciation of a certain ambivalence in Kant's sense of limitation. One might add that Kant often seems to give us a kind of two-way seeing: now dare to know, now respect the limit; now no God, now God as necessary; now restriction to appearances, now necessary reference to the thing in itself; now the law seems given, now it seems we must give ourselves the law. Such a two-way seeing might make us quite cross-eyed, even cross – especially if we have no protocols for negotiating the crossing or transition from one to the other, or no embrace that seems able to hold together the two.

Another Romantic surmise might arise: perhaps we live in neither of these worlds; or perhaps, as Cavell puts it, "we are, as it is said, between worlds" (IQO, 32). I have alluded to such a condition of being between relative to philosophical inheritance, but here it must also mean being able to move between one and the other, mean that the human being is one and the other, or neither one nor the other, or both together. Such an intermediate condition could not be reduced to univocal homogeneity. Cavell underscores the centrality of the issue here.

> Of course, all such notions of worlds and being between them, and dead to them, and living in them, seeing them but not knowing them, as if no longer knowing them, as it were not remembering them, haunted by them, are at most a sheaf of pictures. How seriously one takes them is a matter of how impressed one is by the precision and comprehension of their expression. To test this is a purpose of the texts under discussion here. (33)

Nor is his outlook exclusionary: Wittgenstein and Heidegger can be said to share "this romantic perception of human doubleness."[10] If we have, on one extreme, the feeling of our "worldlessness, or homelessness," on the other we have someone like Wordsworth seeking to arouse men from a "torpor" by making "the incidents of common life interesting," and so to bring them home, give them a world. The extremity of the situation is not to be understated: it is as if the human race had suffered a calamity and we now were in the phase of a convalescence. The calamity is linked to the French Revolution, and to Nietzsche's death of God (33). With such extremities, thoughts of redemption are not far away. Cavell does not focus directly on the Romantic interest in the redemptive possibilities of politics, or in religion or in poetry, but on how such an interest pressures philosophy to "think about its own redemption."

And the ancient mariner? The ancient mariner, Cavell thinks, knows something of Kant's two worlds (45). Perhaps he knows something more than Kant. The ship on which he travels passes below the line, drives to a cold country toward the South Pole. We have to be attentive to the virtual figuration of much of German idealism here. Coleridge himself is quite explicit in *Biographia Literaria*, where his reference to the two polar sciences recalls, I believe, Schelling's efforts to overcome transcendental solipsism by a science that moves from object to subject as well a science that moves from subject to object. Again the recovery of self is inseparable from the recovery of nature. In Spinozist/Hegelian terms, we must move from substance to subject, but also from subject to substance. Thus Coleridge: "The result of both the sciences, or their equatorial point, would be the principle of a total and undivided philosophy." And yet, we must add, such a total and undivided philosophy remains more dream than achievement. Is there something about the desire itself that frustrates the achievement?

While Cavell speaks of being below the line as having to do with the repressed (IQO, 47), one might add that it also has ontological and not just psychological significance. Yet the temptation to knowledge is central here. "The explicit temptation of Eden is to knowledge, which above all means: to a denial that, as we stand, we know." Cavell offers us interesting remarks on the Fall (48–9). If Hegel is mentioned, it is Kant's "extraordinarily interesting document" that is given more attention (50). In fact, Kant's discussion of the Fall is not qualitatively different from Hegel's: both are quite faithful sons of rational enlightenment, in seeing the Fall as telling of our finally laudable transition from animal innocence to what constitutes and will save the human: autonomous reason. Clap your hands, reason, it is all a *felix culpa*. Job's comforters find new friends, though it is less God who guarantees felicity than nature or history, and that son of the serpent, the cunning of reason. Cavell does not dwell on the coils of that serpent, but insists that there is no Hegelian recovery. He finds himself "winding up differently," and yet he winds up only to further navigate what he calls (IQO, Chapter 3) "texts of recovery." Recovery of what?

Kant had the sense that breaching the line creates fanaticism and skepticism; it would be to try to experience what cannot humanly be experienced (IQO, 50). Coleridge's poem shows that what is beyond the line can be experienced (51). The problem of skepticism is not a question of ignorance, but of a repression of knowledge, a denial, a killing. This is what creates the line, hence also want and desire. True to one of his origins, Austin is cited for his version of the original Fall: this is the insistence of philosophers on an epistemologically favored class of sense statements; this is the original sin by which they cast themselves from the garden of the world. And Job's comforters? One can hear them murmuring: If only Job the philosopher had not insisted, if only in his heart, on such epistemologically favored statements, his crops and children would not have been blighted. Something more urgent and hyperbolic than the domesticities of donnish life are here at stake. The theme comes back, like the doom of the ancient mariner. What is finally at stake is bringing the world back to life: a new habitation, a new dwelling (52–3).

We are nothing but something more or less; dead and alive; half-true, half-lie; half and half. How be more than half and half, one again, whole? How come alive again? How be as one, as whole? If creation is gloriously granted, we take it for granted, but not as granted. In taking it, we do not have it anymore; we have its dying double. What of projection? Projection seems to imply that we can breathe life again into what is lifeless. But what if we too, those who breathe, are equally under the spell? We too need to come to life again, but we cannot do it ourselves; the dead may be left to bury themselves, but the dead do not resurrect themselves. Part of the dubious danger of any Romantic project of projection is that it becomes a will to reanimate the world through one's own projection: but in this case, it must be doomed to defeat, since self-projection would be again the spreading of the death-in-life.

What of Cavell's previously mentioned remark: "I want to understand how the other now bears the weight of God, shows me I am not alone in the universe."[11] Can the other bear that weight, resurrect the world – perhaps not create as perhaps God did, but recreate the world? Can the other bear this weight? How so, if the other is also under the same spell as I, in the chiaroscuro of the dead and alive, the half and half. Can two such half-and-halves make a true whole, be truly one, or at one? Or will their being at one rather be the multiplication of the half-and-half life, be the marriage of narcissisms that seems to be intimated in Cavell's discussion of marriage in the *Ancient Mariner*? But having known this death of the world, and perhaps of the God that dies with that half-and-half world, who or what could succeed God? What succession could be a success here?

Cavell had glanced off the theme of animism and the pathetic fallacy in *The Claim of Reason*, but here (IQO, 54) it comes more to the fore with its fuller force. "For an intellect such as Coleridge's, for which objects are now dead, they will not be enlivened by the infusion of some kind of animation from the outside" (55). The issue, or specter, of animism makes a momentary, somewhat disguised or frightened appearance in a late speculation in the final part of *The Claim of Reason* – as does the theme of the

Outsider. In considering Othello, Cavell considers the claim that material-object skepticism derives from other-minds skepticism. He is honest enough to acknowledge that these specters bring their horror and fright, and that one is not always prepared to endure or face it. Perhaps one may have to grow or be dragged into a deeper desperation. "It is understandable that I shrank from that anticipation. It invites the thought that skeptical doubt is to be interpreted as jealousy and that our relation to the world that remains is as to something that has died at our hands. . . . we have killed the world, and specifically out of revenge." The death of the world has to do with obsessive love or hate, and finding oneself in a bewitchment or spell that one has both conjured and yet not lucidly instigated. Hence the puzzle of the fatal happening in the "Ancient Mariner" (IQO, 56). The albatross – the bird loved the man; and yet the mariner killed the thing that loved him. Cavell sees the moral (57) as bearing on one's letting oneself *be loved* (reversing somewhat the usual way). Drifting into the cold country is a consequence of a transgression rather than an original transgression.

Cavell is attentive to the fact that the poem might be seen as about *itself*, about the process of making poems: the old problem that seemed so new with the Romantic's obsession with self-reflection and self-reflexive art. I like what I take as Cavell's declaimers of what pass too easily as the pieties of our claims to poetic power. The word can kill as well as heal, curse as well as bless. Words also are as transgressions: we murder to connect; we stuff nature into words, make points of it (60). It is also true that we can murder to connect by making points about the process of making poems, making points about poetic point. Cavell is himself tempted to think of the redemptive powers of writing itself. When speaking about the Hermit as "shrieving" the Mariner, he connects "shrieve" to script (*schrift*, in Dutch): "Writing is accordingly a kind of self-redemption." (62)

He does not deny entirely the view of such as Robert Penn Warren, for whom the poem cannot be sundered from a sense of the sacramental universe, and most strikingly in relation to the blessing of the sea snakes and the slimy things (61). The Mariner "accepts animals of the slime as also his others – that is, accepts the fact, or you may say, the gift of life. This begins his recovery from the death-in-life of inexpressible guilt." Are some hesitations about the religious to be detected? After all, in more than one place he seems to endorse Austin's denial of the "sacramental" view of language. Here the stress is on the wedding at the end as having its sacramental character "problematized." The Mariner is not seen as reconciled with society (62); he is a disturber of its peace, which is no peace.

And then too for Cavell "the Mariner wanders between Apostleship and Sagehood, as though it is too late for religion, because nothing is any longer common to our gods, and it is too soon for philosophy, because human beings are not interested in their new lives. (No wonder the writer's explicit autobiography will be written in continuous digressions.)," Cavell exclaims (63). I ask: Might this mean that *philosophy is the original sin*; that it is the departure from the common, and that true religion is the true commons, the consummate commons, and the reason why we are not interested in our new lives is because they have become dead without the commons with the divine; and philosophy, no more than art, can not stem the hemorrhage of spirit; though the patient has been bled many times and will say chirpily, I am fine, I feel fine; but it will be the fineness of feebleness; and philosophy will continue the sickness because it can only name self-redemption, even though fitfully, as if in a dream or a fever, images seem to come to it, insurgently, of *being redeemed*, as of *being loved*; but now these fevers are treated as temptations from the new enfeebled commons we have created for ourselves, behind the line? An autobiography in "continuous digression" means there is no digression because there is no main line. In that sense, Cavell is right to tell us that the Mariner is "more a patient than a doctor, more a symptom than a cure." But then what "promise of redemption" can be here, since it seems evident that this ailment of the human cannot heal itself; it can only betray its symptoms; and many ways of betraying these symptoms are themselves betrayals of the promise of redemption.

Does marriage bring some solace? The question is posed by the end of the "Ancient Mariner" (IQO, 64). No more marriages? The Mariner is one who stuns: one who is "permanently, one may say, awaiting redemption. No doubt this can be justified – say, as preparation for philosophy. But it is not philosophy's progress, and neither, I think, is it poetry's or religion's." (64) Marriage is no longer a sacrament, for Cavell, as for Austin language is not (see *Pitch*). And yet Cavell would have more (but how can he have *more?*): marriage as

a new mystery . . . to which outsiders are irrelevant . . . ; a further adventure of aloneness, without solitude but also without society . . . a further investment of our narcissism, as children so typically are. If marriage is the name of our only present alternative to the desert-sea of skepticism, then for that very reason this intimacy cannot be celebrated, or sanctified; there is no outside to it. You may describe it as lacking in poetry; as if intimacy itself, or the new pressure on it, lacked expression. (64–5)

Yet Cavell goes on to suggest that "there is such an intimacy at large, and that poetry is responsible for giving it expression" (65).

A last remark on crossing the line: Are there lines that keep Cavell in, that he cannot or will not cross? That he cannot see? Ask this with respect to redemption as religious. Are there occasions when he keeps himself behind the line, withholding himself from crossing over? For some philosophers, how intolerable if the philosopher crosses the line over to poetry or art. But is it philosophy, then, they ask? But how much more intolerable would it be to cross the line between itself and religion? I anticipate an even more offended apoplexy: But surely it is not philosophy at all then? Has not philosophy in modernity forged its own identity mostly in crossing the road when it sees religion on the same side? Do I rightly detect a hesitation on Cavell's part at this line: he feints, as if crossing a line, or feints, as if not having crossed, but in fact having done so? More (of) the second I would say. See Cavell crossing this line from philosophy to literature, to opera, to film – though, necessarily, he also crosses back: this is not prohibited, be it applauded, or unapproved. Again these lines are not lines but definitions of the spaces of spiritual freedom. But can one say the same, as it were, *out loud*, with regard to the religious? Is this an intimacy that remains intimate: communicated and yet unsaid; unstated, or understated? Is philosophy in hiding here, as if shy of saying certain things, or shying off (away) from them? How hard here it would be to confess without embarrassment, to confide philosophically, to come clean.

ART, RELIGION, AND PHILOSOPHY

Recall now a comparison I made between Cavell and Hegel on absolute knowing: If you protest this as too odd, remember also a contrast previously suggested: *absolute knowing* – attained for Hegel when knowledge no longer needs to go beyond itself, versus *acknowledgment* – where there is a going beyond, or something like it; though it remains wrapped in enigma, we are not locked in the circle of self. By contrast with the circle of Hegel's absolute knowing, one thinks of Cavell's endorsement of Thoreau – to be by oneself, in the sense of a certain wholeness; and to be beside oneself.[12] You say: But is this not reminiscent of Hegel when he speaks of being at home with self (*bei sich*) in one's other? (Rewrite this, if you will, as being at home with oneself in one's other: Hegel's famous phrase, self-recognition in absolute otherness.) And yet the stress falls differently in Cavell. Or perhaps he wants it to fall a bit *more differently*. Does he put enough into the "being beside oneself"? I leave this open for now. Acknowledgment is a kind of absolved knowing, in the sense of being freed from obsessions that, in casting a spell on one, keep one imprisoned, imprisoned indeed in oneself.

Let us take the issue relative to the relation of art and philosophy, and a little further relative to religion. I mean: the relation to the other, who takes the place of God, or assumes the burden of God, might be said to be mediated through a turn to literature, as offering us the imagined occasions in which we are released or absolved to acknowledge the others, even to Lear's extreme of exposing ourselves to feeling as wretches and divinities feel. I underscore that the community of art and philosophy is not at all denied by Hegel, who is here a follower of Schelling, hence a companion along the way with Coleridge. Art too is concerned with absolute knowing. I say follower but also mean dissident, in the sense that Hegel's dialectical concepts are said to do justice to both the form and content of the absolute, while the sensuous form of art binds us to, enchants us with, an otherness, beyond which thought frees us into the purest form, at one, with the concept, by itself. For Hegel there seems too much of "being beside oneself" in the image of art. This is an old complaint against the artist, going back at least to the *Ion*, and perhaps further. What if this "being beside oneself" (*mania*) is just the way "being oneself" comes into the needful openness wherein the access of light is made available for acknowledging? And what if philosophy too entailed "being beside oneself"? Suppose it often conceals this need and instead presents itself as purely being by itself? For were it to confess this, it too would look like madness. Give Plato some at least partial credit for being willing to grant this: the best of the philosophers need to be singled out by a divine madness; otherwise they are competent technicians, or experts, perhaps endowed professors. Nietzsche, as Plato's antagonist, falls in the same line of inheritance, though he presents himself as the black sheep in that family, turning over the traces with a mixture of divine madness and mad madness. This is Hegel's claim and perhaps the Hegelian fraud: that it hides the truth of "being beside itself," and calls the concealment reason, or the counterfeit knowing of self called absolute knowing. What is most at issue here is what I will call *discerning knowing*: knowing that can tell something of the difference between released knowing, genuine acknowledgment of the other as other, and its false doubles that slyly, with great show of argument, actually coil back on themselves, and thus remain in the end by themselves also counterfeit self-knowing.

Does the great power of art call Cavell here? Is not the great power of great art just in its actually calling us out of ourselves: out of ourselves to ourselves, and also to being beside ourselves as beyond ourselves, there out in the glory of creation where we were, strangely, but not as strangers simply, always already. I think of efforts to connect *to kalon* with the call. I think of the figures in the uncut rock that called out to Michelangelo. Suppose that we are the still formless figures in that rock, and that we cannot call ourselves out of that stony existence, and that another must begin to batter that stony existence to loose us, but batter the stone with a love, for otherwise the promise of the rock is betrayed and it shatters. Who is the outsider who hits the rock in love and brings forth life? Not the rock; not us. For we are not hitting the rock; we are the rock being hit.

This power of art or great poetry to stun thought into a different mindfulness names the intimation of the great Romantics. But Hegel, so close, yet so far, came to hate the Romanticism he loved while younger, and hate it because he felt it dissolved in feeling and formlessness; and he could not quite give himself over to the formlessness that, like a return to zero, offered a new interface with creation, in which we are called out of the rock, and not as masters who hammer the world into our mold. Hegel finally wanted an epistemology absolutely in control of itself, if not now, then later, though he could not wait, and even here constructed a historicist monument to his own metaphysical impatience, which at last seemed to allow him to rest in his present. But it is a fraud, if the sources of this being by self are a deeper being beside oneself. Indirect witness to this is the impatience that will not let itself be receptive to the strike that comes from beyond the frozen stone of the unachieved self.[13]

Does this seem rather far from Cavell? Seem, yes, but in truth, no. Remember a third who walks beside us as if unseen, as if unnamed. This is religion. Where is this, this nothing? Present and not present as present. The answer here for Cavell must mimic the answer given for Shakespeare: religion is nowhere because it is everywhere. Religion's importance for Romanticism is not in doubt, even if we want to say here that we are concerned with "secular mysteries." But is this to beg the question, while nodding in the right direction? "Secular mystery" is finally just as incomprehensible as sacred mystery. Why omit to say this? Does our silence make it less offensive, as offensive as sacred mystery, to secular reason? Why not openly admit what is offensive to secular (scientific?) reason, offensive be it secular or sacred? What better protection does the word "secular" give us from the mockery of secular reason that will follow? Either way, sacred or secular, we are exposed. Suppose religion can be a way of *living the exposure*. It can also be a concealment of the exposure from oneself, from others – a way to go to sleep again.

What is a redemptive reading? What would a *saving knowing or acknowledging* be? If one does not come clean on the religious, is it hard to have anything other than an equivocal suggestion here? Who needs redeeming? The text, the reader, the writer. And who redeems or what? The text or the author or the reader. I do not know who the redeemer is. I do not know if this redeemer lives. Should we say, redemption: either absurd or a miracle; or perhaps both?

The matter of being beside oneself is clearly at issue in Hegel's philosophizing about religion, where an analogous appropriation is performed, as with the ecstasis of art. The issue again is the recalcitrance of an otherness that will not be included within a more embracing thought at home with itself. Religion is beside itself; it shows something of the manic, in the Greek sense, as inspiration, as coming from a source that exceeds our self-control, and yet makes ultimate demands on our "mastery" and "self-mastery." Religion as beside itself points to an acknowledging that is a knowing from.

What of that notable feature of post-Kantian culture, namely its granting of a certain autonomy to art, and not least with regard to the religious? There are many complex elements in this. One can understand the granting against the background of a miserable religiosity that fell out of praise of the glory of creation. This is another aspect of the deadening of the earth. And of course, the issue is not confined to the religious: Where is the deep resource for such praise in modern science, then and indeed now? A fidelity to the voices of the earth is needed, you might say. But equally noticeable in post-Kantian culture is that the artistic assumes a metaphysical weight not so strongly accentuated earlier: as a possible revealer or medium of some transcendence even more ultimate than our own self-transcending. In some places, Cavell seems more Kantian than Hegelian; but if he shares companionship with Coleridge, he perhaps should be more Schellingian: art and the religious are inseparable; they pass over into each other; it is hard to disentangle the art of a people from myth, and both from the inheritance of that people; the words a people treasures are the endowment of its sense of ultimacy, and this endowment the true poet keeps and guards; for there is a reticence or reserve about the religious.

Concern about bewitchment cannot be here avoided. Somewhere Pascal speaks about a powerful bewitchment cast over us, as if by the force of some supernatural spell. Cavell toys with something almost the same in *The Claim of Reason*.[14] These may be metaphorical ways of speaking, but if so they are no mere metaphors. If they were, all art would be a colorful baroque surrogate (a merely fantastic double) for what scientific psychology would render in unvarnished truth. But the point is: there is no such un-varnished truth; for always we are in the bewitchment; and the science that claims to dispel the bewitchment is also in the bewitchment, and perhaps even more lost in bewitchment, for it is convinced that it is free of bewitch-ment and the way out of this bewitchment; the shadow that looms over it is the spell cast by the heat of its own self-intoxication, though as always, looking away from itself, it can neither see the shadow nor feel the heat (which takes itself as cold).

The witch is one caught in the mania of religion, be it hot mania or cold. But there is mad madness as much as divine madness; and the issue between the witch and her executioner is the discernment of the difference. How teach, or learn, these differences? This also bears on our waking from the spell. The executioner may also be beside himself in a bewitchment. The one claiming to dispel the bewitchment may be just as spellbound. We do not escape by saying: I am only concerned with art; these deliri-ums of religion I leave behind. We have to deal here with all the darkness of the religious, as much as with the light; and hence we have to deal more honestly than Hegel's idealistic apotheosis of reason did with this dark equivocality. Can we come clean on it? Not by conceptual anorexia, not by conceptual hubris. We seem to need some kind of philosophical confession. But here confession is the hardest. I do note what I take as Cavell's words of admiration for these most capable of confession: those most capable of going into themselves and the recesses of intimacy, or the idiocy of being, and without sacrifice of speaking for what is beyond them, and so beside themselves in a truer sense. Their own voice and the voice of the others somehow match.[15] Can this match happen without some more ultimate source than I and the others? Is this too not the question of God?

Cavell knows that forgiveness and comedy are espoused (see *Pitch*, 87). Comedy is also a way of exposure and perhaps also of absolving sin. He also says: "Philosophy cannot say sin." Might this mean it cannot *laugh*? Is philosophy as a therapy really a catharsis, a purgatory? "Philosophy cannot say sin":[16] But perhaps that is just the laughless sin of philosophy – when it, so to say, withholds itself from its familial attunement with these ex-traordinary others. A worse sin (this is not Cavell's): philosophy goes on to self-exculpation by accusing the others of not managing to be as it claims to be, autonomous self-determining knowing. If to be is to be beside one-self, this preaching of philosophy is a fraudulent form of being beside itself. If we – we professional philosophers – seem to show less of being beside ourselves, this may not be an unequivocal sign of superior sobriety.

BEING BESIDE ONESELF: MUSIC, MADNESS, THOUGHT

Is this to make too much of "being beside oneself"? Yet having written the above, I noticed, as if by accident, the epigraph to *A Pitch of Philosophy*. It is from Thoreau, and here it is: "With thinking we may be beside oneself in a sane sense. *Next* to us the grandest laws are continually being executed."

I am impelled further to ask: beside oneself: What is there besides oneself? What also is it to be "by oneself"? What does "by" mean? "By" whom or what is one effected, affected? Could being by oneself also mean being beside oneself? And what is this *sane sense* of being beside oneself? Is this the temptation: to have one's cake and eat it too? I mean: to be by oneself as a kind of counterfeit of divine madness that cannot let go, though it looks abandoned to what is outside, what is besides, what is other, what is next. And then next: What is this *next*, this nearby, this *nabij*, this *nachbahr*, this neighbor? Who is this neighbor? What other? And why are there *laws* being executed? Who executes? Moira or fate or some other power of the grandest execution? Who is the grand executer? What is being executed? What, if anything, is being granted by the executing grandee? Only laws – and in relation to the neighbor, the ones who are besides one? Given that some *frenzy* is suggested by being beside oneself, how can one be or stay sane? Is this being beside oneself in a sane sense a kind of *grace*? If so, while there might be laws being continually executed, is there more being executed than law can fully express, and is this then the grandest thing?

One wonders also: Is Cavell's own form of being beside oneself, but in a sane sense, connected to *music*? Might one not acknowledge music to have intimate bearing on the happening of being beside oneself, but in a sane sense? I find it intriguing to think of a certain Romantic intonation in *A Pitch of Philosophy*. The idea of voice is central there, obviously, and in a number of senses, the most overt being the finding of a philosophical voice out of philosophical peregrinations, or being on the road.[17] Obviously also there is the power of voice in opera, especially the female voice, and not out of hearing of his own mother. But consider this crucial turning point in Cavell's own becoming. This is his beginning to find himself differently in turning from his ambition to be a composer, turning toward philosophy. He recalls the influence of classes on music taught by Ernest Bloch. (How many echoes of Nietzsche are there muffled in these diverse destinies?) I am taken by Cavell's recounting of his being struck by what he calls the "transcendence of culture" (*Pitch*, 50). It is clear from the story that he is close to being struck speechless, not with lack of thought, but with excess, so much so that at the close of each class he would retreat to guard his thought in the solitude of adjacent rooms. What strikes one here is some echo of the view that music is the Romantic art par excellence (a view we find in Hegel, but one not unique to him). One thinks of the religion of art in the nineteenth century and the absolute importance invested in musical culture, and not only by the musicians themselves. I mean just this sense of the "transcendence of culture," concentrated in music, as most epitomizing that communication from a creative origin on the other side of domesticated determinacy, and passing through genius as the medium in which this other, surpassing source found its voice or articulated release. Can we speak of music as a sane ecstasy? If so, this sane ecstasy of music has been heard too by philosophers before. I mention Schopenhauer, deeply formed in the culture of the Romantics at Jena, the Schlegels, and so on. For him music is the direct embodiment of the Will itself, objectifying it such as to release us from the vehement urgency otherwise marking its tyrannical eros: to be blessed with the voice of music, as singer, player, hearer, was to be blessed with release: redemption. Could we say: Eros as tyrannical is saved from its insane frenzy, its mad bewitchments; music puts us beside ourselves but in a sane sense? And Nietzsche: without music, he held, one might even think life to be intolerable, unbearable; music redeems life, brings us back to life. In the twentieth century, Adorno (close to the Benjamin who holds Cavell's fascination) holds to something of this hope for the redemptive promise of music. And Cavell? Cavell finds himself displaced – speechless first, but beside himself, as he would be by himself; and then his musical hopes turned about in the direction of a philosophical quest that took slow form only in the years to follow, and the struggle for voice. There is nothing overt in Cavell: none of the young enthusiasm, the unguarded ardor, marking something of the religion of music, the religion of art in the nineteenth century. Nevertheless, one is made to wonder if there is here an older, perhaps more calm, passion for a not dissimilar redemption. His story recollects in some tranquility his being beside himself, and so seeks sanity.

I cannot again avoid wondering about a religious displacement. For here we have again a theme most intimate to the Romantics: not just *Kunstreligion*, as in Hegel, but the religion of *Kunst*. If the place falls to art to be the bearer of communicating transcendence, are we not witnessing a migration into art of what previously was religiously named? This is analogous to the point Cavell makes about theater replacing religion: the sacred drama of the ritual is overtaken by a secular and perhaps not less cathartic, or reconciling, ritual. Again I name tragedy and comedy. And again one cannot forget the origins of tragedy and comedy in religious ritual in the ancient world – the great feasts, the festivals of Dionysus – or forget Elizabethan drama inheriting something of the medieval mystery plays. Should one say that there is a replacement in the displacement, or that the redemptive power becomes more incognito, more hidden, the more it claims to be less hidden, less mysterious, in a human(istic) sense? But is there too much of ultimate equivocation here? I see this as a great question put to the culture of post-Kantian aestheticism. The displacement, or replacement, does not change the fact that what we want, want as lacking, want as needing, and needing urgently, is purgation and reconciliation, that is, redemption. Displacing sacred mystery to secular mystery does not elide mystery, surface appearances notwithstanding. When we are stunned by the mystery, we are also made to limp along more in terms of our humanistic confidences: we cannot do it, we do not do it; we participate in the festival. Art alone cannot bear the impossible burden of transcendence.[18]

If we recall the Dionysian festivals, we invariably today call back Nietzsche. The Dionysian festivals were the religious rituals in which Greek society sought to order its being beside itself but in a sane social sense. Redemption seems to ask for madness and sanity together. Can one think of that togetherness in terms of Nietzsche's claim: only as a work of art is the world justified; the only theodicy is an aesthetic theodicy? If so, art can no longer be just art. Was Nietzsche up to the redemptive togetherness of madness and sanity? Can Cavell bear the same question? And Nietzsche does figure very much as a companion in his *A Pitch of Philosophy*, and not least because of the autobiographical exercises of *Ecce Homo*. *Queritur* (as Nietzsche might say): Is Nietzsche not a poet-philosopher for the *young*? Cavell seems to acknowledge as much (*Pitch*, 122). But is there not a different youth of *age* – another spring, a further *primavera*? *Queritur*. And Nietzsche was never quite born to this primavera. One hears Cavell's praise for what is named as the Moral Perfectionism of Emerson (*Pitch*, 50). But then again have we not here the earnestness of the young? – not a mad abandon of age. Moral Perfectionism? But this is not what the mad Lear (51), sane now beyond youth, sought, or saw. And Cavell, if I am not mistaken, would write beyond Nietzsche and Lear. But that beyond cannot be written as "Moral Perfectionism." Nietzsche: the child who cannot, will not, hear the father. Lear: the father who cannot, will not, hear the child. Are both brought to some hearing? Both go differently mad. But to be beyond their different madnesses – or lack of listening – may well seem also to be mad, differently – or to listen and hear, differently. But is it not here that one will find the second spring, begin to find being beside oneself – but in a sane sense?

Notes

1. Ludwig Wittgenstein, *Culture and Value*, 2nd ed., ed. G. H. von Wright with Heikki Nyman, trans. Peter Winch (Chicago: University of Chicago Press, 1980), p. 24e.

2. See, for instance, *Perplexity and Ultimacy* (Albany: SUNY Press, 1995), Chapter 3.

3. Cavell witnesses to a sense of strain between philosophy as a practice of mindfulness and as an institutional practice; hence his touchiness about Emerson, and about the professors at Harvard; and his touchiness at what he takes as Kuklick's claim that the transcendentalists were soundly whipped by the Harvard professionals: good (Christian) organization men (*In Quest of the Ordinary: Lines of Skepticism and Romanticism* [Chicago: University of Chicago Press, 1998], pp. 13–14). (Hereinafter IQO.)

4. Indeed, there is an echo of one of his great guides here: This is the older Wittgenstein, walking in the Phoenix Park, in the autumn of 1948, in conversation with Drury, who asks: What about Hegel? Wittgenstein: "No, I don't think I would get on with Hegel. Hegel seems to me to be always wanting to say that things that look different are really the same. Whereas my interest is in showing that things which look the same are really different. I was thinking of using as a motto for my book a quotation from *King Lear* 'I'll teach you differences.' [Then laughing:] The remark 'You'd be surprised' wouldn't be a bad motto either." In M. O'C. Drury, *The Danger of Words and Writings on Wittgenstein*, ed. and intro. David Berman (Bristol: Thoemmes, 1996), p. 157.

5. See *The Claim of Reason: Wittgenstein, Skepticism, Morality, and Tragedy* (Oxford: Oxford University Press, 1979), p. 189, on language as a bequest, not just an acquirement; on poetry as the second inheritance of language; on Thoreau on the mother and father tongues. "Poetry thereby celebrates its language by making it a return on its birth, by reciprocating." (Hereinafter CR.)

6. He is happy to discover Emerson as a forerunner of Nietzsche: especially with respect to the theme of not finding humans but fragments of men. See *A Pitch of Philosophy: Auto Biographical Exercises* (Cambridge: Harvard University Press, 1994), p. 76, on Cavell's claim about Nietzsche's "transcription" of Emerson's passage about "walking monsters" in "The American Scholar" in *Zarathustra* and in *Ecce Homo*; this in a discussion of Derrida . (Hereinafter *Pitch*.)

7. See CR, Foreword, xviii: He speaks of the "connection of writing and the problem of the other, and the connection of both with my interest in a tradition, anyway an idea, of philosophizing opposed to the tradition in English, as that tradition is represented in the best English-speaking departments." He is and has been concerned with the link and loss of link between English and Continental traditions, and with attempting "to realign these traditions, . . . at least to write

witnessing the loss in that separation. This "has been a formative aspiration of mine from the earliest of the work I refer to here."

8. See CR, xvi, on the difficulty of institutionalizing Wittgenstein. The issue of the esoteric – insiders, outsiders – is also noted. See xvii–xviii on the worry of the philosopher about being "in the right place," about there being any "workable field of philosophy," about "the wrong ground."

9. CR, 470. The words "the other as replacement for God" are used in the table of contents to *The Claim of Reason*: replacement is a strong word. In how strong a sense is one to take it?

10. The theme of limit might be connected with inheritances. The Continental, Romantic sublime can seem a "subliming" that is grandiose, perhaps bombastic, compared to the sometimes primmer English sense of the "ordinary." Is there a "subliming" beyond bombastic aestheticism, that has also seen beyond the don's stiff upper lip, or the scholastic's squeezed lips? As I noted with inheritances, Cavell is between, and more than between, the Continent and England. America is the open space of this other between, where sometimes an empty sublime strikes terror into the lone individual, or gives rise to the freelance predatory self; where sometimes there is a sublime between of a creative opening up, which the constraining limits of Europe, and England, keep damped down. One of the struggles there: to find form, to find a voice in this opening up that seems to lack a *measure* in process itself. Is this not part of Romanticism: the condition of exceeding measure and seeking the measure of such exceeding? Can the human be that measure, even if we are the exceeding? To be at the limit of the ordinary and the marvellous: this is a between at the extremes. Cavell speaks of the *philosophical fantastic*, as somewhere between the everyday and the supernatural (see, for instance, IQO, 181ff.); and of doubleness of the ordinary, with reference to Poe (see IQO, 120ff.).

11. This is offered on p. 470 of *The Claim of Reason*. Twelve pages later, on p. 482, he says: "When I said just now that I wished 'to understand how the other . . .' one cannot but smile at the deferral, or loop of connection! 'Just now . . .' – what specious present is this that holds us with this style of coming and going, sounding and resounding?"

12. See CR, 367; he is referring to *The Senses of Walden* (San Francisco: North Point Press, 1980), pp. 100–4.

13. Clearly, Romanticism is more than a cult of narcissistic feeling, though Cavell is cognizant of this as one of its major dangers. One must wonder if Hegel's claim to have escaped this danger merely reinstates eternal or world-historical narcissism on the heights of absolute knowing: thought thinking itself; Aristotle's old god now historically coming back to itself, itself that it never really left, all appearances notwithstanding.

14. See CR, 143, where he speaks of epistemology and "some power large enough either to keep us in a kind of hypnotic spell, or to arrange the world for our actions as a kind of endless stage-set, whose workings we can never get behind. . . ."

15. See CR, 109, where he speaks of confession, mentioning Augustine, Luther, Rousseau, Thoreau, and Kierkegaard: They "were most convinced they were

speaking from the most hidden knowledge of others," as from the most hidden knowledge of themselves, when to themselves they became a question.

16. Stephen Mulhall devotes an interesting chapter to this in *Stanley Cavell's Recounting of the Ordinary* (Oxford: Clarendon Press, 1994).

17. See, Timothy Gould, *Hearing Things: Voice and Method in the Writing of Stanley Cavell* (Chicago: University of Chicago Press, 1998).

18. "Art and the Impossible Burden of Transcendence: The End of Art and the Task of Metaphysics" to appear in my *Art, Origins, Otherness* (Albany: SUNY Press, 2003), Chapter 8.

7 | Cavell on American Philosophy and the Idea of America

RICHARD ELDRIDGE

Here is a common picture of what American philosophy looks like to and within many American philosophy departments.[1] To a considerable degree, it does not exist at all. Most departments do not feel obliged to teach American philosophy as they do modern philosophy (Descartes to Kant) and ancient Greek philosophy. It is normally not part of the requirements for a major. Of course, writings by Americans are mostly what do get taught, but they are taught as just philosophy, not as *American* philosophy. When it is taught, it is taught as a peripheral history course, typically focusing on the major pragmatist thinkers from the late nineteenth to the mid twentieth century: Peirce, James, and Dewey, with perhaps a turn toward Rorty to round things off. These figures are thought to emphasize the importance of paying attention to what works: to experimental science in the pursuit of knowledge and to liberal reform in politics. The only way to discern what works – in either epistemology or politics – is through trial and error. Epistemology and social theory in any more visionary sense are evaded.[2] Our going practices of experimental science, particularly natural science, have shown themselves to be good enough: neither in need of nor admitting of any further epistemic support from foundationalist theories of justification. In politics, liberal decency, respect for rights, and reliance on markets are about the best we can do. Larger visions of social justice are by and large fantastic and potentially tyrannical, compared to a clear-eyed understanding of how decent people mostly can and do get on socially in order to satisfy their preferences. To the extent that the pragmatist commitment to getting on with what works is taken seriously, it is not so much understood as itself a visionary discovery of the natures of knowledge and justice as it is just taken for granted. Strong voluntarist pictures of human responsibility as including the possibility of getting right what we really ought to do in

Ted Cohen and Richard Schuldenfrei read and commented in detail and very helpfully on a late draft of this paper, under considerable time pressure. Hugh Lacey offered useful remarks about the opening pages.

either the pursuit of knowledge or the arrangement of social life are simply dropped.[3] The naturalist stances of Quine, Rorty, and Dennett, according to which there's little point in making much of a fuss about free will (in anything other than the Humean sense of political liberty or hypothetical freedom) come to the fore. The key notion is *coping*, and emphatically not *achieving our human destiny*.

This picture of American philosophy in turn both rests on and further articulates larger images of America and of philosophy. America is understood as the place in which freedom is construed as a matter centrally, perhaps exclusively, of individual liberty (as opposed to the achievement of the power to do or be something in particular – for example, to be more fully human or properly faithful). Most Americans exercise their liberty by pursuing happiness and satisfaction in the private spheres of family life, consumption, and enjoyment. Larger workplace and public identities are taken to be instrumental to satisfactions in these more private spheres, unless, of course, some people just happen to enjoy political work or quasi-familial workplace friendships or workplace activities. The business of politics in America is the fair reconciliation of competitive individual and factional interests. There are not enough goods to go around to enable everyone to satisfy every preference. Government hence properly sets up rules of fair competition, including centrally the laws of property and person and the laws of contract, fair trade, workplace safety, and nonexploitativeness.

Philosophy is understood in relation to this picture of America as committed to the overcoming of *merely personal* interest. People *do* have idiosyncratic interests. Some people devote themselves to fly-fishing; others to cello playing; others to cooking; still others to building bridges. Some people are Methodists; others are Catholics, Jews, Episcopalians, and nonbelievers. But no set of commitments, practical or religious, works for everyone. Older, premodern philosophies were quasi-theologies that attempted to install a favored set of practical or religious commitments as mandatory. They were failed efforts to make a particular form of devotion rationally obligatory. Happily, we are, in philosophy, beyond that project and its potential and actual tyrannies. Whether as the analysis of concepts, as a defense of the achievements of science (in yielding understandings that anyone might make use of or not, as anyone wishes), or as an outline of fair terms of justice and the rule of law that favors no one set of personal interests, philosophy is, above all, *neutral*.[4]

There is a great deal of both truth and value in these pictures of America and of philosophy. It is, nonetheless, Stanley Cavell's perception that to the extent that these pictures are true, they are *made* true by Americans and philosophers adopting them out of conformism, acquiescence, desperation, and complicity in failures to achieve our best possibilities – as philosophers, as Americans, and as human persons. All too often, Cavell proposes (following Emerson), we fail to dare to exist,[5] fail both personally and socially to live in pursuit and achievement of genuine care and commitment.

According to Cavell, philosophy and politics and America all promise more than this. To the pursuit of happiness as the satisfaction of individual preferences, Cavell – following Emerson and Thoreau, in company with Wittgenstein, Heidegger, Plato, and Rousseau – poses a counterimage of happiness as conversion to and achievement of *freedom*, understood not as liberty, but rather as something more like full mastery in what one does and says.[6] What is needed, then, in this view is a kind of *rebirth*: away from instrumentalism and into accession to transfigured commitment and expressive power. It is naturally difficult to describe the kind of transformation that is in question. It is something like the discovery on the part of the modernist artist in the course of work that her natural talent and instincts can be originally enacted in an intelligible way: to make new sense,[7] against the grain of the old. The thought is that as it stands "we are not free, not whole, and not new, and we know this and are on a downward path of despair because of it; and that . . . for a grownup to grow he requires strangeness and transformation, i.e., birth."[8] The hope is that "we might despair of despair itself, rather than of life, and cast *that* off, and begin, and so reverse our direction."[9]

The idea, by contrast, that philosophy should be neutral and should focus on what works – more or less well and from our present vantage point – is then a betrayal of what philosophy has centrally been and still centrally can be. "Philosophy begins with, say, in the Socratic ambition, and may at any time encounter, an aspiration toward the therapeutic, a sense of itself as guiding the soul, or self, from self-imprisonment toward the light or the instinct of freedom."[10]

The catch, however, is that there are no standing terms available for specifying fully the condition at which transformation or conversion or rebirth aim. A sense of this catch is especially prominent in America, with its founding resistance to any single national religion. This sense also figures in the resistance of certain philosophers, typically the ones Cavell cites as heroes and forebears – Emerson, Thoreau, Rousseau, Plato, and Wittgenstein, most prominently – to academicism and to conclusive formulations of stance, that is, in the drift of these writers toward a certain literariness or poetry. For them the process of discovery of the self to itself takes place in and through an ongoing course of writing. As part of the founding myth of perfection*ism*, as it is exemplified in Plato's *Republic* and then further inhabited by Emerson, Thoreau, and Wittgenstein, Cavell lists the sense that "the self finds that it can turn (convert, revolutionize itself) . . . [in order to achieve] a further state of that self, where the higher is determined not by natural talent [that is, not by birth] but by *seeking* to know what you are made of and cultivating the thing you are meant to do."[11] As it engages in this seeking, the self finds itself caught up in the movement or work of thought and of writing, resistant to what Cavell stigmatizes as "moralism" and dogma and the academic. As vehicle of this seeking, "philosophical *writing* . . . enters into competition with the field of poetry, . . . not to banish all poetry from the just city but to claim for itself the privilege of the work poetry does in making things happen to the soul, so far as that work has its rights."[12] This kind of philosophical writing – both modeled on and in competition with poetry, rather than the treatise or scientific report – expresses both an ambition for conversion in and through process and a distinctly American sense of striking out for the new, of being on the way. Philosophy, from Plato through Emerson through Wittgenstein, then *is* about happiness, but where "the achievement of happiness requires not the perennial and fuller satisfaction of our needs as they stand but the examination and transformation of those needs."[13] What is sought, through transformation, is not the achievement of a final *state*, but rather "a sort of continuous reaffirmation"[14] of self in activity and in relationship. To seek such a continuous reaffirmation, and to see philosophy as seeking it, out of what is perceived as a present state of acquiescence, conformity, complicity, and lack of interest is not neutrally to endorse moderately successful strategies of coping that are already in place. One might say that the perfectionist strain in the thought of Emerson and Thoreau points us toward the possibility and value of falling in love and living in love with what we do, against our present half-heartedness.

Politics, too, then is different, for political thinking and political activity are open to being informed by perfectionist aspirations. "The transformation of the self . . . finds expression in the imagination of a transformation of society . . . , where what is best for society is modeled on what is best for the individual soul."[15] At the beginning of an important essay relatively early in his turn toward Emerson, Cavell cites "the following pair of sentences, attributed . . . to William James" that are set in brass in the lobby of William James Hall at Harvard.

THE COMMUNITY STAGNATES WITHOUT THE IMPULSE
OF THE INDIVIDUAL
THE IMPULSE DIES AWAY WITHOUT THE SYMPATHY
OF THE COMMUNITY[16]

This message, which, Cavell remarks, "may be taken [among other ways] as claiming a transcendental relation among the concepts of community and individual as they have so far shown themselves,"[17] is what politics as the usual business of factional negotiation tends to forget or repress.

An image and practice of politics that embraces this message incorporates, as politics as usual does not, a role for what Cavell, following Kant, calls *reflective judgment*: "the expression of a conviction whose grounding remains subjective – say myself – but which expects or claims justification from the (universal) concurrence of other subjectivities, on reflection."[18] It is this kind of reflective judgment that might best record a perception of our present liabilities and call us to something better – for example, away from present practices of "intolerable inequality or discrimination."[19] The making of reflective judgments and the practice of reflection on them by others point toward politics not as negotiation, but as conversation, a joint exploration of joint possibilities.

The aim of such political conversation is not the satisfaction of individual interests or preferences as they stand, but rather the joining together of the private-erotic with the public-political. This is a tall order; the private and the political do not readily come together. But "while it is the nature of the erotic to form a stumbling block to a reasonable, civilized existence, call it the political, human happiness nevertheless goes on demanding satisfaction in both realms."[20] What we find ourselves engaged in, with one another politically and not just one by one, alone, is "a struggle for mutual freedom."[21]

One immediate consequence of this aim and of our standing failure quite wholly to achieve it is that our sense of being members of our society and culture is likely to take the form of a sense of compromise by and complicity with society as it stands. The social contract as Rousseau and Kant imagine it, as theorists of autonomy (not of preference satisfaction), and as it is lived in America is a matter of *consent*, where "my consent is not . . . modifiable or proportionable (psychological exile is not exile): I cannot keep consent focused on the successes or graces of society; it reaches into every corner of society's failure or ugliness. . . . A compromised state of society, since it is mine, compromises me."[22] This experience of compromise and complicity in American society and culture is all too familiar to Americans – aware of the depth both of their Americanness and of the failures of their society and culture to achieve their promises.

Rightly developed – as Rousseau and Kant (rather than Hobbes, say) develop it – social contract theory focuses this sense of joint membership and complicity. To consent to the social contract is then not to take up an instrument for the pursuit of personal advantage; it is to accept one's responsibility for society and its promise of freedom. Consent implies

> that I recognize the society and its government, so constituted, as *mine*; which means that I am answerable not merely to it, but for it. So far, then, as I recognize myself to be exercising my responsibility for it, my obedience to it is obedience to my own laws; citizenship in that case is the same as my autonomy; the polis is the field within which I work out my personal identity and it is the creation of (political) *freedom*.[23]

As Stephen Mulhall usefully puts it, Cavell's thought is that the story of a social contract makes explicit the idea that "citizenship is [and is to be] not a constraint on my autonomy but an aspect of it."[24] Society is, in the Rousseauian-Kantian form of social contract theory, "an artifact" to which I am "deeply . . . joined,"[25] both bound up in its promises and complicit in its failures.

> The essential message of the idea of a social contract is that political institutions require justification, that they are absolutely without sanctity, that power over us is held on trust from us, that institutions have no authority other than the authority we lend them, that we are their architects, that they are therefore artifacts, that there are laws or ends, of nature or justice, in terms of which they are to be tested. They are experiments.[26]

The image of America that Cavell forwards is then that it is a place of these experiments, perhaps the central place. "It had a mythical beginning, still visible, if ambiguous, to itself, and to its audience."[27] Out of this beginning there arose "a society whose idea of itself requires that it repudiate the hierarchies and enforcements of the European past and make a new beginning."[28] Unlike the countries of Europe, America has been from the beginning and remains the nation of no settled tribe or *Stamm*, of no national religion, not even of any national language. It is a place of immigrancy, a place to come to, in order then to strike off in one's own direction.

No doubt this *is* a kind of myth. The settlement and cultivation of America are in historical fact shot through with violence. There were Native Americans here before there were Europeans, and the Europeans introduced the overwhelming disfiguration of slavery. As Cavell himself remarks,

> It is simply crazy that there should ever have come into being a world with such a sin in it, in which a man is set apart because of his color – *the* superficial fact about a human being. Who could *want* such a world? For an American, fighting for his love of country, that the last hope of earth should from its beginning have swallowed slavery, is an irony so withering, a justice so intimate in its rebuke of pride, as to measure only with God.[29]

Yet despite this withering irony, in the very face of it, this founding mythology – this mythology of a founding, a new beginning – is nonetheless lived imaginatively in America, when Americans dare to dream. It is a central part of "the inner agenda of [our] culture"[30] that America *is* the place where freedom is to be achieved.

Everywhere intertwined with and enacted in these counterimages of philosophy (as transformative thinking, talking, and writing), of politics (as the conversation and cultivation of freedom), and of America (as the new place for the achievement of freedom – its birthplace) is an image of the human person, fit to live in these practices and in this place. The self is not a thing that is simply given, but a power of becoming responsible for and fully invested in what one does, which power is emergent, paradoxically, through its own activity.

> The fate of having a self – of being human – is one in which the self is always to be found; fated to be sought, or not; recognized, or not. My self is something, apparently, toward which I can stand in various relations, ones in which I can stand to other selves, named by the same terms, e.g., love, hate, disgust, acceptance, knowledge, ignorance, faith, pride, shame.[31]

If we do not achieve full investment or what Emerson calls Power or Self-Reliance, but instead accept complicity, conformity, desperation, and dullness, then we fail to (dare to) exist. We face, or in conformity evade,

> the issue ... of the self as a thing of cares and commitments, one which to exist has to find itself, which underlies the myth of the self as on a journey (a path in Plato's image, a stairway in Emerson's, a ladder in others'), a journey to, let us say, the truth of itself (not exhausted by its goods and its rights).[32]

The ideas, first, that we exist in and through our cares and commitments and, second, that we are able to be variously ashamed or proud of them, or faithful in them, or disgusted by them are inflections of the Kantian idea that our consciousness is apperceptively structured. "The *I think*," Kant reminds us, "must *be able* to accompany all my representations; for otherwise something would be represented in me that could not be thought at all, which is as much to say that the representation would either be impossible or else at least would be nothing for me."[33] That is, for any judgment that I make, it is possible for me in reflection to become aware that it is I who have thus judged. The capacity to do this is impersonal, not unique to any individual. It is possessed by all beings who are capable of judgment. That our consciousness has this structure further implies, according to Kant, that we are responsible for our judgments and the actions that flow from them. "The human being, who is otherwise acquainted with the whole of nature solely through sense, knows himself also through pure apperception," so that he is aware of himself as possessing "reason, [which] has causality,"[34] that is, which can give birth to actions, for which we are responsible. When we act out of respect for the moral law, then we exercise our practical reason and power of action appropriately, thereby coming into our own as human agents.

Thoreau picks up this Kantian line of thought, according to Cavell, when he writes, in the "Solitude" section of *Walden*:

> With thinking we may be beside ourselves in a sane sense. By a conscious effort of the mind we can stand aloof from actions and their consequences. . . . We are not wholly involved in Nature. . . . I only know myself as a human entity; the scene, so to speak, of thoughts and affections; and am sensible of a certain doubleness by which I can stand as remote from myself as from another. However intense my experience, I am conscious of the presence and criticism of a part of me, which, as it were, is not a part of me, but a spectator, sharing no experience, but taking note of it, and that is no more I than it is you.[35]

We have, then, an impersonal capacity for reflecting on our judgments, and hence for evaluating what we do – for being proud or ashamed or embarrassed or (culpably) ignorant or accepting of it. Hence we should (dare to) seek to *be* proud, upright, and fully committed in relation to what we venture (never knowing whether the world will cooperate with us or not), rather than timid, acquiescent, or ashamed. Thoroughgoing commitment in and to what one does lures us, or should lure us, as we seek to wed uncertain venture to reflective endorsement. Or, as Cavell furthers Thoreau's thought,

> Our first resolve should be toward the nextness of the self to the self; it is the capacity not to deny either of its positions or attitudes – that it is the watchman or guardian of itself, and hence demands of itself transparence,

settling, clearing, constancy; and that it is the workman, whose eye cannot see to the end of its labors, but whose answerability is endless for the constructions in which it houses itself. The answerability of the self to itself is its possibility of awakening.[36]

Emerson's sense of the human person is similar, as in "Self-Reliance" he develops Descartes' *cogito* into the thought that, as Cavell has it, "if I am to exist I must name my existence, acknowledge it. This imperative entails that I am a thing with two foci, or, in Emerson's image, two magnetic poles – say a positive and a negative, or an active and a passive."[37] That the self in its doubleness or nextness has active and passive sides that might be put together, that it might thus answer to itself in and through its courses of action, is our infinite task and possibility.

Thoreau and Emerson are, for Cavell, the American philosophers who (along with Wittgenstein elsewhere) take up the Kantian image of the human person. In doing so in their specific way, they point us toward the romance of expressive freedom, the romance of the pursuit of full existence, uprightness, pride, self-reliance, and answerability to self. Not that this romance is concluded or even quite concludable: far from it. Thoreau and Emerson are "philosophers of direction, orientation, tirelessly prompting us to be on our way, endlessly asking us where we stand, what it is we face."[38] "Emerson's writing is meant as the provision of experience for these shores, of our trials, perils, essays,"[39] where this experience is not already in place to be smoothly developed into happiness, but instead takes the form of trials, perils, and essays, from and through which conversion of care and commitment are required.

That Thoreau and Emerson seek new direction – a conversion of, and from within, experience as it stands, in which they are themselves all too caught up – lends to their writing (and to Cavell's) qualities of *aversiveness* to the ordinary transmission of a settled message: a certain sense of tentativeness and self-revision, a foregrounding of the writer's own starts and turns and halts. Their writing enacts a sense of *seeking* to be on the way out of present straits and toward happiness, freedom, and self-reliance. As things stand, our getting on the way is enabled, but also inhibited, by imperfect present conditions. Hence for these writers it is a matter (as it typically is for modernist artists) of getting started at all, of figuring out how to "take an interest in our lives"[40] from within present dullness, conformity, and acquiescence.

Thoreau calls this everyday condition quiet desperation; Emerson says silent melancholy; Coleridge and Wordsworth are apt to say despondency or dejection; Heidegger speaks of it as our bedimmed averageness; Wittgenstein as our bewitchment; Austin both as a drunken profundity (which he knew more about than he cared to let on) and as a lack of seriousness. To *find* what degrees of freedom we have *in this condition*, to show that it is at once needless yet somehow, because of that, all but necessary, inescapable, to subject its presentation of necessity to diagnosis, in order to find truer necessities, is the romantic quest I am happy to join.[41]

Getting on our way from where we are requires, in the perception of Emerson, Thoreau, and Cavell, not escape (from the cave) into the abstract, or into scientific procedures, but engagement with the near, the low, the common, the ordinary. Emerson and Thoreau work "out of the problematic of the day, the everyday, the near, the low, the common, in conjunction with what they call speaking of necessaries, and speaking with necessity."[42] They write out of "devotion to the thing they call the common, the familiar, the near, the low."[43] In doing so, the hope – their hope – is that we might hear "how the language we traverse every day can contain undiscovered treasure"[44] that we can work into our lives because it is already worked into our lives (albeit in ways we do not hear), unlike the false promises of ascent of more traditional doctrines.

Out of our present condition, Emerson and Thoreau (and Cavell) propose to teach or provoke us by stumbling ahead of us toward the light of freedom. They are not experts, either in the instruments or means for the satisfaction of desires as they stand or in the specifics of the end to be achieved. There is "no expert knowledge" on offer, "nothing closed to the ordinary human being, once, that is to say, that being lets himself or herself be informed by the process and ambition of philosophy."[45] What we might best do "may not be measurable from outside,"[46] but only from within the ordinary, the cave, America. We are to be, somehow, "guided by our experience but not dictated to by it,"[47] as we seek to put the active (workman) and passive (watchman) sides of the self together and seek to compose selves together into a perfected conversational culture of freedom – all from where we are.

There are, then, no formulae for the achievement of freedom. Advice about means and instruments does not heighten or deepen commitment. Descriptions of ultimate goods to be achieved are tendentious and insupportable, in coming from 'outside' where we are. Because there are no formulae, there are no experts in freedom. Though freedom remains, in this perception, central to the inner agenda of our selves and culture, Americans are also skeptical about prophets. They value expertise and sound advice about coping and getting on with the business at hand. If Thoreau and Emerson and Cavell do not offer that, but instead themselves only stumble as writers toward freedom, then Americans are all too likely to scorn them or, if touched by them at all, to be unsettled but unconvinced. This is pretty much Cavell's sense of the place of Thoreau and Emerson in American culture. Cavell notes what he calls "the extraordinary fact that those I regard as the founders of American thinking – Ralph Waldo Emerson and Henry David Thoreau – are philosophically repressed in the culture they founded."[48] Given the pragmatist strain in American culture, in competition with its inner agendas of freedom and perfection, this fact is perhaps not so extraordinary after all. Americans are generally not terribly attentive to their history, especially to their philosophical history. When they do pay attention to it, they are, as pragmatic individualists, perhaps reasonably inclined to pay attention to Jefferson, Madison (especially *Federalist* No. 10 on faction and the separation of powers), and Lincoln. These thinkers offer political solutions – deep and abstract, but still political – to political problems, not conversion.[49]

Cavell, however, nonetheless argues that Emerson and Thoreau are *specifically* repressed. "I am taking precisely that condition to signify their pertinence to the present: I do not, the culture does not, *repress* the thought of Schopenhauer or Kierkegaard or Spengler; they were simply not part of our formation."[50] Emerson and Thoreau are "threats, or say embarrassments, to what we have learned to call philosophy"[51] and to what in our acquiescence we have come to think of as America. This is *because* the inner agenda of freedom that they forward, and as they forward it in their specific ways (out of allegiance to America, to its future, and to philosophy's) is itself in specific competition with America's pragmatist, competitive individualist, "get on with business" strands of life. They offer "a continuous rebuke to the way we live"[52] from within the contested insides of the way we live (and of themselves).

Cavell's talk of rebuke, prophecy, and conversion to freedom is likely, however, to seem itself empty, tendentious, and "cracker-barrel," especially to Americans naturally suspicious of settled terms of religious and cultural achievement. Such talk seems to monger shame and to do so without telling us much about what, specifically, to do. Emerson and Thoreau seem to undo our sense of ourselves as innocent, without outlining any particular route of recovery or restoration, hence to cast our lives as tragic. Their writings can feel like jeremiads. No doubt we should regret American slavery, and no doubt we face many problems of persistent unfairness and lack of opportunity that should be addressed through political means. But should we feel shame toward our past and our selves, and is conversion the most apt response to the problems we face?[53]

In light, therefore, of this worry about emptiness and shame mongering, it is especially worth noting that in his own faithfulness to the near, the low, and the common Cavell himself traces the achievement of a genuinely honorable American romantic happiness and freedom. In *Pursuits of Happiness* – his happiest book – Cavell follows the careers of the principal pairs in six American movies made between 1934 and 1949. His thought here is that the principal characters in these movies – Jean (Barbara Stanwyck) and Charles (Henry Fonda), Peter (Clark Gable) and Ellie (Claudette Colbert), David (Cary Grant) and Susan (Katherine Hepburn), and so on – "take the time, and take the pains, to converse intelligently and playfully about themselves and about one another."[54] Among the questions that they ask themselves and each other – most explicitly in the case of David in *Bringing Up Baby*, but implicitly throughout – is "What am I doing here, that is, how have I got into this relation and why do I stay in it?"[55] Cavell emphasizes continuously that the asking and answering of this question are figures for consent to the social contract, that the achievement of settlement in the relationship of marriage is a figure for settlement of and with one's country and culture and self (and vice versa). As though, then, to make the rebukes and promises of America's prophets other than empty and tendentious, these pairs *do* achieve a settlement. Among other things, they discover – on their ways with one another and to their continuous surprise (in the sense that what they turn out to want is not what they had thought they wanted) – that "what they do together is less important than the fact that they do whatever it is together."[56] Above all, they talk and acknowledge and have fun with one another. To be sure, at least one of the pair in each case has money, so that these couples are not in the end constrained by the pinch of necessity (though often one of them has been thus constrained). They do not have to get on with business. They have time for conversation and exploration. This can make their careers seem like fairy tales or fantasies for many of us.

But then the question that these movies raise and honorably answer is: What – survival apart – is getting on with business *for*? Most of us, Cavell argues, find their answer to this, their achievement of a kind of ongoing purposiveness (with one another) without settled purpose (no external aim, room left for continuing exploration) to be something worth endorsing. They achieve an "honorable ... happiness"[57] in and through their pursuits. "The pair is attractive, their wishes are human, their happiness would make us happy. So it seems a criterion is being proposed for the success or happiness of a society, namely that it is happy to the extent that it provides conditions that permit conversations of this character, or a moral equivalent of them, between its citizens."[58] Since the criterion of happiness is satisfied by these pairs, and hence proleptically for Americans as a people, the wages of prophecy and conversion need not be only admonishment, rebuke, and shame. Acknowledgment intertwined with fun is possible.

To be sure, even though it anticipates a more general happiness, the happiness achieved by these pairs is achieved pairwise. The stateroom door closes at the end of *The Lady Eve*, leaving Mugsy (and us) outside the happiness of Jean and Charles; at the end of *It Happened One Night*, the camera pulls away from the outside of the cabin as the lights go out and the trumpet sounds, leaving Ellie and Peter inside their happiness, us outside.

Partly, however, this division of the private, erotic happiness and intimacy of these pairs from larger social life is a function of the fact that there is, unlike what Plato imagines the ideal city might accomplish, no one final achievement of happiness and freedom that is possible for us. Each of us must begin from where we are, all at once within our tangled culture, from our individual talents and possibilities, and with certain specific others, in engagement with the near, the low, and the familiar. This is an American pursuit of happiness and freedom, not a Platon*ist*[59] pursuit of a standing good. Both selves and language-culture are, always, on the way, seeking always a further settlement. Improvisation, exploration, and wit are not to be bypassed in this seeking in favor of submission to a final theory. As Stephen Mulhall usefully comments, Emerson and Thoreau (and Cavell) are committed to "writing in a way which acknowledges the relative autonomy of both language and its individual speakers, their simultaneous dependence upon and independence of each other."[60] Between self-speaker and culture-language there will be interaction, always, including possibilities of departure and return.

Writing that acknowledges this condition, as the writing of Emerson and Thoreau does, then "presents itself" not as the statement of a theory but as "the realization of [Friedrich Schlegel's] vision . . . of the union of poetry and philosophy."[61] It will include narratives of departure and return, accounts of rehearsals and efforts, and of partial (or pairwise) successes and failures. The thoughts about our condition and possibilities that occur within such writing will be provisional. They will aim, and will sometimes succeed partly (but only partly), at offering us terms in which to do better from where we are. Cavell captures this point by focusing on Emerson's sentences from "Self-Reliance": "In every work of genius we recognize our own rejected thoughts. They come back to us with a certain alienated majesty." As Cavell goes on to comment, these sentences propose that

> If the thoughts of a text such as Emerson's (say the brief text on rejected thoughts) are yours, then you do not need them. If its thoughts are *not* yours, they will not do you good. The problem [– or possibility? –] is that the text's thoughts are neither exactly mine nor not mine. In their sublimity as my rejected – say repressed – thoughts, they represent my further, next, unattained but attainable self.[62]

To commit oneself, as Cavell does, to the cultivation of such repressed thoughts (of America, of the self, and of their possibilities of freedom) is to adopt what Simon Critchley has usefully characterized as a "weak messianism," wherein one engages in " 'a passive practice', that is, a way of inhabiting the actual everyday with one eye on the eventual everyday."[63]

Are the thoughts to which Cavell (after Emerson and Thoreau) proposes to return us *our* repressed ones? Is freedom – as acknowledgment, and self-reliance, and mutuality, and achieved Power, and happiness in all of this – central to the inner agenda of our selves and our American culture? There *are* some reasons to be doubtful about this. Narratives of possible conversion, however weak, do carry with them risks of authoritarianism, hypocrisy, and the illegitimate repression of our natural and naturally divergent wants and desires. There is good reason, in order not to wallow in guilt and shame, to accept ourselves as just wanting what we want and just getting on with the business of life as best we can. If America promises us no more than the chance to do that, as individuals, perhaps it is not so bad: better this weak promise than the tribalisms and authoritarianisms of Europe and its philosophies and religions. Why should I feel embarrassed that I like, say, Robin Williams, and my wife, and my house, and you don't? Perhaps it is important to me, and should be to you, that these likings are *mine*, not, or at least not necessarily, to be shared.[64] Why should we not, as pragmatism seems to suggest, just go absolutely with what *works*, from where we are, without worrying about mysterious conversion to a higher pursuit of freedom and happiness that might anyway make us too much like one another?

But then – just as with Emerson and Thoreau – it is not clear that this kind of worry is not already internal to Cavell's own perfectionism and commitment to the pursuit of freedom. Perfectionism, as Cavell pursues it, "does not seek to impose itself by power"; "the project of Emersonian Perfectionism demands no privileged share of liberty and of the basic goods."[65] To say

this is to say that democratic equality and fairness and political liberty matter
and, further, that they matter specifically for the sake of the divergences,
explorations, and developments of individual interest and ability and commitment that they enable.

Cavell's sense here – a sense shared with Emerson in his own continuing efforts to join in an American conversation of differing voices, without mastering it – is that there are certain "arguments that must not be
won"[66] – among them the argument between the perfectionist, conversion-
and freedom-seeking voice in American life and the voice of the tolerant,
the divergent, the useful, the acceptance of ourselves as good enough as we
stand. "The conversation over how good [the] justice [of a good-enough
democracy] is must take place and must also not have a victor, . . . not
because agreement can or should always be reached, but because disagreement, and separateness of position, is to be allowed its satisfactions, reached
and expressed in particular ways."[67]

What we seek, as individual selves, as friends and couples, and as
Americans, is "consent to our present state as something we desire, or
anyway desire more than we desire change."[68] Sometimes this will require
just acceptance: acceptance of liberal political arrangements, of divergences
within them, of the sheer difference of people other than oneself or of difference within oneself. Sometimes it will require conversion in the form of
openness to and commitment to a certain route of cultivation and expressiveness – sometimes for oneself, sometimes for several, sometimes for the
nation – in order to overcome present dissatisfactions. After all, "you never
know. I mean, you never know when someone will learn the posture, as for
themselves, that will make sense of a field of movement, it may be writing,
or dancing, or passing a ball, or sitting at a keyboard, or free associating."[69]
Cavell himself expresses some sense of being pulled between his particular
Jewishness and his more general Americaness, as they "inflect each other,"
suggesting that Thoreau and Emerson are of interest to him precisely because they keep open this mutual inflection of particular and national (in
him, and in the nation) by providing "a philosophy of immigrancy, of the
human as stranger"[70] – seeking settlement, but never quite finally arriving
at it.

So you never know. I would not want the American settlement to
continue without furthering America's and our sometimes repressed inner agenda of freedom – without continuing America's romance – just as
I would not want that inner agenda to be administered in comprehensive (nonliberal) political enforcements that would always betray that very
agenda.[71] You never know.

Notes

1. This way of opening the subject is adapted from Russell Goodman, "Cavell and American Philosophy," archived at ⟨http://www.american-philosophy.org/archives/2000%20conference%20papers/Goodman1.htm⟩.
2. See Cornel West, *The American Evasion of Philosophy: A Genealogy of Pragmatism* (Madison, WI: University of Wisconsin Press, 1989), for a reading of a central evasion of epistemology in American philosophy, coupled oddly with the thought that religiously inspired social prophecy is pursued nonetheless. Though West is right that both of these tendencies are in place in American thought, there is more tension between them than he supposes, as the evasion of foundationalist epistemology pushes toward the rejection of social visions and in favor of utilitarianism, while the pursuit of social prophecy seems to require an epistemology of larger visions in order to be credible.
3. Though this is the standard picture in American departments of philosophy, it bears noting that it is in many ways unfair to the richness and visionariness of the actual writings of Peirce, James, and Dewey, among others. On James see, for example, Charles Taylor, *Varieties of Religion Today: William James Revisited* (Cambridge, MA: Harvard University Press, 2002); on Dewey, see Goodman, "Cavell and American Philosophy."
4. Compare Jay Bernstein's similar picture of professional philosophy in his essay in this volume.
5. See Stanley Cavell, "Being Odd, Getting Even: Descartes, Emerson, Poe" in his *In Quest of the Ordinary: Lines of Skepticism and Romanticism* (Chicago: University of Chicago Press, 1988).
6. See Richard Eldridge, *Leading a Human Life: Wittgenstein, Intentionality, and Romanticism* (Chicago: University of Chicago Press, 1997), passim, for an elaboration of the relevant concept of *expressive freedom*, and especially also pp. 108–12 on Cavell in relation to this concept. The pursuit of expressiveness comes to the fore in Cavell's discussion of Thoreau in *The Senses of Walden: An Expanded Edition* (San Francisco: North Point Press, 1981), pp. 55, 57.
7. For a reading of Cavell's understanding of artistic modernism, as the pressure toward it and the possibility of it are described by Wordsworth and by Kant, see Timothy Gould, "The Audience of Originality: Kant and Wordsworth on the Reception of Genius," in Ted Cohen and Paul Guyer, eds., *Essays in Kant's Aesthetics* (Chicago: University of Chicago Press, 1982), pp. 179–93.
8. Cavell, *The Senses of Walden*, p. 60.
9. Ibid., p. 71.
10. Stanley Cavell, *A Pitch of Philosophy: Autobiographical Exercises* (Cambridge, MA: Harvard University Press, 1994), p. 4.
11. Stanley Cavell, *Conditions Handsome and Unhandsome: The Constitution of Emersonian Perfectionism* (Chicago: University of Chicago Press, 1990), pp. 6–7, emphasis and interjection added.
12. Ibid., p. 7.

13. Cavell, *Pursuits of Happiness: The Hollywood Comedy of Remarriage* (Cambridge, MA: Harvard University Press, 1981), pp. 4–5.

14. Ibid., p. 142.

15. Cavell, *Conditions Handsome and Unhandsome*, p. 7.

16. Cavell, "Being Odd, Getting Even," p. 105.

17. Ibid.

18. Cavell, *Conditions Handsome and Unhandsome*, p. xxvi.

19. Ibid.

20. Cavell, *Pursuits of Happiness*, pp. 64–5.

21. Ibid., pp. 17–18.

22. Cavell, *Conditions Handsome and Unhandsome*, pp. 107, 28.

23. Stanley Cavell, *The Claim of Reason: Wittgenstein, Skepticism, Morality, and Tragedy* (New York: Oxford University Press, 1979), p. 23.

24. Stephen Mulhall, *Stanley Cavell: Philosophy's Recounting of the Ordinary* (Oxford: Clarendon Press, 1994), p. 58. Interjection added.

25. Cavell, *The Claim of Reason*, p. 25.

26. Cavell, *The Senses of Walden*, p. 82.

27. Stanley Cavell, "The Avoidance of Love: A Reading of *King Lear*," in his *Must We Mean What We Say?* (New York: Charles Scribners' Sons, 1969), p. 344.

28. Cavell, *Pursuits of Happiness*, p. 156.

29. Cavell, "Ending the Waiting Game: A Reading of Beckett's *Endgame*," in *Must We Mean What We Say?*, p. 141.

30. Cavell, *Pursuits of Happiness*, p. 17.

31. Cavell, *The Senses of Walden*, p. 53.

32. Cavell, *A Pitch of Philosophy*, p. 142.

33. Immanuel Kant, *Critique of Pure Reason*, trans. and ed. Paul Guyer and Allen W. Wood (Cambridge: Cambridge University Press, 1997), B 131–2, p. 246.

34. Ibid., A 546–7 = B 574–5, p. 540.

35. Henry David Thoreau, *Walden*, Chapter 5, para. 11, "Solitude," cited in Cavell, *The Senses of Walden*, p. 102.

36. Cavell, *The Senses of Walden*, pp. 107–8.

37. Cavell, "Being Odd, Getting Even," p. 106.

38. Cavell, *The Senses of Walden*, pp. 141–2.

39. Cavell, *This New Yet Unapproachable America*, p. 92.

40. Cavell, *The Senses of Walden*, p. 67.

41. Cavell, "The Philosopher in American Life," in *In Quest of the Ordinary*, p. 9.

42. Cavell, *This New Yet Unapproachable America*, p. 81.

43. Cavell, "The Philosopher in American Life," p. 4.

44. Cavell, *Must We Mean What We Say?*, p. 43.

45. Cavell, *Pursuits of Happiness*, p. 9.

46. Cavell, *A Pitch of Philosophy*, p. 142.

47. Cavell, *Pursuits of Happiness*, p. 10.
48. Cavell, "The Fantastic of Philosophy," in *In Quest of the Ordinary*, p. 181.
49. Ted Cohen pressed me, rightly, to strengthen this point.
50. Cavell, *This New Yet Unapproachable America*, pp. 82–3.
51. Cavell, "The Philosopher in American Life," p. 14.
52. Cavell, "Emerson, Coleridge, Kant," in *In Quest of the Ordinary*, p. 35.
53. Again, a worry aptly urged on me by Ted Cohen.
54. Cavell, *Pursuits of Happiness*, p. 5.
55. Ibid., p. 130.
56. Ibid., p. 113.
57. Ibid., p. 65.
58. Ibid., p. 32.
59. I specifically note, however, that Plato's texts, with their dramatic structures of conversation, their allegories, and their frequent inconclusiveness are richer and more "literary" than a Plato*nist* doctrine of the good sometimes takes them to be.
60. Mulhall, *Stanley Cavell*, p. 252.
61. Cavell, *This New Yet Unapproachable America*, p. 21.
62. Cavell, *Conditions Handsome and Unhandsome*, p. 57.
63. Simon Critchley, *Very Little . . . Almost Nothing: Death, Philosophy, Literature* (London: Routledge, 1997), p. 130.
64. For an eloquent expression of this thought, balanced against the contrary thought that we also need to and can care about some things together, see Ted Cohen, "High and Low Thinking about High and Low Art," *The Journal of Aesthetics and Art Criticism* 51 (Spring 1993), pp. 151–6.
65. Cavell, *Conditions Handsome and Unhandsome*, p. xxii.
66. Cavell, *A Pitch of Philosophy*, p. 22.
67. Cavell, *Conditions Handsome and Unhandsome*, pp. 24–5.
68. Cavell, *The Claim of Reason*, p. 465.
69. Cavell, "Being Odd, Getting Even," in *In Quest of the Ordinary*, p. 115.
70. Cavell, *A Pitch of Philosophy*, p. xv.
71. Here, along with Russell Goodman, I have the sense that Cavell and Cavell's Emerson and Thoreau are perhaps less far from Dewey and James, and from Rorty's Dewey in *Achieving Our Country*, and from Cornel West's "prophetic pragmatism," than is sometimes thought to be the case. Dewey and James and Rorty and West, rightly read, *do* urge the perfectionist pursuit of freedom, in and through continuing uncertainties, not just "coping." Situating these figures within the tradition of Emerson and Thoreau will mean, however, moderating their voluntarism and utilitarianism and noticing how they remain haunted by skepticism, even when and where they seek to deny this haunting.

8 | "Disowning Knowledge": Cavell on Shakespeare

ANTHONY J. CASCARDI

The limits of my language are the limits of my world.
Ludwig Wittgenstein, *Tractatus Logico-Philosophicus*

By the time Stanley Cavell arrives at his discussion of *Othello* near the end of *The Claim of Reason*, the reader is more than amply prepared for an encounter with the exorbitance of Shakespeare's text. And yet nothing that Cavell writes prior to the conclusion of that book suggests in any particular way that an analysis of Shakespeare is in the offing. *The Claim of Reason* is hardly systematic enough for its itinerary to be predicted; but even more important, it seems to prove that one need not read Shakespeare in order to drive language to its limits: one need only possess an unstinting attention to, and ear for, the weight of what we say. The disclosure of our commitments in what we say, together with an account of what it means to honor or to skirt them, is as important as anything in Cavell's work. It is this project of disclosure and of accounting that led him, in the early essays that comprise the volume *Must We Mean What We Say?*, to take the language of sight in *King Lear* as the basis for a breathtakingly broad discussion of the problem of acknowledgment and the avoidance of love in that play. The issues of skepticism, knowledge, and the efforts of human beings to avoid acknowledgment are among the most prominent themes in his Shakespearean essays. But rather than regard any of his encounters with Shakespeare either as unforeseeable or as dictated by a specific philosophical agenda, it might be better to say that Cavell portrays his engagements with Shakespeare as unavoidable because it is Shakespeare who, above all writers, explores the full range of the commitments that language entails. The power of Shakespeare's work rests on his ability to envision characters who live out the fate of their words relentlessly, without compromise or escape, or who suffer disastrously from their failure to do so.

My thanks to Richard Eldridge for especially insightful comments on an earlier version of this essay.

190

Shakespearean tragedy, as it is epitomized in plays such as *Macbeth*, *Othello*, *Hamlet*, and *King Lear*, is a form of drama in which language is drawn to extremes, but the force of Cavell's work is to magnify the intensities that are present within Shakespeare's work rather than to submit them to anything like a "philosophical" point of view extraneous to it. Cavell himself is supremely aware of the fact that his aims may be interpreted otherwise. As he writes in the Preface to *Disowning Knowledge*,

> The misunderstanding of my attitude that most concerned me was to take my project as the application of some philosophically independent problematic of skepticism to a fragmentary parade of Shakespearean texts, impressing those texts into the service of illustrating philosophical conclusions known in advance. Sympathy with my project depends, on the contrary, on unsettling the matter of priority (as between philosophy and literature, say) implied in the concepts of illustration and application. The plays I take up form retrospective interpretations of skepticism as they yield to interpretation by skepticism.[1]

Indeed, Cavell's essays on Shakespeare gain their power from the fact that Shakespeare seems to have anticipated the philosophical engagements that Cavell subsequently uncovers in them.

The relative historical proximity of Shakespeare and Descartes helps to solidify the case for Shakespeare's involvement with questions of skepticism, but Cavell's arguments hardly rest on historical grounds, and the fact that Descartes' seminal statement of the skeptical problematic comes *after* Shakespeare would quash a historical claim anyway. If temporal coincidence is the issue, then Montaigne is a far more likely candidate for comparison. But Montaigne's version of skepticism lacks something that Cavell finds in Descartes, and that turns out to be central to Cavell's own engagement with the problematic: the development of an epistemological stance "against" skepticism. Insofar as that stance has subsequently been incorporated as part of philosophy's identity, Cavell's encounter with Shakespeare is part of his larger engagement with the modern philosophical tradition.

There Cavell's work is to dismantle the opposition between skepticism and epistemology rather than to oppose skepticism by proposing an alternative to epistemology. Descartes stands on the near side of a division within the history of philosophy that makes such work necessary, whereas in Montaigne the contrast between skepticism and epistemology had not yet emerged in anything like its fully formed modern version. In Shakespeare, Cavell finds the resources for testing the validity of what the

philosophical tradition since Descartes has made of the Cartesian formulation of the problem of skepticism, and of the answers to it. In Cavell's
readings, Shakespearean tragedy and romance are interpreted as presenting openings into the problems of skepticism and knowledge that take these
issues to domains that lie beyond, or beneath, what philosophy conventionally imagines to be at stake in them. Or, perhaps better said after a consideration of Cavell's essays, Shakespeare's texts ask us to take account of the
full measure of what skepticism means and thereby challenge us to confront
those things for which epistemology has come to be a cover

To be sure, it could be complained that Cavell gives us a Shakespeare
whose thought appears mannered, or whose characters seem to be involved
in intricacies of plotting that require motives far more recherché than they
themselves might imagine. But whether or not one reads Cavell's approach
to Shakespeare as the source of such mannerism, or his account of motives
as extravagant and implausible, will depend in large measure on how one
distinguishes mannerism from self-reflection, or extravagant speculation
from the extremes of consciousness that expose themselves under the dire
conditions of tragedy. There is, at the very least, a relentlessness about the
logic that Cavell puts to Shakespeare's texts, a commitment to follow and
test the textual and psychological links that the plays seem to demand we
make. Moreover, what Shakespeare's characters may be aware of, or what
they may deny, are issues that Cavell hardly fails to confront. And yet in the
end nothing beyond the kinds of judgments that literary critics customarily
make is likely to settle these matters. Cavell's judgments must ultimately
be tested against one's experience of what the plays themselves hold. The
issues that bear further commentary here are the train of Cavell's thinking
on Shakespearean drama and its relationship to skepticism, as well as the
intersection between his work and the history of criticism of Shakespearean
drama.

Cavell's engagement with Shakespeare begins in his essay on *King Lear*
published in *Must We Mean What We Say?* (1969) with what was then a
familiar conundrum in Shakespeare studies: the relationship between an
older kind of criticism centered on Shakespeare's characters (the form of
criticism that had reached something of a high-water mark in A. C. Bradley's
1904 book, *Shakespearean Tragedy*) and a newer kind of criticism centered on
Shakespeare's language (the criticism that was considered valid among the
"New Critics," such as William Empson). To reconstruct this particular
shift in the history of Shakespearean criticism may now seem purpose-
less, not so much because we have come to regard Shakespeare's characters
and their words as inextricably linked but because Shakespearean criticism

seems to have shifted to other grounds and to have found other routes into, or around, Shakespeare's texts. The "New Historicism," cultural poetics, psychoanalysis, and gender studies would be the names of but a few of these newer approaches. And yet Cavell's early work makes claims on our attention, even today. Let me sketch one of the most important reasons why that work is still worth reading, which may in turn help to introduce some of the issues more broadly at stake in Cavell's thinking about Shakespeare.

Simply put, the question of a disjunction between Shakespeare's characters and their words is an issue that still haunts Shakespearean criticism – or that ought to. Contemporary criticism leaves some of the central questions that Cavell poses wide open: *How* do the characters in a play mean what they say? How can they *not* mean what they say? What are we to make of the meaningfulness of their words? Cavell's analyses of Shakespeare are all rooted in a conviction that Shakespeare's characters *must* mean what they say, and mean it thoroughly, unless of course they are in a posture of avoidance, in which case their words may reveal whatever it is they might wish to disown. It bears upon us as readers and critics of these plays to suppose this and nothing less. And yet recent Shakespearean criticism raises the possibility that historical context, repressed desires, ideological structures, and the like might account for the meaningfulness of what Shakespeare's characters say. Thus it is especially interesting to find that Cavell later sought to bridge the apparent gaps between his work and certain of the directions in Shakespearean criticism just mentioned. Cavell became increasingly interested in drawing parallels between his own work and other contemporary critical methods (deconstruction and psychoanalysis come first to mind), but this rapprochement is also an indication of developments in Cavell's own thinking about Shakespeare over the course of nearly thirty years, and of his increasing openness to certain branches of psychoanalysis and political theory. The conjuncture is validated, in part at least, by a remark of Freud's that Cavell cites, viz., that the "poets" – Shakespeare prominent among them – preceded psychoanalysis in its insights. Looking back at the course of Cavell's development from the vantage point of his essays on *Coriolanus* and *Hamlet*, it is possible to recognize that the distinctions we sometimes make among works of philosophy, psychoanalysis, literary criticism, and political theory are artificial products of a modern division of the world of human experience into separate discursive realms, a division that is bound to seem artificial. Certainly Cavell shows that Shakespeare's plays are far more encompassing than the insights that any one of those disciplines can possibly provide.

For reasons that should become clear over the course of the following pages, the central point of reference for Cavell's work on Shakespeare, both philosophically and literarily, is the genre of tragedy. Nothing that he has to say about the other genres that interest him – romance and comedy (though comedy in a secondary way)[2] – makes sense without first knowing his relationship to Shakespearean tragedy. Tragedy is the genre that Cavell first and most consistently confronts, and it is also the one that grounds his discussion of a romance play such as *The Winter's Tale*. But to know Cavell's relationship to Shakespearean tragedy requires an informed perspective both on tragedy as a genre and on some of the interests that Cavell cultivates outside of the literary sphere.

At least since the time of Aristotle, critics and philosophers have regarded tragedy as grounded in action and in the categories directly related to action, such as character and plot. Virtually all of the philosophical questions that have been asked about tragedy have matters of action at their core. This holds true whether the issue is the injustice of the tragic hero's suffering, the relative freedom of the protagonist's actions, the role of fate, or the workings of the tragic emotions. It is hardly the work of this brief chapter to outline these matters in anything like the full scope they warrant. And yet Cavell's contribution to Shakespeare studies cannot be understood without some reference to them, because, unlike that of so many of his predecessors, Cavell's interest in tragedy does *not* revolve around questions of action. Without forsaking the issues just mentioned, Cavell's work on Shakespeare shifts the ground of the analysis of tragedy to the questions of knowledge and doubt, which in turn point to the problems of acknowledgment and avoidance. Although the issues of knowledge and recognition have been at stake in tragedy ever since *Oedipus Rex*, tragedy as a genre reflects something much more than what epistemology takes "knowledge" to be. Indeed, Cavell grounds his claims about Shakespearean tragedy on his philosophical analysis of what epistemology *avoids*. What precisely might that be? In *The Claim of Reason*, Cavell devotes massive efforts to the derivation of what he calls "the moral of skepticism," namely, "that the human creature's basis in the world as a whole, its relation to the world as such, is not that of knowing, anyway not what we think of as knowing."[3] What epistemology *avoids* must be something that "knowing" cannot provide. Indeed, knowing serves as the excuse, the cover, or the alibi for what ought to be acknowledged.

This is also to say that just as Cavell shifts the analysis of tragedy away from the problems of action, he also shifts the philosophical ground on which the problem of skepticism had conventionally been addressed. In his work, an adequate diagnosis of skepticism as a condition of mind requires breaking its sometimes-concealed attachment to paradigms of knowledge. There are, on Cavell's philosophical account, certain facts that neither philosophical skepticism nor epistemology is able to recognize – psychological facts about motives; anthropological facts about shame, exposure, and concealment; dramatic facts about the performance of actions and the elaboration of fictions within a space that is only partially congruous with the one that we usually accept as "real." Philosophical skepticism typically relies on fictional tales or "thought experiments" to move its arguments forward. These are tales of the kind that Cavell frequently cites when referring to Descartes, and they often turn on some fantastical supposition: that I have no body, that I am made of glass, that I am a brain in a vat, and so forth. Such examples ought to make the move to the "fictions" of drama easy enough. And yet there is something quite distinctive about Cavell's use of these philosophical fictions that proves significant for the way he treats literature. Whether in literature or in philosophy, the task he sets is not to judge what truths a given example might illustrate, what claims it might falsify, or what general principles it might challenge us to defend or to accept. The task is rather to make some more reflective assessment of the role that a given fiction plays for the thinker who invokes it, or for the one who speaks it: to judge its role in revealing or concealing motives, in pointing to things that may remain unsaid, or in exposing what may be avoided or concealed. But this is just to say that Cavell's work on Shakespeare is consistent with his approach to other philosophical issues. For in Shakespeare – certainly no less than in philosophical epistemology – the most basic questions revolve around a character's relationship to his or her words, the relationship between those words and the character's actions, and the sometimes-veiled links between what is spoken and what is not.

Keeping such things in mind may help explain how it is that Cavell can provide an adequate analysis of tragedy *without* taking action as the central concern. But questions nonetheless remain. Does the shift in focus away from matters of action somehow mean that the essentially *dramatic* quality of Shakespeare's plays is neglected? Does the attention to characters and words mean that Shakespeare's texts are being treated as dramatic poems (which they may well be, though most plausibly if we give special meanings to the words "dramatic" and "poem")? Or, in Aristotelian terms, does Cavell make the mistake of privileging the "thought" (*dianoia*) of Shakespeare's works over and above matters of character and plot? Perhaps the best response that can be given to these questions is one that reveals them as relying on assumptions that are false. In Cavell's analysis, drama is not simply the representation of incidents in the form of a plot; rather, it is a mode of "poetry" that brings out as *dramatic* forms of human consciousness and experience that may not initially strike us as dramatic at all. These qualities include the sense of the impendingness or unavoidability of an action, or the feeling of necessity that can seem built into a sequence of events, or the urgency of the present as a temporal moment. Understanding the dramatic qualities of Shakespeare's plays thus means understanding what drama is. For Cavell, this is revealed best via a comparison between Shakespeare's works and music – especially Beethoven, whose late compositions convey a powerful sense of necessity, even urgency.

> It is not uncommon to find Shakespeare's plays compared to music, but in the instances I have seen, this comparison rests upon more or less superficial features of music, for example, on its balance of themes, its recurrences, shifts of mood, climaxes – in a word, on its theatrical properties. But music is, or was, dramatic in a more fundamental sense, or it became so when it no longer expanded festivals or enabled dancing or accompanied songs, but achieved its own dramatic autonomy, worked out in its progress in its own terms. Perhaps this begins with Monteverdi (born three years after Shakespeare), but in any case it is secured only with the establishment of tonality and has its climax in the development of sonata form. The essence of the quality I have in mind has to do with the notion of *development*: not, as in early sonata forms, merely with an isolated section in which fragments of earlier material are re-colored and reassembled, but with the process, preeminent in late Beethoven and Brahms, in which the earlier is metamorphosed into new stabilities, culminating in a work like the "Hammerklavier" Sonata, in which *all* later material can be said to be "contained" in the rising and falling interval of a third in the opening two bars. The question I wish to raise here is: how is music made this way meant to be perceived? *What* are we to perceive in order to understand and respond to what is said? . . . I will say that the quality we are to perceive is one of *directed motion*, controlled by relation of keys, by rate of alteration, and by length and articulation of phrases. We do not know where this motion can stop and we do not understand why it has begun here, so we do not know where we stand nor why we are there. The drama consists in following this out and in finding out what it takes to follow this out. (DK, 91–2)

Cavell's analysis of the emotions treats them as likewise "dramatic." They establish expectations, respond to motives, and draw us to make responses that follow from feelings that are no less strong than the force of logic. They can be imagined as working themselves out by means of a grammar and a syntax as complex and coherent, in its way, as anything that might be said with words. Along with states of mind, the emotions (jealousy and shame, in particular) play a prominent role in Cavell's discussions of Shakespeare. In Shakespeare, "states of mind" project themselves out onto the world through the designs and the fears that characters display. The emotions take an active role in shaping this world and in moving the action toward whatever conclusion it may eventually or inevitably reach.

As for skepticism, the particular analysis of this problematic that drives Cavell's reading of Shakespearean tragedy will be familiar enough to readers of his works and has already been hinted at here. I would nonetheless recall two of its most distinctive features, both of which illustrate the deeper issues covered by the umbrella title of his collected Shakespearean essays, *Disowning Knowledge*. The first of these is that Cavell regards skepticism not as rooted in doubt but as stemming from the avoidance of truths that we are unwilling to accept. Doubt is a cover for this. It provides a way of "disowning" knowledge that would bear too heavily upon us, that would leave us too exposed, or without defense: ". . . finding, so far, in the cases of Lear, and of Othello, and of Coriolanus, and of Leontes, that tragedy is the result, and the study, of a burden of knowledge, or an attempt to deny the all but undeniable (it may begin, or seem to, as a simple wish to test it) – that a loving daughter loves you, that your imagination has elicited the desire of a beautiful young woman, that however exceptional you may be you are a member of human society, that your children are yours" (DK, 179). Cavell's diagnosis of the skeptic's hyperbolic form of doubt is epitomized in Descartes' precipitous shift from the things he *sometimes* doubts to the things he thinks he must *always* doubt. The second is that in Cavell's analysis, skepticism remains in thrall to the standards of cognition and of evidence by which epistemology proceeds. Those standards are, respectively, *certainty* in matters of knowledge, and tangible, *ocular proof* in matters of evidence.

The various themes and motifs through which Cavell tracks these issues in Shakespeare's drama lend considerable nuance to the claims that he makes about skepticism. In *Lear*, for instance, the language having to do with matters of sight, insight, and blindness leads to questions about moral visibility and physical vulnerability. In *Othello*, the telltale bloodstained handkerchief takes the protagonist from a relentless demand for evidentiary proof to a form of rage, fueled by jealousy, that cannot be satisfied by *any* form of proof. There is a force at work in such passions that carries human consciousness beyond what evidence can prove; and likewise, the search for evidence simply aids in the denial of truths more significant than it could support.

Cavell's essay on *Hamlet* nonetheless shifts the ground away from the issue of acknowledgment as played out in the dramas of love and jealousy to what seems to be the limit case for all matters of knowledge and acknowledgment: the ability to take responsibility for one's existence as such, that is, for one's birth. But this shift represents a continuation and deepening of two of the themes already present in Cavell's work. One is the idea that if skepticism is the denial that one's relationship to the world as such goes beyond knowing, then taking full responsibility for that relationship must entail something as radical as taking responsibility for the fact that one exists. The second is that the things denied in epistemological responses to skepticism nonetheless persist, though in some hidden or repressed relationship to consciousness. Hence the opening for the questions of psychoanalysis that had long been waiting in the wings. As Hamlet's plotting is conventionally understood, and as he himself presents it, it is driven by the desire to establish the facts that would in turn enable him to take revenge – moral, political, and otherwise – against his uncle Claudius. The dumb show bears a "burden of proof" that Cavell adopts as the focal point of his essay and provides the most visible point of contact with the problem of skepticism: "In speaking of a 'burden of proof' in *Hamlet* I refer of course to Hamlet's declared purpose in simultaneously testing the Ghost's honesty and Claudius's conscience by means of the play-within-the-play, which stages the story of murder by poisoning. At the same time I allude to the problem of skepticism that has prompted me in each of my amateur forays into Shakespeare...." (DK, 179) Also within conventional understandings of Hamlet's actions is the recognition that when Shakespeare sets the play that Hamlet stages inside his own play, the effect is to create a doubling of form that brings the artifice of theater to consciousness without fully breaking its illusion. Cavell's long and intricate remarks on this topic are worth quoting in full, because they epitomize his views of the play just as they mark a moment of transition from his interest in matters of acknowledgment to matters of Freudian psychology:

> On his deciphering of the dumb-show as primal scene – enciphering young Hamlet's delayed sense of Gertrude's power to annihilate all Hamlets – I see Hamlet's question whether to be or not, as asking first of all not why he stays alive, but first of all how he or anyone lets himself be born as the one he is. As if human birth, the birth of the human, proposes the

question of birth. That human existence has two stages – call these birth and the acceptance of birth – is expressed in religion as baptism, in politics as consent, in what you may call psychology as what Freud calls the diphasic character of psychosexual development. In philosophy I take it to have been expressed in Descartes' *cogito* argument, a point perfectly understood and deeply elaborated by Emerson, that to exist the human being has the burden of proving that he or she exists, and that this burden is discharged in *thinking* your existence, which comes in Descartes . . . to finding how to say 'I am, I exist': not of course to say it just once, but every instant of your existence, originate it. To exist is to take your existence upon you, to enact it, as if the basis of human existence is theater, even melodrama. To refuse this burden is to condemn yourself to skepticism – to a denial of the existence, hence the value, of the world. (DK, 187)

To take existence as a "burden," so that it requires enacting (as opposed, say, to mere being), is to recognize that one's stance toward the world cannot adequately be accepted as a matter of cognition – that cognition, in fact, does not allow for such acceptance. Rather, it requires activating one's own existence, allowing oneself to be called into being by the world, hence also accepting the world and one's finitude. Though Cavell does not point to the fact, the conclusion is consistent with what one finds in certain Greek tragedies, such as in Sophocles' *Antigone*, where Creon's tragic suffering follows from his efforts to place man-made laws on a par with those the gods have established, hence to deny the conditions that the gods (and the Oedipal past) have set in place. The fact of human finitude is hardly a discovery of Shakespeare's, and yet his tragedies, especially in Cavell's readings, do give a distinctive color to this fact. Consider, for example, the fact that Shakespeare's tragedies stage these burdens as bearing overwhelmingly upon men rather than women. The reasons why this might be so must remain speculative, but those speculations are nonetheless revealing of the particular weight that Cavell gives to matters of the body and of the certainties and uncertainties that attach, respectively, to motherhood and fatherhood. The idea, not inconsistent with some feminisms, is that men are rather less certain than women of their bodily existence and continuity with others, and in the face of those uncertainties are drawn to what the world has come to call "heroism," "achievement," or "originality."

Such speculations ought to help explain why such an important focus of Cavell's interest in Shakespeare lies in what he calls "the fate of the body under skepticism." Though the reference immediately at hand is to *Othello*, Cavell's interest in this question runs throughout his Shakespearean essays. His psychoanalytic treatment of *Hamlet* hardly weighs against it. On the contrary, part of Cavell's insight into the "fate of the body" lies in the discovery of the effect that certain fears and fantasies have upon the body, and likewise in the recognition that the fantasies and fears exposed in psychoanalysis have recognizable connections to the body – whether as the archaeological site of experiences that may later manifest themselves fantasmatically, or as itself the place where symptoms show themselves.

Cavell's interest in the body begins with his essay on *King Lear*, in which he aims to recover the literal meaning and function of the eyes, as they are used for seeing (and blinding) and for weeping. The motif of the eyes and of blinding points to the visible human facts that one might wish to shield from sight: that one is an embodied creature and exposed, that one is finite, that one is a creature vulnerable to rejection by others and to feelings of shame. The issues unearthed in the reading of *King Lear* resurface in Cavell's work on *Othello*, but here questions of the body and its fate under skepticism are far more central. The reasons are numerous, and among them is the fact that Othello is a blackamoor and Desdemona white – he with a body suggestive of a romantic hero, she with a body suggestive of innocence and purity, but also of stone. Cavell rightly notes the affinities, by way of inversion, between the situation in *Othello*, where a white woman meets her death, and the scene in *The Winter's Tale* where a marble-white statue is returned to life. But beyond this, there is the tremendous uncertainty in *Othello* about whether Desdemona has remained a virgin after, or in spite of, the nuptials. The wedding night is cut short, interrupted by shouts of alarm and a storm. And later, in Act III, while in Cyprus, Othello speaks these words: "come, my dear love, / The purchase made, the fruits are yet to ensue, / The profits yet to come 'twixt me and you" (III. iii. 8–10). Cavell glosses one possible reading of the passage as follows: "It seems to me possible that the purchase, or price, was her virginity, and their fruits or profit pleasure. There could hardly be greater emphasis on their having had just one shortened night together, isolated from this second night by a tempest." (DK, 132) If this reading is a possibility among others, it is in part because the play opens with a sexual scene that we do not see (thus opening as a normal comedy would conclude, "as if turning comedy inside out," DK, 132). The idea that Othello's characterization of Desdemona as "alabaster" is bound up with his denial of her – of what it would cost to love her, of her finitude – is magnified by the other denials, perhaps less easily detected, of which Cavell writes. Othello's great speech ("It is the cause, it is the cause, my soul . . . Put out the light, and then put out the light,") is, Cavell comments, so filled with mystery and grandiloquence as to suggest that it might be in the service of "some massive denial" (DK, 133). Just what might this be? The greatest task in assessing such a thing is to avoid assuming that Othello knows relatively little of Desdemona, and that we know more. Rather, the question of Othello's denial must be asked in the full light of the things that he does in fact know. To acknowledge this is to take the full measure of his words.

> By "denial" I do not initially mean something requiring psychoanalytical, or any other, theory. I mean merely to ask that we not, conventionally but insufferably, assume that we know this woman better than this man knows her – making Othello some kind of exotic, gorgeous, superstitious lunkhead; which is about what Iago thinks. However much Othello deserves each of these titles, however far he believes Iago's tidings, he cannot just believe them; somewhere he also *knows* them to be false. This is registered in the rapidity with which he is brought to the truth, with no further real evidence, with only a counterstory (about the handkerchief) that bursts over him, or from him, as the truth. Shall we say he recognizes the truth too late? The fact is, he recognizes it when he is ready to, as one alone can; in this case, when its burden is dead. . . . Othello's eager insistence on Iago's honesty, his eager slaking of his thirst for knowledge with that poison, is not a sign of his stupidity in the presence of poison but of his devouring need of it. I do not quite say that he could not have accepted slander about Desdemona so quickly, to the quick, unless he already believed it; but rather that it is a thing he would rather believe than something yet more terrible to his mind; *the idea of Desdemona as an adulterous whore is more convenient to him than the idea of her as chaste.* But what could be more terrible than Desdemona's faithlessness? Evidently her faithfulness? But how? (DK, 133; italics added)

The answers to these last questions are central to Cavell's understanding of the relationship between skepticism and tragedy:

> I wish to keep suspicion cast on what it is we take to express skepticism, and here especially by casting suspicion on whether we know what it means to know that another exists. Nothing could be more certain to Othello than that Desdemona exists; is flesh and blood; is separate from him; other. This is precisely the possibility that tortures him. The content of his torture *is* the premonition of the existence of another, hence of his own, his own as dependent, as partial. . . . [H]is professions of skepticism over her faithfulness are a cover story for a deeper conviction; a terrible doubt covering

a yet more terrible certainty, an unstatable certainty. But *this is what I have throughout kept arriving at as the cause of skepticism – the attempt to convert the human condition, the condition of humanity, into an intellectual difficulty, a riddle.* (To interpret "a metaphysical finitude as an intellectual lack.")[4] (DK, 138, italics added)

If these are the conditions and concerns that dominate Cavell's engagement with Shakespearean tragedy, then what of his work on romance? The question is especially important because romance has sometimes been thought of as occupying a place in the logic of Shakespearean drama that sets it beyond or after tragedy, as if romance were an aid in the recovery from tragedy. Indeed, Cavell helps to solidify the intuition that romances such as *The Winter's Tale* are written from a perspective that already knows of the devastations of tragedy and finds that there is still more to be said, thought, and felt. If tragedy provides Cavell with a basis for exploring the matter of skepticism and doubt, and if the "truth" of tragedy revolves around what it costs to avoid love and acknowledgment, then the first task of romance is to avoid a naive response to the conditions that tragedy works so hard to expose. To be sure, there are some who will keep on paying those costs of avoidance (all of us, perhaps, at certain times) by cultivating the false sense of mastery over the world that "knowledge" pretends to give. By contrast, romance of a "mature" sort takes place in full view of the problem of skepticism, and likewise in view of what skepticism may seek to avoid. But beyond skepticism, romance provides Cavell with a wide canvas for the exploration of issues that have to do with belief, including matters requiring extraordinary belief, such as revival, rebirth, and reawakening. Cavell's initial musings about such matters shift the question of a post-tragic awareness into a distinctively Freudian register:

Apart from any more general indebtedness of the romantics to Shakespeare, *The Winter's Tale* is particularly apt in relation to their themes of reawakening or revival, as for example entering into the figure of the six-year-old boy of Wordsworth's *Intimations* ode and the ode's idea of the adult's world as 'remains,' as of corpses. I associate this figure, especially in view of his difficulties over remembering, with Freud's report of a phobia in a five-year-old boy, partly simply to commemorate Freud's acknowledgment that he was preceded in his perceptions by the poets, more specifically because of Freud's consequent perception in this case of adult human life struggling toward happiness from within its own 'debris.' Now here at the end of *The Winter's Tale* a dead five- or six-year-old boy remains unaccounted for. (DK, 193)

Clearly, there are hopeful fantasies – wish-fulfillment dreams – that romance entertains: fantasies about the recovery of childhood, or of the recovery of innocence that goes with it. But in Cavell's reading there are also darker, tragic sides to romance, such that romance remains tinged with tragedy, and tragedy serves as "commentary" upon romance. Leontes from *The Winter's Tale* and Othello seem inevitably paired.

> Both plays involve a harrowing of the power of knowing the existence of another (as chaste, intact, as what the knower knows his other to be). Leontes refuses to believe a true oracle. Othello insists on believing a false one. Second, in both plays the consequence for the man's refusal of knowledge of his other is an imagination of stone. It is not merely an appetite for beauty that produces Othello's most famous image of his victim, as a piece of cold and carved marble (". . . whiter skin of hers than snow / And smooth, as monumental alabaster" [IV. ii. 4–5]). Where does his image come from? (DK, 125–6)

We know enough about Cavell's views concerning the fate of the body in skepticism to know something about the answer to this question in the case of *Othello*. But what about *The Winter's Take*? Here it is a case of asking what it is that Leontes avoids, and why; of probing the motives behind his jealousy, which is usually seen as itself the motive for what he does; and of asking about what his disowning or denial of knowledge might mean: "Why would the father fear being the true father of his children? One reason might be some problem of his with the idea that he has impregnated the mother, I mean of course the *son's* mother. Another might be that this would displace him in this mother's affection, and moreover that he would himself have to nurture that displacement. Another might be that this would ratify the displacement of his and his friend Polixenes' mutual love. . . ." (DK, 195). The matter goes beyond Leontes' denial of knowledge to his disowning his own issue. What Cavell in fact suggests is that Leontes disowns something that is "more fundamental than, or causes, his jealousy of his friend and brother rather than the other way around" (DK, 195).

While acknowledging his interest in the myth criticism of Northrop Frye in works such as *The Secular Scripture*, Cavell's approach to romance is hardly myth-critical in the conventional sense. And yet he does seem to ask us to recognize that we have not overcome myth, even to ask us to forsake the idea of ever overcoming it fully, and to acknowledge Shakespeare and Freud as the mythmakers whose work is indispensable to an understanding of the "modern age." They tell truths that otherwise might go unnoticed because they lie so deeply embedded, even buried, in our culture. Moreover, myth and romance provide the opportunity for Cavell to amplify some of the issues that run at a subsurface level throughout much of his other literary-critical work: the question of belief in relation to the fate of religion in modernity, and both of these in relation to a culture that has staked much of its claim on the possibility of finding epistemological answers to skepticism.

But it would be wrong to think that the recourse to or sympathy for myth (including the myths of psychoanalysis) provides Cavell with a key to the interpretation of the human condition – as if the stories of myth, some of which are recast in psychoanalysis and romance, offer us the master narratives in terms of which human lives ultimately make sense. Indeed, part of the reason to insist on the buried or "underground" nature of these myths is to suggest that our relationship to them is one of inaccessibility, or of incomplete or untimely accessibility. If these myths *were* fully accessible, then the problem of human existence would in the end be solvable, and skepticism would be brought to an end. But that is hardly Cavell's view. In it he finds support from a critic no less acute than Northrop Frye, whose remarks about virgin-baiting as sustaining a false idea of human integrity Cavell aptly adduces in the course of his reading of *Othello*. (Frye: "Deep within the stock convention of virgin-baiting is a vision of human integrity imprisoned in a world it is in but not of, often forced by weakness into all kinds of ruses and stratagems, yet always managing to avoid the one fate which really is worse than death, the annihilation of one's identity.")[5] Moreover, Cavell's reading of human culture as not having fully overcome myth calls into question the assumption that there is such "overcoming" to be had. Likewise, there is no reason to think that Cavell proposes a return to myth – or to romance – as a way to solve the problems that epistemology has left. No less than myth, tragedy and romance dramatize the fact that we are fated to move within the finite world, to make choices on the basis of knowledge that is bound to be partial, and to live with the awareness that we are finite and embodied creatures who may be incapable of knowing others in the ways that epistemology demands. To acknowledge these things may well be to recognize something greater, or truer, than what "knowledge" was meant to provide.

Notes

1. Stanley Cavell, *Disowning Knowledge in Six Plays of Shakespeare* (Cambridge: Cambridge University Press, 1987), p. 1. Further references to this book will be incorporated into the text as DK.

2. Mainly through the affinities between Shakespearean comedy, Roman "new comedy" and the subgenre of film that Cavell calls the Hollywood "comedies of remarriage."

3. Stanley Cavell, *The Claim of Reason: Wittgenstein, Skepticism, Morality, and Tragedy* (New York: Oxford University Press, 1979), p. 241.

4. Here Cavell cites himself, from the earlier essay in *Must We Mean What We Say?* entitled "Knowing and Acknowledging."

5. Northrop Frye, *The Secular Scripture* (Cambridge, MA: Harvard University Press, 1976), p. 86. Cavell cites this passage in DK, p. 130.

9 | Cavell on Film, Television, and Opera

WILLIAM ROTHMAN

Writing about movies has been strand over strand with Stanley Cavell's philosophical life, from *The World Viewed*, published between *Must We Mean What We Say?* and *The Senses of Walden*, to *Pursuits of Happiness: The Hollywood Comedy of Remarriage*, a companion piece to *The Claim of Reason*, to *Contesting Tears: Hollywood Melodramas of the Unknown Woman*, his most recent book about film. Film has also figured importantly in numerous other essays and occasional pieces. And he has also reflected, philosophically, on other artistic media, such as television and opera, which bear an intimate relationship to film.

Cavell is the only major American philosopher who has made the subject of film a central part of his work. Yet to many philosophers, the relation of his writings on film to his explicitly philosophical writings remains perplexing; and within the field of film study, the potential usefulness of philosophy – as he understands and practices it – remains generally unrecognized. It has long been one of Cavell's guiding intuitions that a marriage between philosophy and film is not only possible but also necessary. Over the years, his vision of such a marriage has been an unfailing source of inspiration for me, and for the authors whose writings about film I find most fruitful. What follows is an account, at times unavoidably sketchy, of some of the leading thoughts in Cavell's three books about film, in "The Fact of Television," and in "Opera and the Lease of Voice" (Chapter 3 of *A Pitch of Philosophy*) and the recent "Opera in and as Film." By providing such an account, I hope to illuminate, above all, why Cavell aspires to a marriage between philosophy and film, and how he achieves it.

THE WORLD VIEWED: REFLECTIONS ON THE ONTOLOGY OF FILM

The World Viewed incorporates reflections on diverse matters pertaining to the origins of film, its historical development, its characteristic genres, the myths and human types around which those genres revolve, the medium's ability (until recently) to employ unselfconsciously traditional techniques that tap naturally into the medium's powers, and so on. Although there are few of the remarks about philosophy everywhere to be found in *Must We Mean What We Say?*, philosophy is no less central to Cavell's brilliant and beautiful little book about film. *The World Viewed* declares that it is not possible to think seriously about film apart from philosophy, and that philosophy cannot avoid the subject of film.

The World Viewed begins by acknowledging that Cavell's "natural relation" to movies has been broken. In investigating his experience of film, his goal is not to restore the relation to movies that once came naturally, but to achieve a new philosophical relation to movies, to others, and to ourselves.

The World Viewed argues that movies project and screen reality rather than representing it, as (some) paintings do. The ontological difference between film and painting is a central theme that the book develops by addressing the mysterious relationship between a photograph and the thing(s) and/or person(s) in that photograph.

The mystery of photographs resides in their capacity to allow persons and things to reveal themselves, without human intervention. Yet it is misleading to suggest, as did André Bazin, that the automatism of the making of photographs enables them to satisfy painting's obsession with realism. This is because, first, painting's obsession was with reality, not realism. So far as photography satisfied a wish, it satisfied the human wish – intensifying in the West since the Reformation – to reach this world, to achieve selfhood, by escaping the metaphysical isolation to which our subjectivity has condemned us. "Apart from the wish for selfhood (hence the always simultaneous granting of otherness as well), I do not understand the value of art," Cavell writes.[1] Second, photographs are not more realistic than paintings. Realistic as opposed to what? Only what exists in the world can be subject to photography's displacements of things and people. But the world already bears the stamp of our fantasies.

The objects and persons projected on the movie screen *are* real. Yet they do not exist (now). The role reality plays in movies makes the world on film a moving image of skepticism, as Cavell puts it in "More of *The World Viewed*" (a lengthy addendum included in the 1979 enlarged edition), but the possibility of skepticism is internal to the conditions of human knowledge. That we do not know reality with certainty is a fact about what knowledge, for human beings, is. It does not follow that we cannot know the world, or ourselves in it.

To read *The World Viewed* in a way that acknowledges Cavell's philosophical perspective, though, one must free oneself from prejudicial theories as to how philosophy has to *look*. In an interview with James Conant, Cavell remarks that if you give up

> something like formal argumentation as the route to conviction in philosophy, and you give up the idea that either scientific evidence or poetic persuasion is the way to philosophical conviction, then the question of what achieves philosophical conviction must at all times be on your mind. . . . The sense that nothing other than this prose just here, as it's passing before our eyes, can carry conviction, is one of the thoughts that drives . . . what I do. Together with . . . the sense that . . . if there is any place at which the human spirit allows itself to be under its own question, it is in philosophy; that anything, indeed, that allows that questioning to happen *is* philosophy.[2]

A further key may be found in *Disowning Knowledge*, where Cavell observes that his readings work out his intuition that Shakespeare's plays interpret the skeptical problematic.

> In calling my guiding theme an intuition I am distinguishing it from a hypothesis. . . . An intuition . . . does not require, or tolerate, evidence but rather, let us say, understanding of a particular sort. . . . Emerson says in 'Self-Reliance': 'Primary wisdom [is] intuition, whilst all later teachings are tuitions.' He is accordingly called, not incorrectly, a philosopher of intuition. For some reason it is not typically noticed that he is at the same time a teacher of tuition. I read him as teaching that the occurrence to us of intuition places a demand upon us, namely for tuition; call this wording, the willingness to subject oneself to words, to make oneself intelligible.[3]

Cavell, too, may be called a philosopher of intuition, as long as we notice that he is also a teacher of "tuition." All of his writings seek both to exemplify the importance of intuition and to teach the discipline of finding words that lead to a certain sort of understanding.

One of *The World Viewed*'s guiding intuitions is that American Westerns, musicals, romantic comedies, and melodramas of the 1930s and 1940s, no less than European masterpieces such as Vigo's *L'Atalante* and Renoir's *Grand Illusion* and *The Rules of the Game*, are about the human need for society and the equal need to escape it, about privacy and unknownness, about the search for community. But a number of intuitions crucial to his later work had not yet occurred to Cavell: for example, that the combination of popularity and seriousness of American movies of the 1930s and 1940s was a function of their inheritance of concerns for society, for human relationship generally, in the works of Emerson and Thoreau. Nor had his own inheritance of their concerns fully dawned on him. Those intuitions awaited the publication (all in 1979) of his first essay on Emerson ("Thinking of Emerson"); his reading of *The Lady Eve*, a cornerstone of *Pursuits of Happiness*; and the monumental *The Claim of Reason*.

In *Pursuits of Happiness*, the intuition that Hollywood movies have inherited the concerns of American transcendentalism – conjoined with the intuition that he has, too – leads to the further intuition that Cavell's own philosophical procedures are underwritten by the ways in which American movies "think." Apart from the role Hollywood movies played in his education, how could this philosopher – who received his professional training within an Anglo-American analytical tradition that, like its Continental counterpart, has never acknowledged Emerson's writing as (simply) philosophy – have inherited Emerson's thinking at all?

Without achieving a perspective of self-reflection, one cannot acknowledge *The World Viewed*'s achievement of such a perspective. But there is no *system* for acquiring the requisite understanding. Attending to *The World Viewed*'s utterly specific words ("to this prose just here, as it's passing before our eyes") can be difficult. Without facing this difficulty, one cannot know what makes the book worth reading.

In "More of *The World Viewed*," Cavell acknowledges that even admirers of *Must We Mean What We Say?* have told him that *The World Viewed* is difficult to read. In accounting for its *special* difficulty, he writes, "I persist in the feeling asserted in the book's Preface, that its difficulty lies as much in the obscurity of its promptings as in its particular surfacings of expression" (WV, 162). In *Must We Mean What We Say?*, the procedures of ordinary language philosophy assure that what prompts each assertion is anything but obscure. In *The World Viewed*, too, every assertion claims to exemplify something that we too would or could say in his circumstances. But insofar as his assertions are prompted by memories of movies, we are not in Cavell's circumstances. Memories are private.

"A certain obscurity of prompting is not external to what I wished most fervently to say about film," Cavell suggests in "More of *The World Viewed*" (WV, 163). This remark's aptness can already be glimpsed in the obscure, fervent opening of *The World Viewed*'s Preface:

Memories of movies are strand over strand with memories of my life. During the quarter of a century . . . in which going to the movies was a normal part of my week, it would no more have occurred to me to write a study of movies than to write my autobiography. Having completed the pages that follow, I feel that I have been composing a kind of metaphysical memoir – not the story of a period of my life but an account of the conditions it has satisfied. (WV, xix)

What prompts this paragraph is the entirety of the book that it opens, the book whose completion it announces, the book its author has made out of material he has woven, strand over strand, from memories of movies and memories of his life. Placed at the beginning, not the end, how can it not be obscure in its promptings?

What prompts this paragraph also prompts the entirety of *The World Viewed*: the book's subject, film. The paragraph's "obscure promptings" cannot be separated from what the book is about, in other words. *The World Viewed* is about film, its singularly obscure subject. It is also about film's singular obscurity. What prompts its writing, what the book is about, cannot be separated from what this writing *is*, the material out of which it is made. This fact about its writing, "More of *The World Viewed*" suggests, accounts for the book's special difficulty, its special challenges and rewards.

In this metaphysical memoir, Cavell commemorates a world of movies and moviegoing that has slipped into memory. The final paragraph at once closes the book on his "natural relation" to movies and raises the writing to its highest plane. "A world complete without me which is present to me is the world of my immortality," the paragraph begins (WV, 160). That immortality "is an importance of film – and a danger." Viewing from outside, we haunt the world on film, rather than staking our existence within it. But no harm could come from haunting the world on film were it not for the massive way in which we involve movies in our lives.

If we accept the world on film as complete without us, and accept it *as* the world, we also accept that there *is* no world apart from the world on film, that the world complete without us, the world we haunt, is the one existing world. So he has reason, Cavell confesses, to want his "natural relation" to film to be broken, to want the world of movies and moviegoing, whose loss *The World Viewed* mourns, to be past. Without recanting this confession, the book's final words enable a new aspect to dawn. "There is equal reason to want it affirmed that the world is coherent without me. That is essential to what I want of immortality: nature's survival of me. It will mean that the present judgment upon me is not yet the last." (WV, 160)

It is a central thrust of *The World Viewed* that what movies have always promised, their way of "speaking the being of the world directly," is as much as ever to be wished for, and that it is still possible for film's promise – letting the world and its children achieve their candidness – to be kept. Cavell wants film to affirm, specifically, that nature has survived *him*, has survived his turnings away from nature, from his own nature. If nature has survived his violence and betrayals, that means that human nature has survived. It is not yet too late for him, for us, to reach this world and achieve selfhood. That this possibility still exists means, as the final line of *The World Viewed* puts it, that "the present judgment upon me" – the judgment he has brought upon himself by writing this book, the judgment he has brought upon the world, the judgment the world has brought upon itself – "is not yet the last" (WV, 160). The Last Judgment is not yet at hand.

At the end of Carl Dreyer's *Passion of Joan of Arc*, Joan, at the stake, sees a flock of birds wheeling above her. She knows that, in Cavell's words, "[t]hey are waiting, in their freedom, to accompany her soul" (WV, 159). Knowing that these birds will survive her, Joan knows that nature will survive her. Flames are consuming her body, but she knows that she too is free.

For years, going to the movies was a normal part of Cavell's week, as it was for millions of Americans. The breaking of his "natural relation" to movies seems so particular to Cavell, *The World Viewed* makes clear, because he is the one prompted by that loss to write this book, to achieve a philosophical perspective on the loss that it mourns. He is the one who must now fall silent in order to acknowledge that he is outside this writing, as he was outside the world on film. That is, these words, which give voice to his experience of movies, are complete without him, autonomous, free to acknowledge the reality of the unsayable.

That is Cavell's faith.

PURSUITS OF HAPPINESS

In *The Postman Always Rings Twice* and *Double Indemnity*, Cavell remarks in *The World Viewed*, "the lovers die because they have killed, but also [because] they transgress the deeper law against combining sex and marriage. In a thousand other instances the marriage must not be seen, and the walk into the sunset is into a dying star: they live happily ever after – as long as they keep walking." (WV, 48)

Tellingly, Cavell invokes Thoreau's image, in the punning last sentence of *Walden*, of "the sun as but a morning [and *mourning*] star." For *Walden*'s writer, the morning of mourning, the dawning of grieving, is the only alternative to what he calls "our present constitution," which must end.[4] Movies that end with a man and woman abandoned to a sexless marriage do not make explicit the necessity to transform ourselves that Thoreau insists upon. In *The World Viewed*, the invocation of the thousand movie couples walking into the sunset provides the penultimate image of a paragraph that culminates by singling out *The Philadelphia Story* and *The Awful Truth* as instances of films in which "the marriage is established from the beginning and is worth having at the end" (WV, 49). It is hardly an exaggeration to say that all of *Pursuits of Happiness* can be glimpsed in *The World Viewed*'s inspired gesture of linking *The Philadelphia Story* and *The Awful Truth* – prominent members of the genre of romantic comedy that Cavell will come to call "the comedy of remarriage" – to the culminating image of Thoreau's *Walden*.

In *Pursuits of Happiness*, Cavell singles out seven films of the 1930s and 1940s that he takes to be definitive remarriage comedies – *It Happened One Night*, *The Awful Truth*, *Bringing Up Baby*, *His Girl Friday*, *The Lady Eve*, *The Philadelphia Story*, and *Adam's Rib*. Remarriage comedies recount a story or myth that hinges on the romance of a woman and a man who arrive at happiness not by overcoming social obstacles to their love, as in a classical comedy, but by facing divorce and coming back together.

Cavell understands the women of these films, played by the likes of Katharine Hepburn, Claudette Colbert, Irene Dunne, and Barbara Stanwyck, to be on a spiritual quest, like Emerson in his journals or the author in Thoreau's *Walden*. A non-American source that Cavell cites is Nora in Ibsen's *A Doll's House*. Nora leaves her husband in search of an education that he says she needs, but that she knows he cannot provide. Unlike Nora, the woman in a remarriage comedy is lucky that her once and future husband is a man, a Cary Grant or a Spencer Tracy, with the capacity to embrace her creation as a new woman. She is also lucky to have a father who, unlike the woman's father in classical comedy, wishes to award her to a man who really loves her, a modern hero to whom she might freely award herself.

Hollywood remarriage comedies of the 1930s and 1940s, *Pursuits of Happiness* claims, exemplify a stage in the development of the consciousness of women at which what is at issue is a mutual acknowledgment of the equality – without denying their difference – of the sexes. The films' criteria for what makes a marriage worth having – mutual trust and desire, as reflected in the quality of the couple's conversation – have nothing to do with perpetuating the patriarchal line. Nothing outside the marriage – not church, or state, or society's need for children – is capable of validating the exemplary marriage that the genre envisions, a marriage between a woman and a man that also "marries" the realities of the day and the dreams of the night, the public and the private, and city and country. This last point is registered in the genre's insistence that the man and woman at a certain moment find themselves in a location conducive to a new perspective. Shakespearean criticism calls this the Green World, and it is typically located, like Walden Pond, just outside a major city. Remarriage comedies usually call this place Connecticut. "Connecticut" here means a perspective that discovers happiness in our lives here and now, a perspective attained by living every day and night in a spirit of adventure.

Each chapter of *Pursuits Happiness* presents what Cavell calls a "reading" of one comedy of remarriage. These readings are guided by two claims. The first is that these films constitute a genre. The second is that this genre inherits the preoccupations of late Shakespearean romance (*The Winter's Tale, The Tempest*).

The first of these claims concerns logical connections among the films of the genre, the second their origins or sources. In specifying features of the genre, Cavell's readings at the same time concern themselves with matters that we might think of as historical. For the genre's historical origins, and how film transforms the genre's sources, are matters *internal* to the genre. How film transforms classical comedy reveals something about what remarriage comedies are, what film genres are, what films are, what film is.

To put it in *The World Viewed*'s terms, the comedy of remarriage is one of film's artistic media. The genre's material basis is film's material basis. In turn, the range of film's artistic possibilities is available to members of the genre, which are also bound by film's *necessities*. In *The World Viewed*, it is a leading idea that each possibility of a medium is what it is only in view of all its other possibilities. Like a language (in which, Emerson and Thoreau claim, each word is what it is only in view of all the other words of the language), and like a world (in which "nothing less than everything is new in a new period"), a medium is a *whole* (WV, 47).

Pursuits of Happiness develops this idea when it asserts that instances of a genre do not share a set of features that can in principle be completely specified. We may say that they share *every* feature, so long as we remember, first, that what counts as a feature is not determinable apart from critical analysis and second, that a member may account for a feature's apparent absence by articulating a compensating circumstance. (*It Happened One Night* compensates for lacking a Green World, for example, by the role played by the couple's being on the road.) Cavell prefers to think of a genre's members as versions of a story or myth, or as sharing "the inheritance of certain conditions, procedures, and subjects and goals of composition." Each member *studies* those conditions, interprets them, revises the ways in which they have been interpreted, and thereby earns membership in the genre by bearing the *responsibility* of its inheritance.[5]

Pursuits of Happiness specifies certain of the features – certain of the clauses of the story, certain of the conditions, procedures, and subjects and goals of composition – that remarriage comedies share. But what Cavell takes a genre of film to be is also a matter that receives specification. What a genre of film is, *Pursuits of Happiness* claims, is a matter internal to what remarriage comedies are, internal to what film is. What a reading of a film is, too, is such a matter.

These last two facts bring home two further facts. First, although *Pursuits of Happiness* rarely refers to *The World Viewed*, it takes as its starting point, and develops further, that book's reflections on the ontology of film. Second, *Pursuits of Happiness*, like *The World Viewed*, has a self-reflective dimension. What these readings enable us to know about film cannot be separated from what they enable us to know about themselves, about readings of films, about this writing. Not coincidentally, remarriage comedies, as they emerge in Cavell's readings, themselves possess a self-reflective dimension.

In *The World Viewed*, Cavell argues that on film it is the human condition to be embodied, hence that film's emphasis on the bodies of women reveals that the medium singles women out as exemplars of the human, not that it systematically objectifies women. This idea is further developed in *Pursuits of Happiness*, where Cavell insists that each comedy has a way of "harping on the identity of the real woman cast in [the film], and each by way of some doubling or splitting of her projected presence" (PH, 64). This doubling or splitting is at once the narrative's emphasis on the heroine's identity and "an emphasis taken by the cinematic medium on the physical presence, that is, the photographic presence, of the real actress playing this part, an emphasis that demands . . . some occasion for displaying or suggesting the naked body of the woman to the extent the Production Code will allow" (PH, 140). And each comedy also finds a way to declare that its own attention to the splitting or doubling of the woman's projected presence is itself split or doubled.

For example, the sequence in *The Lady Eve* in which Jean (Barbara Stanwyck) first lays eyes on Hopsy (Henry Fonda) virtually identifies the images on the screen with the images she sees in a mirror. "One plausible understanding of our view as Jean holds her hand mirror up to nature – or to society – . . . is that we are looking through the viewfinder of a camera," Cavell writes. "We are informed that this film knows itself to have been written and directed and photographed and edited. (Each of our films shows its possession of this knowledge of itself. *The Lady Eve* merely insists upon it most persistently.)" (PH, 66) Cavell claims that *The Lady Eve* presents the man as a stand-in for the viewer, the woman a stand-in for the director, and that "as this surrogate she informs us openly that the attitude of the film begins with is one of cynicism or skepticism." By the end of the film, however, this skeptical woman/artist becomes a member of the man's species, "the sucker sapiens, the wise fool; she has found what Katharine Hepburn at the end of *The Philadelphia Story* calls a human being; she has created herself, turned herself, not without some help, into a woman."

The Lady Eve thus emerges as a story about a woman's (or a couple's) overcoming or transcending of skepticism. This helps us appreciate Cavell's observation, in *Contesting Tears*, that looking back he sometimes sees "the issuing of *Pursuits of Happiness* as an expression of the relief in completing the study of skepticism and tragedy in *The Claim of Reason* (1979)."[6]

The Claim of Reason's culminating reading of *Othello* fleshes out Cavell's discovery of the affinity between Cartesian skepticism and its near-contemporary, Shakespearean tragedy – as if what philosophy interprets as skepticism *is* what Elizabethan theater interprets as tragedy. Shakespeare's late romances discover within the conditions of Elizabethan theater a way of overcoming or transcending skepticism and thereby of avoiding a tragic fate whose possibility is inherent in the condition of being human. In inheriting – but also transforming, for film is not theater – the preoccupations and discoveries of Shakespearean romance, remarriage comedies discover their own ways – ways that film makes possible – of overcoming or transcending skepticism.

Cavell writes, in *Pursuits of Happiness:*

> It is not news for men to try, as Thoreau puts it, to walk in the direction of their dreams, to join the thoughts of day and night, of the public and the private, to pursue happiness. Nor is it news that this will require a revolution, of the social or of the individual constitution, or both. What is news is the acknowledgment that a woman might attempt this direction, even that a man and a woman might try it together.... For this we require a new creation of woman, call it a creation of the new woman.... It is a new step in the creation of the human. (PH, 140)

Calling upon us to embrace their "romantic flights of fantasy," comedies of remarriage declare their own participation – declare film's participation – in this revolutionary enterprise. Is not this news, too? The genre that *Pursuits of Happiness* studies is committed to a philosophical way of thinking that affirms the possibility, and necessity, of radical change. Cavell, too, is committed to such a philosophy. Hence it is one of his book's pivotal moments when Cavell identifies the Cary Grant figure in *The Philadelphia Story* as a philosopher. Part therapist, part Emersonian sage, he is Stanley Cavell's kind of philosopher.

Remarriage comedies affirm truths about the world, and about film, that Cavell himself affirms. And, in holding these truths to be self-evident, Cavell understands himself to be representative of the films' audience. Hence the special charm of the readings that comprise *Pursuits of Happiness* – the sense that their author is enjoying a conversation with the reader as "meet and happy" as the conversations in a marriage worth having (even as the films, as they emerge in these readings, enjoy such conversations with their – our – culture).

Nonetheless, Cavell anticipates that these readings will encounter resistance. For the comedies that *Pursuits of Happiness* addresses are (mostly) assumed to be nothing more than escapist fairy tales for the Depression. And movie genres are (mostly) assumed to be nothing more than formulas. But Cavell is claiming that the films may themselves "be up to reflecting on what it is that causes them, hence that they have some bearing, for instance, on our experience and understanding of the Depression." "We seem fated to distort the good films closest to us, exemplified by the seven concentrated on in this book," he writes in a splendid passage.

> Their loud-mouthed inflation by the circus advertising of Hollywood is nicely matched by their thin-lipped deflation by those who cannot imagine that products of the Hollywood studio system could in principle rival the exports of revolutionary Russia, of Germany, and of France. This view... expresses, it feeds on, a pervasive conflict suffered by Americans about their own artistic accomplishments, a conflict I have described elsewhere as America's overpraising and undervaluing of those of its accomplishments it does not ignore. (PH, 39)

But something beyond that conflict keeps the good films closest to us inaccessible as food for thought. Remarriage comedies are films that many

> bear in their experience as memorable public events, segments of the experience, the memories, of a common life. So that the difficulty of assessing them is the same as the difficulty of assessing everyday experience, the difficulty of... making oneself find the words for what one is specifically interested to say, which comes to the difficulty of finding the right to be thus interested.... This poses... the specific difficulty of philosophy and calls upon its particular strength, to receive inspiration for taking thought from the very conditions that oppose thought. (PH, 41–2)

Each reading in *Pursuits of Happiness* is at once an interpretation of a *film* and an account of Cavell's *experience* of a film, at once criticism and philosophy, at once an experiential and a conceptual undertaking that requires a commitment to being "guided by our experience but not dictated to by it," to letting "the object or the work of your interest teach you how to consider it," to subjecting a given experience and its object "to the test of one another," and to educating "your experience sufficiently so that it is worthy of trust." The philosophical catch: the education cannot be achieved in advance of the trusting. (PH, 10)

In his reading of *It Happened One Night*, for example, Cavell finds the film to be about hungering, where "hungering is a metaphor for imagining, in particular imagining a better, or more satisfying, way to live." Is Frank Capra seriously to be thought of as taking the occasion of the Depression "to ask what we as a people are truly depressed by, what hunger it is from which we all are faint? And wouldn't that be like saying 'Man does not live by bread alone' to a man in a breadline?" (PH, 6) Cavell's answer is worth quoting at length.

> Around the middle of *Walden* Thoreau shows himself offended by the impoverished, inefficient lives of a certain John Field and his family.... I do not know that this passage takes upon itself a greater hardness ... than Emerson's saying in "Self-Reliance," as he pictures himself going off to write, "Do not tell me, as a good man did to-day, of my obligation to put all poor men in good situations. Are they *my* poor?" That is, it is not I who make them and who keep them poor; and so far as I can better the situation of whoever is poor, I can do it only by answering my genius when it calls. But to give that sort of answer one must have a healthy respect for the value of one's work, let us say for its powers of instruction and redemption. (PH, 6-7)

"Is it obvious," Cavell asks, "that the makers of the films we will read through are in principle not entitled to such claims for their work?"

> These films *can* be appropriated ... as fairy tales rather than, let us say, as spiritual parables. But so can Scripture ... ; so can Emerson and Thoreau; so can Marx and Nietzsche and Freud. But from what better writers can one learn, or have companionship in knowing, that to take an interest in an object is to take an interest in one's experience of the object, so that to examine and defend my interest in these films is to examine and defend my interest in my own experience. (PH, 7)

In order to give that sort of answer, Cavell too must have a healthy respect for his own work's powers of instruction and redemption. Is it obvious that the author of *Pursuits of Happiness* is in principle not entitled to such claims for his work?

"THE FACT OF TELEVISION"

In 1982, the year in which *Pursuits of Happiness* was published, Cavell was asked to contribute to an issue of *Daedalus* devoted to television. The resulting essay, "The Fact of Television," begins by observing that television, like the electric light, the automobile, and the telephone, has "conquered." Yet there has been a lack of critical attention to television too complete to be a simple lack of interest; it is a *refusal* of interest. The disapproval of television evinced in educated circles suggests a *fear* of television for which Cavell has heard no credible explanation.

Although he too has sometimes felt such disapproval of television, Cavell cannot accept the view that the medium has not yet come of age, or that it is inherently impoverished. He argues that television's "poverty" lies in our failure to grasp "what the medium is for, what constitutes its powers and its treasures."[7]

It is a guiding thesis of *The World Viewed* that major films are those in which the medium is most richly or deeply revealed. In the case of television, however, revelation of the medium is not primarily the business of the individual work, this episode of *I Love Lucy*, but of *I Love Lucy* itself, the program as such, the *format*.

Most film critics think of a genre as a category whose criteria for membership are as unproblematic as the exemplification of a serial in its episodes. Cavell calls this way of thinking about genre "genre-as-cycle," and contrasts it with *Pursuits of Happiness*'s way of thinking about genre, which he here calls "genre-as-medium."

When a remarriage comedy diverges from the other members of the genre, it compensates for this divergence. The genre undergoes revision as new members introduce new points of compensation. When other films *negate* a feature shared by a genre's members, those films comprise an "adjacent" genre. Compensation and negation, however, are not pertinent to genre-as-cycle, or to the serial – episode relationship. The episodes of a sitcom exemplify a format that can be unproblematically called a formula. But in a film genre like the remarriage comedy, "what you might call the formula, or what in *Pursuits of Happiness* I call the myth, is itself under investigation, or generation, by the instances" (TOS, 248).

If film as an artistic medium is primarily revealed by a genre-member mode of composition, and television primarily by a serial-episode mode, this difference must reflect a difference between their material bases. *The World Viewed* characterizes film's material basis – what it is apart from which there would be nothing to call a movie, as without color on a delimited two-dimensional support there would be nothing to call a painting – as a "succession of automatic world projections" (WV, 72). "The Fact of Television" characterizes television's material basis as a "current of simultaneous event receptions" (TOS, 251). The intimacy of the difference between these formulations registers Cavell's sense of the intimacy of the difference, hence affinity, between film and television. This intimacy is reflected, as well, in the difference, and affinity, between viewing, the mode of perception that film calls for, and "monitoring," the mode that television calls for. ("The mysterious sets or visual fields, in our houses, for our private lives, are to be seen not as receivers, but as monitors" [TOS, 252].) Television's successful formats – the sitcoms, game shows, sports, talk shows, news, weather reports, specials, and so on – are, he argues, "revelations (acknowledgments) of the conditions of monitoring" (TOS, 252).

A notable feature of such formats, Cavell notes, is the amount of talk they incorporate.

> This is an important reason . . . for the . . . descriptions of television as providing 'company.' But what does this talk signify, how does it in particular signify that one is not alone; or anyway, that being alone is not unbearable? Partly . . . this is a function of the simultaneity of the medium, or of the fact that at any time it might be live and that there is no sensuous distinction between the live and the repeat, or the replay; the others are *there*, if not shut in this room, still caught at this time. One is receiving or monitoring them, like callers. (TOS, 253)

Each format for talk incorporates opportunities for improvisation, hence preserves the quality of the live that seemed threatened when television switched to primarily taped production. The exchanges of pleasantries that have become common on news shows, for example, demonstrate that "our news is still something that can humanly be responded to, in particular, responded to by the human power of improvisation" (TOS, 256). But, Cavell wonders, what news "may be so terrible that we will accept such mediocre evidence of this power as reassuring?"

Before answering this question, Cavell ponders the fact that television monitors the *uneventful* (the repeated, the repetitive, the utterly familiar) as readily as it monitors events. Each television format can be thought of as "the establishing of a stable condition punctuated by repeated crises or events that are not developments of the situation requiring a single resolution, but intrusions or emergencies . . . each of which runs a natural course and thereupon rejoins the realm of the uneventful" (TOS, 258). A tree branch, viewed on a movie screen, is in the world, *The World Viewed* argues; the world is in the viewed branch, in "*that* thing *now*, in the frame of nature" (WV, 200). But the world is not in a *monitored* branch, "whose movement is now either an event (if, say, you are watching for a sign of wind) or a mark of the uneventful (a sign that the change has not yet come)" (TOS, 259).

But, again, what change would be so fearful that we turn to television for reassurance that it has not yet happened?

Television's "conquering" began just after the Second World War, Cavell reminds us – just after "the discovery of concentration camps and the atomic bomb," the discovery of "the literal possibility that human life . . . is *willing* to destroy itself" (TOS, 266–7). And it continued with "the decline of our cities and the increasing fear of walking out at night, producing the present world of shut-ins." What television monitors is often a setting of the shut-in, "a reference line of normality or banality so insistent as to suggest that *what* is shut out, that suspicion whose entry we would at all costs guard against, must be as monstrous as . . . the death of the normal, of the familiar as such."

Cavell's guiding hypothesis, then, is that we seek the "company" of television to "overcome the anxiety of the intuition the medium embodies" (TOS, 267). The fear large or pervasive enough to account for our fear of television, according to his hypothesis, is the fear that what television monitors is "the growing uninhabitability of the world, the irreversible pollution of the earth, a fear displaced from the world onto its monitor. This is a hypothesis the concluding paragraph of *The World Viewed* prepares for by intimating that the breaking of our "natural relation" to movies may spell the end of film's ability to reassure us that nature will survive our turning away from nature, from our own nature.

The real possibility that nature will not survive us, hence that our anxiety may well have a fitting object, in Cavell's view, does not rule out a "psychological etiology for our anxiety, say in guilt, toward that same object." And he ends "The Fact of Television" with an expression of guarded optimism.

> Who knows? – if the monitor picked up on better talk, and probed for intelligible connections and for beauty among its events, it might alleviate our paralysis, our pride in adaptation, our addiction to a solemn destiny, sufficiently to help us allow ourselves to do something intelligent about its cause. (TOS, 268)

That would mean, to paraphrase the ending of *The World Viewed*, that the present judgment upon us is not yet the last.

CONTESTING TEARS

"Is it true in movies that virtue is always rewarded and vice vanquished?" Cavell asks in *The World Viewed* (WV, 48). Someone who draws the morals of movies too hastily might assume that movies condemn the "woman outside" for luring men to stray. Yet such a woman is "outside" because she rejects a marriage that would deny her nature, not because she is unworthy. It is a crucial datum in pondering the morals of movies that in films it is a moral imperative to pursue happiness. What Cavell discovered, in discovering this, is the depth of film's commitment to what his later writings will call "moral perfectionism." In *The World Viewed*, it is already a central theme that there is a serious moral philosophy internal to the stories that movies are forever telling. In *Pursuits of Happiness*, Cavell does not yet use the term "perfectionism," but that way of thinking about morality is an implicit subject throughout. It becomes an explicit (if still unnamed) subject when he invokes Matthew Arnold's idea of the "best self" existing in each of us.

> [M]ore natures are curious about their best self than one might imagine, and this curiosity Arnold calls the pursuit of perfection. "Natures with this bent," Arnold says, "emerge in all classes . . . and this bent tends to take them out of their class, and to make their distinguishing characteristic not their Barbarianism or their Philistinism, but their *humanity*." (PH, 157–8)

Cavell understands perfectionism not as a theory of morality but as "a dimension or tradition of the moral life."[8] His goal is to develop what he calls "an open-ended thematics" of perfectionism, not a theory or a definition of the idea. "That there is no closed list of features that constitute perfectionism follows from conceiving of perfectionism as . . . embodied in a set of texts spanning the range of Western culture" (CHU, 4).

A Doll's House is one. Nora's "imagination of her future, in leaving, turns on her sense of her need for education whose power of transformation presents itself to her as the chance to become human. In Emerson's terms, this is moving to claim one's humanness . . . , to follow the unattained" (CHU, 115). Moral perfectionism is as internal to comedies of remarriage as it is to Shakespeare's late romances, Emerson's and Thoreau's writings, *A Doll's House*, and to *Pursuits of Happiness* itself.

Cavell most fully develops the theme of a woman's rejecting marriage in order to "follow the unattained" in *Contesting Tears: The Hollywood Melodrama of the Unknown Woman*. In the films that the book "reads" – *Gaslight, Letter from an Unknown Woman, Now, Voyager,* and *Stella Dallas* – the woman seeks fulfilment outside marriage. Marriage is not reconceived and provisionally affirmed; marriage is overcome or transcended.

In comedies of remarriage, it is the man who claims the woman; he needs only prodding, while she needs to undergo a metamorphosis; and the woman's mother is absent, her absence underscored both by her father's role and by the fact that the woman herself is not a mother. In short, the creation of the woman is the business of men, even though the creation is that of the so-called new woman, the woman of equality – as if there were a taint of villainy inherent in maleness. "This so to speak prepares the genre for its inner relation to melodrama," Cavell remarks in his Introduction to *Contesting Tears*, where he points out that *Pursuits of Happiness* predicted the discovery of a genre of melodrama adjacent to the comedy of remarriage in which that genre's themes are negated in a way that hinges on the threats of misunderstanding and violence that dog the happiness of the comedies. (CT, 5)

It is a claim central to *Contesting Tears* that the genre therein called the Melodrama of the Unknown Woman is derived from the remarriage comedy by the mechanism of negation. For example, in these melodramas

> the woman's father, or another older man (it may be her husband), is not on the side of her desire but on the side of law, and her mother is always present (or her search for or loss of or competition with a mother is always present), and she is always shown as a mother (or her relation to a child is explicit).... [I]n the comedies the past is open, shared, a recurring topic of fun, no doubt somewhat ambiguous; but in melodramas the past is frozen, mysterious, with topics forbidden and isolating. Again, whereas in remarriage comedy the action of the narration moves ... from a setting in a big city to conclude in a place outside the city, a place of perspective, in melodramas of unknownness the action returns to and concludes in a place from which it began or in which it has climaxed, a place of abandonment or transcendence. (CT, 5–6)

In both genres, the woman's goal is creation. But in the melodramas, she "achieves existence (or fails to), apart from or beyond satisfaction by marriage (of a certain kind) and with the presence of her mother and of her children, where something in her language must be as traumatic ... as the conversation of marriage is for her comedic sisters – perhaps it will be an aria of divorce, from husband, lover, mother, or child" (CT, 117). The "something" in her language that negates the conversation of the pair in remarriage comedy is *irony*. Irony isolates the woman. That is one reason Cavell characterizes the genre as studying the *unknownness* of the woman.

The World Viewed claims that the most significant films are those that most significantly reveal the medium of film. *Pursuits of Happiness* develops this claim by arguing that comedies of remarriage reveal film's power of transfiguration, as expressed in the woman's suffering creation, where this refers both to the character's metamorphosis and to the transfiguration of the flesh-and-blood actress into projections of herself on a screen.

Contesting Tears develops the claim further by reflecting on the fact that the Melodrama of the Unknown Woman registers the woman's transfiguration less by revealing her body than by tracing its changes of costume and circumstance. Whatever role such a woman chooses to play at a given moment, in playing that role she declares that her identity is not fixed. And she declares that in this role she is, and is not, herself, with that "flair for theater, that theater of flair, exaggeration it may be thought, call it melodrama," that these films require of their leading women. Their star quality resides not in their beauty but in their "dangerous wish for perfect expressiveness," their flair for declaring their distinctness, their freedom, their human *existence* (CT, 128). This last point registers Cavell's intuition that these women emblematize the fact about human identity that "every single description of the self that is true is false, is, in a word, or a name, ironic" (CT, 134). So "one may take the subject of the genre of the unknown woman as the irony of human identity as such" (CT, 134–5).

In his Introduction to *Contesting Tears,* Cavell describes both the remarriage comedies and the melodramas of unknownness as "working out the problematic of self-reliance and conformity as established in the founding American thinking of Emerson and of Thoreau" (CT, 9). In an earlier essay ("Being Odd, Getting Even"), Cavell linked Emerson's idea of self-reliance with the self-consciousness demanded in the Cartesian *cogito ergo sum* (I think, therefore I am), Descartes's answer to philosophical skepticism.[9] Emerson's work, that essay claimed, proposes a new proof of human existence. And it linked Emerson's revision of Descartes's *cogito* to melodramas like *Now, Voyager.*

The Melodrama of the Unknown Woman, *Contesting Tears* argues, is an expression of a stage in the development of the skeptical problematic at which the theatricalization of the self becomes the main proof of the self's existence. And the book develops this suggestion further by linking the invention of film with the simultaneous emergence of psychoanalysis. While men in movies primarily appear in contexts of mutual competition and of uniform or communal efforts, as *The World Viewed* had argued, it is individual women who have given film its depth. It is as if the role of women in originating both psychoanalysis and film – in psychoanalysis as suffering subjects, in film as subjects of the camera – reveals that by the turn of the twentieth century, psychic reality – the existence of minds – had become believable primarily in its feminine aspect. A melodramatic star such as Bette Davis reveals the affinity between film's interest in the "difference of women" and that of psychoanalysis, insofar as she

> taps a genius for that expressiveness . . . in which Breuer and Freud, in their *Studies in Hysteria*, first encountered the reality of the unconscious, the reality of the human mind as what is unconscious to itself, and encountered first in the suffering of women; a reality whose expression they determined as essentially theatrical, a theatricality of the body as such. (CT, 105)

In remarriage comedies, the woman's happiness depends on her choosing the right man to educate her. The Melodrama of the Unknown Woman, too, presses the question of the woman's interest in knowledge, but "within their mood of heavy irony, since her knowledge becomes the object – as prize or as victim – of the man's fantasy, who seeks to share its secrets (*Now, Voyager*), to be ratified by it (*Letter from an Unknown Woman*), to escape it (*Stella Dallas*), or to destroy it (*Gaslight*), where each objective is (generically) reflected in the others" (CT, 13–4).

In remarriage comedies, the "war between the sexes" is a struggle for mutual recognition. In the Melodrama of the Unknown Woman, the man struggles *against* recognizing the woman. The woman's struggle, as Cavell puts it, "is to understand why recognition by the man has not happened or has been denied or has become irrelevant, hence may be thought of as a struggle or argument (with herself) over her gender" (CT, 30). In each melodrama, the woman, unrecognized, isolated, is torn not simply over the conflicting desires or demands between being a mother and being a woman, say, but over questions "as to what a mother does and what a woman is, what a mother has to teach, what a woman has to learn, whether her talent is for work or rather for the appreciation of work, whether romance is agreeable or marriage is refusable, how far idiosyncracy is manageable" (CT, 198).

Early and late in "Stella's Taste," the final essay in *Contesting Tears*, there are moments of autobiography, as we might put it, that construct a bridge to *A Pitch of Philosophy*, Cavell's next book, where he takes autobiographical expression further than ever before in his work. Here is the first of these moments:

> When my mother asked for an opinion from my father and me about a new garment or ornament she had on, a characteristic form she gave her

question was, "Too Stella Dallas?" The most frequent scene of the question was our getting ready to leave the apartment for the Friday night movies, by far the most important, and reliable, source of common pleasure for the three of us. I knew even then, so I seem always to have remembered it, that my mother's reference to Stella Dallas was not to a figure from whom she was entirely dissociating herself. (CT, 200)

In this passage, Cavell all but explicitly declares that his reading is guided by an intuition of his mother's, by his intuition of her intuition, his recollection of knowing, even as a boy, that she identified with Stella. The (male) voice that "speaks" in this writing is attuned to his mother's way of thinking – and to Stella's.

Thus this moment of autobiography is pertinent to what Cavell calls a "presiding question" in his writing about film melodramas and comedies: whether a male voice such as his is "well taken into a conversation with women" on the issues he finds raised in such films (CT, 200). This question of the pertinence of the male voice, as it emerges in "Stella's Taste," is a way of articulating the subject of *Stella Dallas* (and hence of each of the Melodramas of the Unknown Woman).

In his reading of *Now, Voyager* in *Contesting Tears*, Cavell anticipates – and contests – the charge that he appropriates, or wishes to appropriate, Charlotte Vale's voice. But why is it only now, writing the book's final chapter, that he finds himself "willing to confront more systematically the provenance and pertinence" of *his own voice* in these matters? (CT, 200) He attributes this willingness, or links it, to his "willingness for taking further steps in autobiographical expression" – the mode in which, he is increasingly convinced, his "encounter with feminism must take place."

It is in the context of his questioning of the pertinence of his own (male) voice in thinking about *Stella Dallas* – and his linking of this question to the question of autobiography's pertinence to philosophy – that Cavell mounts a devastating brief against the theory – it is all but a dogma within academic film study – that "film seems to be the perfect agent for generalizing the Freudian fetishistic process, extending it to the masculine gender as such – a generalizing ratified somehow by taking on at the same time a Marxian development of the idea of the universal commodification (in capitalist society) of women" (CT, 207–8). According to this theory, Freud's concept of fetishism explains Stella's victimization and utter lack of self-knowledge, and confirms an essentially male stake in viewing a film such as *Stella Dallas*. Cavell contests this fashionable theory, first, because the film itself contests a fixed view of the woman's victimization, and second, because "the details of Freud's description of fetishization do not account for what becomes of things and persons on film" (CT, 209).

The second of Cavell's arguments amounts to the idea

> that film assaults human perception at a more primitive level than the work of fetishizing suggests; that film's enforcement of passiveness, or say victimization, together with its animation of the world, entertains a region not of invitation or fascination primarily to the masculine nor even, yet perhaps closer, to the feminine, but primarily to the infantile, before the establishment of human gender. (CT, 209)

Up to this point in *Contesting Tears*, Cavell has formulated the subject of the Melodrama of the Unknown Woman as the irony of human identity, and alternatively, as the question of the pertinence of the male voice. Having now insisted on the dimension of infantilization in the viewing of film, and in light of *Stella Dallas*'s closing (Stella looks through the lit window behind which her daughter's wedding is taking place, then turns away from that window and jauntily walks toward us), Cavell further articulates the genre's subject: "Stella's gaze before the window, as the camera gives it to us, is the mother's, backed by mothers; and as Stella turns to walk toward us, her gaze, transforming itself, looms toward us, as if the screen is looming, its gaze *just* turned away, always to be searched for. (For what it grants; for what it wants.)" (CT, 216)

Thus Cavell formulates the field of feminine communication effected by the film screen, as allegorized in *Stella Dallas* by the screen-within-the-screen of the lit window, as "the search for the mother's gaze – the responsiveness of her face – in view of its loss, or of threatened separation from it" (CT, 214–15).

The ratifying of Stella's reliance on her own judgment, her own taste – of her "taking on the thinking of her own existence, the announcing of her *cogito ergo sum*" – happens without her yet knowing who this thinker is who is proving her existence (as in Descartes's presenting of the *cogito*, which happens without his yet knowing who he is) (CT, 219). This woman's "walk toward us, as if the screen becomes her gaze, is allegorized as the presenting or creating of a star." As an interpretation of stardom, it "is the negation, in advance so to speak, of a theory of the star as fetish. This star, call her Barbara Stanwyck, is without obvious beauty or glamour. . . . But she has a future." Not only do we now know that this woman was to become the star of *The Lady Eve*, "she is presented *here* as a star (the camera showing her that particular insatiable interest in her every action and reaction), which entails the promise of return, of unpredictable incarnation" (two features of stardom singled out in *The World Viewed*).

What is Cavell's stake in insisting that Stella is self-knowing, that she puts herself in the way of a transfiguration that he associates with the teachings of Emerson and Thoreau? "The Emersonianism of the films I have written about as genres," Cavell writes, "depict human beings as on a kind of journey . . . from what he means by conformity to what he means by self-reliance; which comes to saying (so I have claimed) a journey, or path, or step, from haunting the world to existing in it; which may be expressed as the asserting of one's *cogito ergo sum* . . . , call it the power to think for oneself, to judge the world, to acquire – as Nora puts it at the end of *A Doll's House* – one's own experience of the world" (CT, 220). For Cavell, acceptance of this woman's transfiguration would provide "a certain verification of this philosophy, hence, of philosophy as such," as he cares about it most.

Cavell's *publication* of this reading, in the company of the other readings in *Contesting Tears*, can thus be seen as part of his effort "to preserve that philosophy, or rather to show that it *is* preserved, is in existence, in effect, in works of lasting public power – world-famous, world-favored films – while the Emerson text itself, so to speak, is repressed in the public it helped to found" (CT, 220). Yet these films too are repressed in that public. For all their popularity, their thinking remains unhonored and unsung (if hardly unwept).

> I assume that movies have played a role in American culture different from their role in other cultures, and more particularly that this difference is a function of the absence in America of the European edifice of philosophy. And since I assume further that American culture has been no less ambitious, craved no less to think about itself, than the most ambitious European culture, I assume further still that . . . American film at its best participates in this Western cultural ambition of self-thought or self-invention that presents itself in the absence of the Western edifice of philosophy, so that on these shores film has the following peculiar economy: it has the space, and the cultural pressure, to satisfy the craving for thought, the ambition of a talented culture to examine itself publicly; but its public lacks the means to grasp this thought as such for the very reason that it naturally or historically lacks that edifice of philosophy within which to grasp it. (CT, 72)

Like the difficulty of grasping a remarriage comedy, the difficulty of grasping a Melodrama of the Unknown Woman, assessing its thought, is the same as the difficulty of assessing everyday experience. Again, this difficulty calls for philosophy's capacity to receive inspiration for taking thought from the conditions that oppose thought. "Nothing much to me would be worth trying to understand" about a melodrama like *Now, Voyager*, Cavell writes, "unless one cares for it, cares to find words for it that seem to capture its power of feeling and intelligence, in such a way as to understand why we who have caused it (for whom it was made) have also rejected it, why we wish it both into and out of existence." (CT, 117–18)

In the Introduction to *Contesting Tears*, Cavell observes that despite most critics' condescension, *Stella Dallas, Gaslight, Now, Voyager*, and *Letter from an Unknown Woman* are worthy companions of the remarriage comedies. "They are of course less ingratiating," he adds. Indeed, they "are so often the reverse of ingratiating that it becomes painful to go on studying them. A compensating profit of instruction must be high for the experience to be justified." (CT, 7) The readings in *Contesting Tears* are worthy companions of those in *Pursuits of Happiness*, too, although they are less ingratiating, are indeed at times painful to go on studying. In each melodrama, the woman suffers an isolation so extreme "as to portray and partake of madness," as Cavell puts it, "a state of utter incommunicability, as before the possession of speech" (CT, 16). A woman like Stella has a capacity to judge the world as a place fit to live in or not, a power that comes from the extremity of her isolation. But isolation so extreme is painful to think about. Less painful is to deny this woman's power of judgment and fixate on the idea that she is pathetically oblivious to her own inadequacy. Not shrinking from the pain of thinking about Stella's thinking, and calling on us too to face that pain, Cavell's writing seeks to undo that fixation, to understand what is of value in such a woman, in such a film. What, then, is the "compensating profit of instruction" in the understanding, the pain, that is to be exchanged in the writing, and reading, of *Contesting Tears*? This is a question that guides Cavell's reading of *Stella Dallas* and, indeed, the book as a whole.

In *Contesting Tears*, Cavell writes about these melodramas "as though the woman's demand for a voice, for a language, for attention to, and the power to enforce attention to, her own subjectivity, say to her difference of existence, is expressible as a response to an Emersonian demand for thinking" (CT, 220). What authorizes this supposition is his interpretation of Emerson's authorship "as itself responding to his sense of the right to such a demand as already voiced on the feminine side, requiring a sense of thinking as reception . . . , and as a bearing of pain, which the masculine in philosophy would avoid. To overcome this avoidance is essential to Emerson's hopes for bringing an American difference to philosophy."

(CT, 221) Overcoming this avoidance, bearing the pain, is no less essential to Cavell's hope to inherit philosophy, as received, and founded, in America by Emerson's (and Thoreau's) writings – essential to his hope to preserve that philosophy, or rather to show that it *is* preserved, that it does exist.

Cavell ends the body of his reading of *Stella Dallas* by posing three questions. Does Emerson's idea of the feminine philosophical demand serve to prefigure the "difference of women" that film lives on? Does it articulate or blur the difference between the denial to women of political expression and a man's melancholy sense of his own inexpressiveness? And is the relation of the Emersonian and the feminine demand for a language of one's own a topic for a serious conversation between women and men? "It is ... the logic of human intimacy, or separateness," Cavell writes, "that to exchange understanding with another is to share pain with that other, and that to take pleasure from another is to extend that pleasure. And what reason is there to enter this logic in a particular case?" (CT, 221)

"No reason," Cavell concludes, with an echo of Wittgenstein. ("Reasons come to an end somewhere.") This invocation of Wittgenstein is followed by a typographical break and, in turn, by a page-long coda, another autobiographical moment, which brings *Contesting Tears* to a close with a haunting image of isolation and pain. (*The World Viewed*, too, ends with an invocation of Wittgenstein, a typographical break, and a haunting image of isolation and pain.)

> Now I am recognizing another of my mother's moods, somehow associated with the demand to be noticed (perhaps with its explicit failure, perhaps with the implicit failure of having to demand it). She named this state migraine – definable, I assumed, assume, through her therapy for it, which was to play the piano, in a darkened room (her eyes were evidently affected), alone. (I am interpreting the mood, after the fact, from the few times I came home from school late in the afternoon to enter such a scene.) What music she would play then (mostly Chopin, her favorite composer), and how she became a prominent pianist in Atlanta, then largely a culturally unprominent part of the country, and hence what her relation was to a certain stardom, and to her refusal of the chance for more, are pertinent matters. They must concern the relation between searching for the mother's gaze and being subjected to her moods. Hence they concern the question of what her moods are subjected to, to what scenes of inheritance. Was the music filling the loss or impoverishment of a self-abandoned ego (so speaking to melancholia), or was it remembering, say recounting, the origins,

hence losses, of her reception of her glamorous talent for the world of music (so speaking of dispossession and nostalgia)? Music, moods, worlds, abandonment, subjection, dispossession – of course, we are speaking of melodrama. (CT, 222)

Suffering the pain she called "migraine," Cavell's mother was playing the piano, alone, in a dark room, on the occasions when her son happened to "enter" such a scene. Are we to think of the writing of *Contesting Tears* as comparable to her piano playing on those occasions? No less than hers, the extremity of his isolation can be glimpsed in these words. But so can the way, in all his writings, philosophy overcomes or transcends that isolation, finds its way to locate its author within the world, enables him to suffer creation, to perform his own *cogito ergo sum*.

A PITCH OF PHILOSOPHY: "OPERA AND THE LEASE OF VOICE"

In the Melodrama of the Unknown Woman, *Contesting Tears* argues, the woman's flair for theater declares her dangerous wish for perfect expressiveness. Chapter 4 ("Postscript") stresses the condition that, Cavell finds, grounds the desire to express all, "the terror of absolute inexpressiveness, suffocation, which at the same time reveals itself as a terror of absolute expressiveness, unconditioned exposure." These extreme states of voicelessness, he observes, "are the polar states expressed in the woman's voice in opera" (CT, 43). With such remarks, *Contesting Tears* provides another bridge to *A Pitch of Philosophy*, in whose culminating third chapter ("Opera and the Lease of Voice") opera joins film as a central subject of Cavell's philosophical reflections.

Early in "Opera and the Lease of Voice," as in "Stella's Taste," Cavell introduces a moment of autobiography. ("Twice I remember asking my mother, 'Why are operas always sad?' She tried no answer, but she was someone to whom I could direct such a perplexity.")[10] Cavell goes on, responding continuously to the answer that another woman, Catherine Clement, gives in her book *Opera, or the Undoing of Women*. Her answer is, in effect, that "opera is about the death of women, and about the singing of women, and can be seen to be about the fact that women die *because* they sing" (PP, 112).

In "Opera and the Lease of Voice," Cavell puts together what he characterizes as "jigsaw shapes of intuition" about what it is that singing in opera betokens, about what operas have revealed about the powers, and limitations, of the human capacity to raise the voice (PP, 155).

As Cavell had argued in *The World Viewed*, the medium of film reverses the priority that theater gives to character over actor. On film, as he puts it in "Opera and the Lease of Voice,"

> the actor is the subject of the camera, emphasizing that this actor could (have) become other characters (that is, emphasizing the potentiality in human existence, the self's journeying), as opposed to theater's emphasizing that this character could (will) accept other actors (that is, emphasizing the fatedness in human existence, the self's finality or typicality at each step of the journey). In opera the relative emphasis of singer and role seems undecidable in these terms, indeed unimportant beside the fact of the new conception it introduces of the relation between voice and body, a relation in which not this character and this actor are embodied in each other but in which this voice is located in – one might say disembodied within – this figure, this double, this person, this persona, this singer, whose voice is essentially unaffected by the role. (PP, 137)

The fact that Monteverdi's *Orfeo*, the first masterpiece of the new medium, is a rendering of the story of Orpheus and Eurydice "is almost too good to be true," Cavell writes, "in establishing the myth of opera, of its origins – the story of the power of music, epitomized as the act of singing" (PP, 139). That Orpheus ultimately looks back and fails to redeem Eurydice for their everyday life together also makes this a story of the limitations of the powers of the voice. The question of whether this story, transformed by the medium of opera, is to end happily or sadly – a bone of contention between Monteverdi and his librettist – provides us with two interpretations of the expressive capacity of singing: "ecstasy over the absolute success of its expressiveness in recalling the world, as if bringing it back to life; melancholia over its inability to sustain the world, which may be put as an expression of the absolute inexpressiveness of the voice, of its failure to make itself heard, to become intelligible – evidently a mad state" (PP, 140).

The first operas, contemporaneous with Shakespeare's major tragedies, marked the crisis of expression engendered by the traumatic discovery that human language no longer assured connection with reality, a discovery that Descartes articulated philosophically in the radical skepticism which heralds modern philosophy. As Cavell observes, a "Cartesian intuition of the absolute metaphysical difference between mind and body, together with the twin Cartesian intuition of an undefined intimacy between just this body and only this spirit, appears to describe conditions of the possibility of opera" (PP, 138).

The significance of the fact that assaults on marriage are narrative figures for skepticism, Cavell adds, has been a central theme of his own writings since his studies of film and Shakespearean theater prepared him to recognize marriage, in "its idea of mutual, diurnal devotion," as a "figure for the ordinary" (PP, 141). Before going on to consider instances of such marriage, or their avoidance, in opera, Cavell develops further the concept or condition of the voice raised in song by relating the duality of the singer – the figure of the human as both necessarily and accidentally body and spirit – to the Orpheus myth, which pictures this doubleness as the spanning of two worlds. "I am counting here on an intuition of opera which . . . I imagine as widely shared," Cavell writes, as the "intervention or supervening of music into the world as revelatory of a realm of significance that either transcends our ordinary realm of experience or reveals ours under transfiguration" (PP, 142).

In Kant, the passage from one realm to the other – perfectionism's upward path of education – takes place in every moral judgment, "every time you stop to think, to ask yourself your way." Perfectionism's journey "has been cut short – to a half-step – you see how to take it, where it lies, or you do not" (PP, 143). Emerson's contribution to perfectionism, which Cavell finds decisive, is that "the moral constraint upon the human can be expressed not, as for Kant, as an obligation, but as an attraction. . . . Attraction as the basis of commitment – as paradoxical as taking narcissism as the basis of altruism."

These "Kantian/Emersonian modifications of perfectionism," Cavell suggests, help to explain why in most operas – The Magic Flute is exceptional – there is little elaboration of perfectionist journeys. "Rather we may leap," he writes in one of his inimitable sweeping summations,

> from a judgment of the world as unreal, or alien, to an encompassing sense of another realm flush with this one, into which there is no good reason we do not or cannot step, unless opera works out the reasons. Such a view will take singing . . . to express the sense of being pressed or stretched between worlds – one in which to be seen, the roughly familiar world of the philosophers, and one from which to be heard, one to which one releases or abandons one's spirit (perhaps to call upon it, as Donna Anna and Donna Elvira do; perhaps to forgo it, as the Marschallin and as Violetta do; perhaps to prepare for it, as Desdemona and Brünnhilde do; perhaps to identify it with this one, as Carmen does), and which recedes when the breath of the song ends. (PP, 144)

Cavell's image of singing as abandonment draws on Emerson's use of the concept of abandonment "to name a spiritual achievement (of, let us say, neutrality) expressed as a willingness to depart from all settled habitation, all conformity of meaning" (PP, 144). Cavell's passage also draws on Thoreau's idea that being beside oneself in a sane sense – the dictionary definition of ecstasy – is that which proves one's humanity. Thus singing is to be understood "as an irrupting of a new perspective of the self to itself," an "ecstatic response whose self-reflectiveness suggests the structure of narcissism" (PP, 145).

In bringing the concept of narcissism into play in order to articulate a double intuition of singing as ecstasy and as abandonment, Cavell is registering the sense that singing is at once primitive (the "spectacular vocality of opera in its aspect as orality") and sophisticated ("in its aspect as exposure or display, sometimes named seductiveness") (PP, 144–5).

With regard to singing's "sophisticated" aspect, Cavell argues that if we reformulate Clement's "women die because they sing" to say that "women's singing exposes them to death, the use of the voice to the stopping of the voice," we have also to ask what the woman's singing *exposes* (PP, 145–6). Cavell's answer: It exposes her as thinking, as performing the *cogito*, the thinking that confirms existence. Thus it exposes her to "the power of those who do not want her to think, do not . . . want autonomous proof of her existence." He cites, as opera's "most precise, appropriately defiant, announcement of the fact of thinking as narcissism, of its exposure in or as defiant seduction," Carmen's "*Seguidilla*" ("Don José: I forbid you to speak to me; Carmen: I didn't speak to you . . . I sing for my own pleasure / And I'm thinking . . . It's surely not forbidden to think") (PP, 146).

On the "primitive" side too, Cavell argues, the woman's singing reveals her intellectual agency, her autonomous existence. Cavell cites Freud's claim that judgment has an oral, primitive basis in the original process by which the ego took things in or expelled them, which "amounts to the judgment of the world, as affirmation or negation in each utterance or outcry" (PP, 148). In the fact that singing, in its breaths, "incessantly draws in and lets out the world as such," Cavell suggests, lies a hint as to why opera "so attunes itself to moments of separation, as if this is the founding trauma of human experience."

According to Kant, ideas that assure us of a moral universe (for example, the moral law and freedom of the will), like concepts that assure us of a world (substance and causation, for example), are grounded in the a priori conditions of reason or of understanding. Aesthetic judgments, by contrast, claim universal assent upon no more than subjective grounds. "The feeling," as Cavell puts it, "comes first (Emerson calls it Intuition or Instinct), and its putative grounded concepts (the reasons for the judgment)

await determination in . . . acts of criticism (Emerson calls them Tuitions)"
(PP, 149). Inverting Kant's formulation that aesthetic judgments rest on
"the predication of pleasure without a concept," Cavell proposes, in one of
his own most elegant – and provocative – formulations, that "we think of
the voice in opera as a judgment of the world on the basis of, called forth by,
pain beyond a concept." Opera cannot demand that we "take events as hard,
and as far, as Desdemona, Aida, Verdi's Leonora, Carmen, Brünnhilde, the
Marschallin, and Mélisande do." But opera can make it irresistible for us
"to listen and to understand beyond explanation."

In the remainder of the chapter, Cavell provides sketches – each a gem of
criticism – of moments from five masterpieces of opera: Mozart's *Marriage
of Figaro*, Verdi's *Il Trovatore* (and the Marx Brothers' grand burlesque and
homage of *Il Trovatore* in *A Night at the Opera*) and *La Traviata*, Wagner's
Götterdämmerung, and Debussy's *Pelléas and Mélisande*). In each of these instances, Cavell finds that the woman, in singing, is, like Carmen, performing the thinking that confirms existence. Not coincidentally, each woman
is thinking specifically about "how to manage a marriage, that is, how to
keep its idea intact; or how to avoid one" (PP, 151–2). Cavell's task, in these
critical sketches, is not to *explain* the woman's thinking, to enable us to
know what she knows; it is to listen to her voice, and to his own voice, in
order to enable a certain sort of understanding – an understanding beyond
explanation – to take place.

Cavell concludes "Opera and the Lease of Voice," and with it *A Pitch
of Philosophy*, by posing questions that seamlessly join his concerns with
the powers and limitations of the human voice, with philosophy's capacity
to receive inspiration for taking thought from the conditions that oppose
thought, and with the provenance and pertinence of his own voice.

> Am I ready to vow . . . that I know my mother's mother tongue of music
> to be also mine? The hills are different ones now, but the world is, I'm
> glad to say, the same when I have to catch my breath at such promises.
> Are they mine? Have I, throughout these pages, been asking anything else?
> (PP, 169)

As in his reading of *Stella Dallas*, Cavell stakes this writing's right to exist
on his own claim to a double inheritance – the inheritance of Emerson's (and
Thoreau's) thinking, which itself claimed to inherit philosophy for America,
and the inheritance of his own mother's powers of thought – whether they
be called, as they are here, her "mother tongue of music" or, as in "Stella's
Taste," "migraine."

CODA: "OPERA IN AND AS FILM"

When Cavell proposes, in "Opera and the Lease of Voice," that we think of the voice in opera as a judgment of the world on the basis of, called forth by, pain beyond a concept, the question of what is comic in opera briefly comes up. "Perhaps it lies in affirming the thought that whatever causes happiness does not occur in the absence of pain, or the thought that the world may for a moment be found to escape judgment altogether," Cavell observes (PP, 149). Marking a region for future exploration, he adds, "Such thoughts would suggest the affinity of Shakespearean romance with opera." Hence they would also suggest opera's affinity with the comedy of remarriage, as well as with the Melodrama of the Unknown Woman. That is, they would suggest opera's affinity with film itself – an affinity so intimate, Cavell testifies, that it has led him in recent years to experiment with the thought that what has happened to opera, as an institution, is that it has "transformed itself into film, that film is, or was, our opera" (PP, 136).

As I was in the midst of composing the present remarks, Stanley Cavell sent me his as-yet-unpublished "Opera in and as Film." This latest of his ongoing reflections on film, on opera, and on their thought-provoking relationship does indeed explore this region of the affinity between opera and film.

This relatively brief piece begins by considering a moment in Frank Capra's *Mr. Deeds Goes to Town* (1936) that Cavell reads as confessing "film's sense of affinity with opera, often expressed in an impulse of competition with opera." Assaulted by proposals for ways to spend his newly inherited fortune, Mr. Deeds (Gary Cooper) is informed that he has been elected to replace his uncle as president of the Friends of the Opera, "an immediate privilege of which is for him to continue his uncle's annual subsidy of the opera's productions." Told that ticket sales alone cannot support opera productions, he replies, "Well, maybe you're putting on the wrong kind of shows." Clearly, Cavell remarks, "the film is proposing that the right kind of shows for them to put on are movies, and that it is offering itself as an example." And, he adds, "I read the moment of Mr. Deeds refusing a use of his inheritance to support opera as an argument of film with opera generally about its claims to inherit from opera the flame that preserves the human need, on pain of madness of melancholy, for conviction in its expressions of passion."

It is, Cavell observes, an old argument. During the silent era, Cecil B. DeMille made a film of the opera *Carmen* – one of several silent *Carmens*, in fact – "as if to declare that the expressive powers of silent film are equal to those of music." Evidently, DeMille believed in film "to the extent that he would measure its power of, let's say, the magnification of gesture against music's intensification of speech in making human expression lucid." (Already in *Pursuits of Happiness*, Cavell drew a connection between film and opera by suggesting that the camera's powers of transfiguration, and music's, are in some sense comparable.)

Tracing some of the vicissitudes of the old argument, Cavell distinguishes three principal ways, citing several instances of each category, in which "opera and film have intervened in one another." Films can (1) realize the full performance of an opera, or (2) incorporate an opera essentially within the film's structure, or (3) briefly or intermittently allude to an opera. Cavell dwells, in particular, on two instances of the second of these categories: *Moonstruck* (1989, directed by Norman Jewison) in connection with *La Bohème*, and *Meeting Venus* (1991, by the Hungarian director Istvan Szabo) in connection with *Tannhäuser*. In these instances, as Cavell puts it, "the competition between an opera and the attention given it in the film becomes an essential part of the film's subject, or, to say it otherwise, to understand the relation between the film and the opera to which it weds itself sets the primary task of the understanding of the film."

We will not trace here the sublime details of Cavell's accounts of these films, but will only note one salient point that repeatedly resurfaces: the tendency for film, when it incorporates an opera into its narrative, to seek to divert death – as if, by providing "a happier, anyway less fatal, ending," the film is declaring its own powers in opposition to those of opera.

Cavell develops this point further when he concludes "Opera in and as Film" by remarking on a reference to *Tannhäuser* that occurs near the end of Preston Sturges's *The Lady Eve*, one of the definitive remarriage comedies.

> If we may say that *Tannhäuser* is about two women who are opposite aspects of a woman's powers of love, where each promises redemption and each proves to be lethal, then we may say that *The Lady Eve* is about one woman who plays two opposite women, each of whom pretends, and cons the man into believing, that she is not someone she is.

Sturges's insertion of a "Wagnerian air of profundity," which has become so famous that it "inevitably risks banality," is designed, Cavell suggests, to shock us

> into posing necessary and banal questions, such as how this man can fail to recognize the woman he has married as the woman he loves, or loved. One answer is that while she has not disguised her appearance she has

altered her voice. . . . But what about that voice does the man not want to hear? Presumably that he has placed his desire where he loves and that this singular woman is prepared to become an object for him in whom the currents of passion and tenderness can flow together. Such is this woman's proposal of the reality which prolongs life, or say which diverts death. It is frightening, but the man allows himself foolishness and bewilderment and persistence enough perhaps to welcome it. But why is it through film that such a proposal becomes credible?

Cavell answers this last question, or draws its moral, by responding to Mr. Deeds's dismissal of opera in favor of film.

> Even when what were called movie palaces increasingly put on what he implied were the right shows, those picture shows more often than perhaps they knew demanded an inheritance from opera's transcendent powers of communication. And some of us find that movies have proven to deserve that inheritance. To think about the conditions of the inheritance, principally about how film's reflections provide further chapters of opera's life, has afforded me pleasures to which, while strength lasts, I see no end.

Viewed from *The Lady Eve*'s philosophical perspective, the old argument between film and opera, like the far older "war between the sexes," takes on the aspect of the "meet and happy" conversation in a marriage worth having. Film's proposal of the reality that prolongs life, or diverts death, is frightening, but Cavell allows himself enough "foolishness and bewilderment and persistence" to welcome it. Affirming the thought that whatever causes happiness does not occur in the absence of pain, and the kindred thought that the world may for a moment be found to escape judgment altogether, Cavell expresses his passionate belief in opera's, and film's, transcendent powers of communication, and in philosophy's expressive powers as well. This happy session of thought about opera and film and philosophy ends, not with a haunting image of isolation and pain, but with a tribute to the pleasure – and the promise of pleasure – that makes philosophy so humanly attractive.

Notes

1. Stanley Cavell, *The World Viewed: Reflections on the Ontology of Film*, enlarged edition (Cambridge, MA: Harvard University Press, 1979), p. 22. Hereinafter WV.
2. James Conant, "An Interview with Stanley Cavell," in Richard Fleming and Michael Payne, eds., *The Senses of Stanley Cavell* (Lewisburg, PA: Bucknell University Press, 1989), p. 59.

3. Stanley Cavell, *Disowning Knowledge: In Six Plays of Shakespeare* (Cambridge: University Press, 1987), pp. 4–5.

4. Stanley Cavell, "The Politics of Interpretation," in his *Themes Out of School: Effects and Causes* (San Francisco: North Point Press, 1984; reprinted Chicago: University of Chicago Press, 1988), p. 54.

5. Stanley Cavell, *Pursuits of Happiness: The Hollywood Comedy of Remarriage* (Cambridge, MA: Harvard University Press, 1981), p. 28. Hereinafter PH.

6. Stanley Cavell, *Contesting Tears: The Hollywood Melodrama of the Unknown Woman* (Chicago and London: University of Chicago Press, 1996), pp. 11–12. Hereinafter CT.

7. Stanley Cavell, "The Fact of Television," *Daedalus* 11 (Fall 1982), pp. 75–96; reprinted in *Themes Out of School*, pp. 235–68, at p. 236. Hereinafter TOS.

8. Stanley Cavell, *Conditions Handsome and Unhandsome: The Constitution of Emersonian Perfectionism* (Chicago and London: University of Chicago Press, 1990), p. 2. Hereinafter CHU.

9. Stanley Cavell, "Being Odd, Getting Even," in his *In Quest of the Ordinary: Lines of Skepticism and Romanticism* (Chicago: University of Chicago Press, 1988), p. 10.

10. Stanley Cavell, *A Pitch of Philosophy: Autobiographical Exercises* (Cambridge, MA, and London: Harvard University Press, 1994), p. 132. Hereinafter PP.

Brief Annotated Bibliography of Works by and about Stanley Cavell

Books by Stanley Cavell

A full bibliography, "Stanley Cavell: A Bibliography, 1951–1995" by Peter S. Fosl, of Cavell's books, articles, and anthology contributions (including original appearances of articles later reprinted in Cavell's own collections), interviews and discussions, and recorded lectures up through 1995 appears in Stephen Mulhall, ed., *The Cavell Reader* (Oxford: Basil Blackwell, 1996), pp. 390–414.

Cavell has regularly referred to his essay "Must We Mean What We Say?," *Inquiry* 1 (Autumn 1958), pp. 172–212, as "the oldest piece of mine which I still use." It appears as the title essay of his collection *Must We Mean What We Say?* (New York: Charles Scribner's Sons, 1969; reprinted Cambridge: Cambridge University Press, 1976). In this collection, and beginning with the title essay, Cavell announces many of the themes that were to dominate his career: our responsibility for what we say, both in relation to and in all-too-human repudiation of ordinary language; artistic modernism and the pursuit of originality of voice and stance (and their repression) as problems in and *for* modern philosophy; the intertwining of the pursuit of knowledge (and knowledge of knowledge) with avoidance and acknowledgment of others; Shakespeare as an investigator of responsibility, voice, avoidance, and acknowledgment; and Austin and, especially, Wittgenstein as themselves writers concerned with and caught up in these themes.

The World Viewed: Reflections on the Ontology of Film (New York: Viking, 1971; enlarged edition Cambridge, MA: Harvard University Press, 1979).

> Cavell's discovery of film and philosophy as subjects for one another, in relation to his discovery or recovery of (mostly) American popular films as embodiments of thoughts worth following about subjectivity, happiness, intimacy, pleasure, grace, and so on.

The Senses of Walden (New York: Viking, 1972; expanded edition San Francisco: North Point Press, 1981; reprinted Chicago: University of Chicago Press, 1992).

Cavell's first investigation of a distinctly American attempt to achieve full voice and selfhood, both in criticism of American culture as it stands and in continuing relation to that culture, seeking its perfection and redemption.

The Claim of Reason: Wittgenstein, Skepticism, Morality, and Tragedy (Oxford: Oxford University Press, 1979; reprinted with a new preface 1999).

The centerpiece of Cavell's work, incorporating widely circulated material on Wittgenstein and on morality from Cavell's 1961 Harvard Ph.D. dissertation, but going well beyond that. Cavell develops a systematic reading of Wittgenstein's engagement with (rather than refutation of) skepticism, seeing Wittgenstein as both investigating and enacting a standing plight of mind and of human relationship. Cavell pursues this plight as it is variously expressed in political judgment, in one's relation (typically both intimate-necessary and alienating) to one's culture and language, and in genuine moral conversation and criticism (as opposed to so-called metaethics). Part IV, "Skepticism and the Problem of Others: Between Acknowledgment and Avoidance," is a kind of "limited philosophical journal" (xxiii) of Cavell's engagements with Shakespeare, Blake, Kleist, Hemingway, Mann, Freud, and others as he, following them, sees the central plight of mind – the bearing of responsibility, together with the impossible wish to "sublime it away" – enacted nearly everywhere.

Pursuits of Happiness: The Hollywood Comedy of Remarriage (Cambridge, MA: Harvard University Press, 1981).

Readings of six Hollywood romance comedies from the period 1934–49, dwelling on how romantic pairs may come through conversation and play to discover that "what they do together is less important than the fact that they do whatever it is together" (113). This discovery embodies acknowledgment of one another, and it is urged as something we might hope for generally in the making of an American culture. Perhaps Cavell's happiest book.

Themes Out of School: Effects and Causes (San Franciso: North Point Press, 1984; reprinted Chicago: University of Chicago Press, 1988).

Occasional essays from the period 1978–84, extending Cavell's investigations into film, television, American culture and its prospects, and Shakespeare.

Disowning Knowledge: In Six Plays of Shakespeare (Cambridge: Cambridge University Press, 1987; reissued 2002).

> Collects all of Cavell's prior readings of Shakespeare (from *Must We Mean What We Say?*, *The Claim of Reason*, and *Themes Out of School*) plus new essays to form a unified whole dwelling on Shakespeare's diagnoses of the motive to refuse acknowledgment of others and of one's own motivations.

In Quest of the Ordinary: Lines of Skepticism and Romanticism (Chicago: University of Chicago Press, 1988).

> Following on *The Claim of Reason*, deepens the themes of "the truth of skepticism," and "the uncanniness of the ordinary" as both home and provocation to departure. These themes are traced as they are enacted in texts by a variety of Romantic writers (Coleridge, Wordsworth, Hoffman) and American writers (Poe, Emerson, Thoreau), among others. The essay "The Uncanniness of the Ordinary" is perhaps the best highly compact summary of his concerns that Cavell has produced.

This New Yet Unapproachable America: Lectures after Emerson after Wittgenstein (Chicago: University of Chicago Press, 1988).

> Develops the theme of Wittgenstein as having a "vertical sense" of our human "form of life" as awaiting and permitting cultivation and perfection. Philosophizing as involving a "spiritual struggle with oneself" to achieve such perfection is connected with the itinerary of Emerson in seeking the enlargement and transfiguration of "Power," "Experience," and America.

Conditions Handsome and Unhandsome: The Constitution of Emersonian Perfectionism (Chicago: University of Chicago Press, 1990).

> A sustained investigation of perfectionist aspirations: as they are expressed by Emerson, taken up from Emerson by Mill, Nietzsche, and Heidegger, among others; then as they are repressed in Kripke's reading of Wittgenstein (in whom they are pervasively present) and in Rawls's *A Theory of Justice*. Argues that perfectionist aspirations are pursued through "aversive thinking," "the argument of the ordinary," and "the conversation of justice" – practices that are sideways to normal academic-theoretical activity.

A Pitch of Philosophy: Autobiographical Exercises (Cambridge, MA: Harvard University Press, 1994).

> An account of provocations and inheritances on Cavell's part: of his parents' pasts, aspirations, and lines of interest; of music; of Judaism;

of J. L. Austin and his teaching; and of (identification with) achievements of voice, especially female voice, in dramatic opera.

Philosophical Passages: Wittgenstein, Emerson, Austin, Derrida (Oxford: Basil Blackwell, 1995).
   Further readings of the figures named in the subtitle.

Contesting Tears: The Melodrama of the Unknown Woman (Chicago: University of Chicago Press, 1996).
   Close readings of four Hollywood melodramas in which female protagonists seek perfection, education, equality, and transfiguration but find themselves isolated in their quests, in ways that invert the careers of the pairs examined in *Pursuits of Happiness*.

Interviews

Cavell has given several interviews in which he has described the development of his work and interests. Especially useful are:

James Conant, "An Interview with Stanley Cavell," in Richard Fleming and Michael Payne, eds., *The Senses of Stanley Cavell* (Lewisburg, PA: Bucknell University Press and Cranbury, NJ: Associated University Presses, 1989).

Michael Payne and Richard Fleming, "A Conversation with Stanley Cavell on Philosophy and Literature, in their *The Senses of Stanley Cavell*, pp. 311–21.

Richard Fleming, "The Self of Philosophy: An Interview with Stanley Cavell," in Cavell, *Philosophical Passages*, pp. 91–103.

Seminar on "What Did Derrida Want of Austin?" in Cavell, *Philosophical Passages*, pp. 66–90.

Books about Stanley Cavell

Stephen Mulhall, *Stanley Cavell: Philosophy's Recounting of the Ordinary* (Oxford: Clarendon Press, 1994).
   A comprehensive survey of Cavell's work, organized to follow Cavell from the topic of responsibility in and for what we say, to aesthetics and morality, to skepticism and romanticism, to Shakespeare, psychoanalysis, and movies, and finally to American philosophy, religion, and the female voice.

Timothy Gould, *Hearing Things: Voice and Method in the Writing of Stanley Cavell* (Chicago: University of Chicago Press, 1998).

> A thematic survey and assessment of Cavell's central preoccupation with the tension between voice (originality) and method (confirmable results), as Cavell moves from the method of ordinary language philosophy into the later method of reading.

Richard Fleming and Michael Payne, eds., *The Senses of Stanley Cavell* (Lewisburg, PA: Bucknell University Press and Cranbury, NJ: Associated University Presses, 1989).

> A valuable collection of articles on Cavell's work.

Ted Cohen, Paul Guyer, and Hilary Putnam, eds., *Pursuits of Reason: Essays in Honor of Stanley Cavell* (Lubbock Texas Tech University Press, 1993).

> A volume of essays, many treating Cavell's own work, by Cavell's colleagues and former students.

William Rothman and Marian Keane, *Reading Cavell's The World Viewed: A Philosophical Perspective on Film* (Detroit: Wayne State University Press, 2000).

> A comprehensive reconstruction and defense of Cavell's basic commitments to and strategies for the study of film.

Michael Fischer, *Stanley Cavell and Literary Skepticism* (Chicago: University of Chicago Press, 1989).

> An extension and application of Cavell's work on skepticism and meaning to controversies about literary meaning provoked by poststructuralism.

Richard Fleming, *The State of Philosophy: An Invitation to a Reading in Three Parts of Stanley Cavell's The Claim of Reason* (Lewisburg, PA: Bucknell University Press and Cranbury, NJ: Associated University Presses, 1993).

> A reading of *The Claim of Reason*, focusing on Cavell's "pursuit of self-knowledge" through strategies of voice, confessional and conversational, throughout the text as a whole.

Richard Eldridge, *Leading a Human Life: Wittgenstein, Intentionality, and Romanticism* (Chicago: University of Chicago Press, 1997).

> Contains a central chapter comparing Cavell's reading of Wittgenstein to those of Kripke, Rorty, Dummett, Kenny, and Baker and Hacker (among others), followed by a continuous reading of *Philosophical Investigations*, §§1–308, in engagement with Cavell's work.

Richard Eldridge, *The Persistence of Romanticism: Selected Essays in Philosophy and Literature* (Cambridge: Cambridge University Press, 2001).

>Includes two essays on Cavell's work in the context of a general characterization and defense of Romanticism.

Ronald L. Hall, *The Human Embrace: The Love of Philosophy and the Philosophy of Love: Kierkegaard, Cavell, Nussbaum* (University Park: Pennsylvania State University Press, 1999).

>Comparisons of these three philosophers on love, commitment, marriage, and luck.

Espen Hammer, *Stanley Cavell: Skepticism, Subjectivity, and the Ordinary* (Oxford: Polity Press, 2002).

>Argues that Cavell's account of the relations between skepticism and subjectivity uncovers resources for self-transformation in relation to going practices.

Index

245